CONTINENTAL
PHILOSOPHY
IN
AMERICA

CONTINENTAL PHILOSOPHY IN AMERICA

edited by

Hugh J. Silverman
John Sallis
Thomas M. Seebohm

DUQUESNE UNIVERSITY PRESS
PITTSBURGH, PA   1983

Published by:
Duquesne University Press
600 Forbes Ave.
Pittsburgh, PA 15282

Distributed by:
Humanities Press
Atlantic Highlands, New Jersey 07716

PRINTED IN THE UNITED STATES OF AMERICA

Library of Congress Cataloging in Publication Data
Main entry under title:

Continental philosophy in America.

  Includes bibliographical references.
  1. Husserl, Edmund, 1859-1938—Addresses, essays, lectures.
2. Heidegger, Martin, 1889-1976—Addresses, essays, lectures.
3. Merleau-Ponty, Maurice, 1908-1961—Addresses, essays,
lectures. I. Silverman, Hugh J. II. Sallis, John, 1938-
II. Seebohm, Thomas M.
B3279.H94C65 1983   190   83-1628
ISBN 0-8207-0160-2

CONTENTS

ABOUT THE EDITORS AND CONTRIBUTORS

The Editors

HUGH J. SILVERMAN is Associate Professor of Philosophy and Comparative Literature at the State University of New York at Stony Brook. He taught previously at Stanford University and has been visiting professor at New York University, Duquesne University, and the University of Warwick (England). He is author of over twenty-five articles in continental philosophy, translator of Merleau-Ponty's *Consciousness and the Acquisition of Language* (1973) and "Philosophy and Non-philosophy since Hegel (1976), and editor of *Jean-Paul Sartre: Contemporary Approaches to His Philosophy* (1980) and *Piaget, Philosophy and the Human Sciences* (1980). He is Executive Co-Director of the Society for Phenomenology and Existential Philosophy.

JOHN SALLIS holds the Chair of Philosophy at Loyola University of Chicago. He is author of *Phenomenology and the Return to Beginnings* (1973), *Being and Logos: The Way of Platonic Dialogue* (1975), and *The Gathering of Reason* (1980). He is editor of *Heidegger and the Path of Thinking* (1970), *Radical Phenomenology: Essays in Honor of Martin Heidegger* (1978), and *Heraclitean Fragments* (1980). He edits the annual journal *Research in Phenomenology* and the new book series Contemporary Studies in Philosophy and the Human Sciences with Humanities Press and Macmillan International.

THOMAS M. SEEBOHM is Professor of Philosophy at the Pennsylvania State University in State College, Pennsylvania and currently Visiting Professor of Philosophy at the New School for Social Research in New York City. He is author of *Die Bedingungen der Möglichkeit der Transzendentalphilosophie* (1962), *Zur Kritik der hermeneutischen Vernunft*, and numerous articles in phenomenology, hermeneutics, and Kant-studies. He is also co-editor of *Bewusst sein: Gerhard Funke zu eigen* (1975) and a member of the Editorial Board of the Ohio University Press series in Continental Thought.

*   *   *

List of Contributors

ELIZABETH A. BEHNKE holds a doctorate from Ohio University in Comparative Arts.

WALTER BIEMEL is currently professor at the Staatliche Kunstakademie, Düsseldorf, West Germany. He was previously Professor of Philosophy at the University of Aachen.

RICHARD COBB-STEVENS is Associate Professor of Philosophy at Boston College.

JOSÉ HUERTAS-JOURDA is Associate Professor of Philosophy at Wilfred Laurier University in Ontario, Canada.

THEODORE KISIEL is Professor of Philosophy at Northern Illinois University in DeKalb, Illinois.

GRAEME NICHOLSON is Associate Professor of Philosophy at the University of Toronto, Canada.

DENNIS T. O'CONNOR is Associate Professor of Philosophy at the Loyola Campus of Concordia University, Montreal, Canada.

ROBERT D. ROMANYSHYN is Associate Professor of Psychology and member of the Graduate Faculty at the Institute of Philosophic Studies, University of Dallas, Irving, Texas.

THOMAS M. SEEBOHM is Professor of Philosophy at the Pennsylvania State University and Visiting Professor at the New School for Social Research in New York City.

THOMAS SHEEHAN is Associate Professor of Philosophy at Loyola University, Chicago and currently teaching at the Loyola University Center in Rome, Italy.

ELISABETH STRÖKER is Professor of Philosophy and Director of the Husserl-Archives at the University of Cologne, West Germany.

STEPHEN H. WATSON is currently Post-Doctoral Fellow at the Center for Twentieth Century Studies at the University of Wisconsin, Milwaukee and will be Assistant Professor of Philosophy at Colgate University in Hamilton, New York.

INTRODUCTION

IN RESPONSE TO A GROWING NEED for special attention to particular areas of continental philosophy in America, an annual Heidegger conference was established in 1966. Two years later another group of scholars initiated a society devoted to the study of Edmund Husserl's phenomenology. Ten years later the Merleau-Ponty Circle was formed. The purpose of these societies has been to devote careful consideration to the important work initiated by Edmund Husserl (1859–1938), Martin Heidegger (1889–1976), and Maurice Merleau-Ponty (1908–1961). However, none of these societies sees its task as the simple reiteration of views established by each of the three European philosophers. The respective members of the societies are more concerned with a clarification of fundamental philosophical issues and with the development of thought in the general direction appropriated by the particular philosopher in question. Often such a concern involves the rereading and reinterpretation of primary texts in the phenomenological tradition.

In recent years, a number of excellent papers have been presented at the annual meetings of the Husserl, Heidegger, and Merleau-Ponty Circles. Because there is only minimal overlap in the memberships of the three societies and because the members of each circle would not wish to be subsumed under any umbrella organization, each group has formed its own publications committee. The committees individually determined which papers presented at recent meetings would be available for publication.

Each committee then evaluated and accepted the four best papers for the volume. Since these annual meetings typically last three days each year, a wide range of possibilities was available. The respective publications committees made their selections of the prize essays on the basis of excellence. Within this framework they sought to offer balance and diversity of topics. The chairmen of the three publications committees have served as editors of this volume since they have been responsible for collecting the papers, requesting appropriate revision in several cases, and coordinating the separate efforts of the three individual societies. As editors, we are particularly grateful to the other members of the publications committees, to the coordinators of particular annual meetings, and to the members of the individual societies for their cooperative efforts.

All of the essays in this volume are being published for the first time. They have been organized in groups of four; the studies of Husserl are followed by those of Heidegger and Merleau-Ponty. They include essays both by well-recognized scholars and by younger members of the philosophical community. They represent some of the best work in continental philosophy presented and discussed in America. They will be useful to anyone wishing to pursue the interpretation and implications of phenomenology as articulated by three of its dominant figures. Above all they represent new perspectives developed out of working groups with common interests, common concerns, and a common philosophical tradition. The particular formulations, orientation, and interpretations themselves vary, as they must. In returning to Husserl, Heidegger, and Merleau-Ponty, each of whom took phenomenology along a new path in Europe, the authors of these essays have offered a picture of the contemporary status of continental philosophy for the American context. They have shown how this reassessment opens the way for new directions in American philosophical thinking.

Hugh J. Silverman
MERLEAU-PONTY CIRCLE

John Sallis
HEIDEGGER CONFERENCE

Thomas M. Seebohm
HUSSERL CIRCLE

PART I

Husserl

ONE

THE ROLE OF PSYCHOLOGY
IN HUSSERL'S PHENOMENOLOGY

I.

HUSSERL'S FIRST WORK IN PHENOMENOLOGY was the *Logical Investigations*, originally published in German at the turn of our century. In it he passed harsh judgment on psychologism and overcame the long psychologistic tradition that was influential in Germany and other countries in the nineteenth century. This tradition involved above all the contention that logic and mathematics are about psychic acts and experiences of knowledge. In contrast, Husserl showed that any attempt to give these sciences or indeed knowledge in general such a basis was doomed to failure. In the specific objectivity of the formations (*Gebilde*) of logic and mathematics (e.g., numbers, propositions, truths, proofs, theories) there is nothing like subjective acts or psychic experiences (*Erlebnisse*) to be found.

For Husserl, these formations belong to a specific realm of objects in their own right which, it is true, are not real objects like things but are nevertheless objects inasmuch as (a) they are identical unities over and against the multitude of psychic acts through which they are "given"; and (b) they are ideal unities (i.e., matters that are significant and to which validity is ascribed). No real psychic acts or events occur in this timeless realm. With this alternative view of the subject matter of logic and mathematics, Husserl justified the subtitle of the first volume of his *Logical Investigations*, namely: "Prolegomena to Pure Logic." Because virtually any reference to psychology is labeled "psychologism" within some contemporary philosophic tendencies, it is imperative to clarify that which Husserl opposed in his critique of psychologism and that which he proposed to replace it.

On the basis of the "Prolegomena" of 1900 there was wide-spread expectation that especially the "Elements of a Phenomenological

Elucidation of Knowledge," announced for the second part of the second volume of the *Logical Investigation*, would at least sketch an epistemology devoid of psychologistic implications. Afterward, however, Husserl was repeatedly reproached for relapsing into psychologism. While this objection is unfounded, Husserl is partly responsible for it as a result of his misleading self-interpretations and emphases. It is unfounded because in Husserl's phenomenology there is, from the beginning, nothing to be found of a renewed attempt to reduce knowledge formations to psychic events. Nevertheless the reader could become confused because in the Vth and VIth "Investigations" Husserl for the first time takes up the question of how the subjectivity of knowing acts, on the one hand, and the objectivity of the achievements of knowledge, on the other hand, are to be related, and in so doing he lays the major emphasis on the analysis of the acts of knowledge.

Husserl's early phenomenological analyses were thus taken to be nothing more than a psychology of mental acts. Husserl himself also led readers into a misconstrual of his purposes and achievements by taking several sections over *verbatim* from his "Psychological Studies in Elementary Logic" (1894) into the IIIrd, Vth, and VIth "Investigations." He furthermore unfortunately characterized his phenomenology as "descriptive psychology," a characterization that he later withdrew. Hence the mistake was almost inevitable that Husserl was only continuing and elaborating the sort of psychology that his teacher, Brentano, had inaugurated and was using the title "phenomenology" to contrast it with the genetic and causal research concerning consciousness predominant in the psychology of that era.

As a matter of fact, however, in their very methical procedures (which are not well presented by Husserl in his early methodological discussions), the phenomenological analyses of the *Logical Investigations* do not involve empirical psychological analyses of events of consciousness at all. Rather they are purely eidetic analyses of the essence of conscious experiences. Conceived as a doctrine of essence and endowed with procedures for grasping essences, this phenomenology is focused exclusively on the ideal possibilities of acts of knowledge and their essential traits and thus plainly is not in any way an empirical psychology. Insofar as an eidetic phenomenology takes concrete acts and experiences into account at all, it is not aiming, as was done in the psychology of the time, at generalizations about features of actual consciousness but only using actual cases of consciousness as examples, on the basis of which eidetic insights into the apriori structures of consciousness could be obtained.

II.

Up to this point the theme of this study has hardly been hinted at. It may be that Husserl could have defended himself against all charges of psychologism in his earlier phenomenology because psychology was actually not used there as a basis for knowledge. Nevertheless, there is still a question of relations between phenomenology and psychology. The chief task of this paper will be to take up various difficulties and even contradictions in Husserl's thought about the relationship of these two disciplines and, through a close analysis of certain trains in that thought, to attempt to resolve these difficulties.[1]

From his typical starting point Husserl cannot help but face incessantly the relationship in question since it is of the nature of his epistemological problem that knowledge can be elucidated only with reference to how cognitive achievements are constituted in the intentions of consciousness. Husserl was always concerned with the relations of phenomenology and psychology. While he normally ignored criticism, Husserl very decidedly tried to refute psychologistic distortions of his position. The relationship was of central concern in all the different lectures of the 1920s under the title of "Phenomenological Psychology." Husserl's article, "Phenomenology," in the *Encyclopedia Britannica* of 1927 also thematized the connection and cohesion of phenomenology and psychology. Finally, the Amsterdam lectures of 1929, which were an expanded version of the *Britannica* article, again had the main title "Phenomenological Psychology." (That Husserl now and then also used "psychological phenomenology" need not confuse us. He did this mainly in manuscripts and preliminary studies. It is substantially the same as that which in the lectures and publications of the 1920s is called "phenomenological psychology.")

But what does "phenomenological psychology" signify? Are we now confronted with an entirely new psychology, which will be pur-

[1]Husserl's questions of the constitution of the psychic (cf. *Ideas II*) and of transcendental psychologism (cf. *Formal and Transcendental Logic*, Ch. 6) are beyond the scope of this study.

Numbers between parentheses in the text refer to the volumes and pages of the "Husserliana" edition of Husserl's works.

sued with phenomenological methods and which is to replace the
old psychology referred to above? Are we faced with a new phenomenological discipline alongside "pure" phenomenology, probably in
the sense of "applied" phenomenology and analogous to pure and
applied logic and mathematics? Or has Husserl finally come to the
conclusion that his phenomenology is after all nothing but a
psychological approach taken to intentional events of consciousness
and its constitution of objects? There are other questions that the
term "phenomenological psychology" raises, and if, to clarify this
title, we study what he advances we can become somewhat bewil-
dered.

To begin with, in 1925—and quite obviously in contrast to *Ideas I* of
1913 and to Husserl's self-criticisms—the term "descriptive psychology" is accepted as applying to the *Logical Investigations* (IX 27). As
Husserl now states, where the analysis and description of the facts of
consciousness are concerned, the *Investigations* tended toward psychology. But, as Husserl also pointed out repeatedly later on, we are
already confronted there with analyses of essences (IX 38). The
procedure for analyzing essences had, however, been explicitly
characterized by Husserl thus far as "pure" phenomenology to set it
off from the procedures of psychology. Could it be then that "pure"
phenomenology is a kind of psychology after all, something like a
psychology of essence or an eidetic psychology?

This is just what Husserl came to maintain. From about 1925
onwards, he took the *Logical Investigations* as exhibiting a modification or transformation of the idea of descriptive psychology by
means of a new method, the eidetic method (IV 34f & 39); he speaks
of a transition to a new apriori eidetic-intuitive psychology. This is
what the title of the 1925 lectures, *Phenomenological Psychology*, hints
at. To differentiate it from psychology as an empirical science, Husserl sometimes calls it "pure" psychology and contends that "pure
phenomenology" might also be defined as "pure psychology"
(IX 217). Moreover, the course of these lectures shows that
phenomenological psychology had already been dealt with in part
and provisionally in *Ideas I* of 1913. And since Husserl described the
task of *Ideas I* as that of offering a first systematic approach to pure
phenomenology, one could be led to take the later phenomenological psychology as the continuation of *Ideas I* and at least part of the
completion of its program.

However, the danger of a deep confusion lurks here. It is explicitly denied that the "pure phenomenology" of *Ideas I* has any
thing to do with psychology. In the "Introduction" to *Ideas I* (III 4),

Husserl emphasizes that pure phenomenology is not psychology and that, in addition to terminological conventions, there are reasons of principle for excluding phenomenology from psychology, even though it also deals with consciousness and its acts. Psychology, even if descriptive, is there said to be concerned with the analysis of real events of consciousness in empirical subjects and hence is an empirical science, a science concerned with facts. It might seem that the manifest contradiction between the works of 1913 and 1925 about pure phenomenology and psychology might be overcome in the following way:

Phenomenology is not empirical psychology, but later Husserl outlined something like a nonempirical (i.e., an eidetic or pure psychology [IX 224]) and consequently could identify this psychology with pure phenomenology or at least with one part of it. Unfortunately things are not that simple, as appears from the very fact that as early as 1913 Husserl at least used the idea of an eidetic psychology in saying that phenomenology was the eidetic fundament of psychology (III 41). Yet it is also in *Ideas I* that one is repeatedly informed that, strictly speaking, this eidetic fundament of psychology is by no means psychology itself. Consequently it cannot be "pure psychology," as was nevertheless maintained in 1925.

III.

Now the confusions seem perfect. How are we to escape such inconsistencies? Can there be any success at all in defining the role Husserl attributes to psychology for phenomenology? It is my thesis that a most impure and even ambiguous usage of the term "pure" and its derivatives lurks in Husserl's phenomenology and that a clear understanding of the role of psychology for his philosophy can be obtained only if a sharp distinction can be made, notwithstanding their close connection, between pure and transcendental phenomenology. Then it is not by chance that when pure phenomenology shows up in 1925 as pure psychology this pure psychology or pure phenomenology is contrasted with transcendental phenomenology (IX 44, 222, & 247) and they are considered to be two sciences within phenomenology *qua* transcendental philosophy.[2] The distinction between pure and transcendental phenomenology is of the utmost

---

[2]IX 34 f. For a clear contrasting of pure (i.e., eidetic) and transcendental phenomenology, cf. the various sketches for the *Britannica* article published in IX 235 ff.

importance. That Husserl failed to make this distinction in *Ideas I* is a
flaw that makes at least parts of this early expression of transcendental phenomenology difficult to understand. Flaws of this sort become clearly visible only in the light of his later works.

In *Ideas I* Husserl makes constant and not merely casual use of the
expression "pure and transcendental phenomenology," or even that
of "pure or transcendental phenomenology," as if the two qualifiers
were identical or equivalent. This confusion—if not identification—of "pure" and "transcendental" in 1913 had hidden the true
signification of "transcendental" in that founding text. It also involved the sharp rejection, indicated above, of psychological trains
of thought, for the precise signification of "pure" is equally blurred
by its combination with "transcendental." To bring the role of
psychology in Husserl's phenomenology into focus thus requires
first of all attempting to clarify these terms. As is well known, Husserl starts out in *Ideas I* with two basic and intersecting distinctions,
namely that between fact (*Tatsache*) and essence (*Eidos, Wesen*), on the
one hand, and, on the other hand, that between real (*real*) and irreal
(*irreal*). The "pure or transcendental" phenomenology is not concerned with "facts" of "reality" such as are to be found when reflecting in the natural attitude but rather "reduces" such matters in a
twofold respect: (a) it employs eidetic reduction to get from "fact" to
"essence"; and (b), through transcendental reduction, it reduces
what is given in the natural attitude to the so-called "phenomena" of
transcendentally "pure" consciousness.

One must remember that these two reductions (both of them
called by Husserl, in a broad sense, "phenomenological reductions")
can be performed in whichever sequence one chooses and that the
final results either way are the same. It is also true, however, that
there will be phenomenologically different intermediary results
along the two different ways.[3] If eidetic reduction is performed on

---

[3]The difference between the two Husserlian reductions in terms of a "parallegram
of forces" was first emphasized by O. Becker in "Die Philosophie Edmund Husserls"
(*Kant-Studien*, Vol. 35 [1930], pp. 119 ff.). Becker does not mention the problem
arising from this diagram of whether or not the transcendental *eidos* of a fact can be
identified with the *eidos* of a transcendental fact. For example, let the individual
consciousness be the "fact"; then the transcendentally reduced consciousness (all
naive belief in the world inhibited), taken in its eidetic structures only, must be
regarded as the same as the eidetically purified consciousness (the consciousness
freed from all merely occasional features) functioning within the epoché. This view
can be established on the basis of various statements in Husserl, such as when he
postulates not only a transcendental fundament for the doctrine of all essences but
also an eidetic doctrine (e.g., of the transcendentally purified consciousness [V 75]).
This subtle question need not be pursued on the present occasion.

empirical facts (e.g., on cogitations pertaining to an empirical consciousness) one grasps their essence and—whatever the phenomenological complications might be—the essential genus (*generelles Eidos*) of the fact—in our example the essence "cogitatio"—and, finally, the *eidos* "intentional consciousness."

Husserl repeatedly defended the right of such an inquiry into essence against nominalistic attacks and later improved his description of the procedure (IX 72ff.), which was still quite inadequate in *Ideas I*, where he could continue to make the linguistic mistake of speaking of "seeing essences (*Wesensschau*)." Nevertheless, *Ideas I* already brought a number of eidetic data into focus; especially those concerning consciousness, which were later taken over into phenomenological psychology. To these eidetic data belongs, for example, the intentional structure of consciousness in general (i.e., its "being directed" toward something objective that is not an integral part of the consciousness itself). This leads to the fundamental difference between immanence and transcendence in general and between real (*reel*) and intentional immanence, specifically. Furthermore, "intentional consciousness" essentially implies the difference between actuality of understanding (*Erfassen*) and the inactuality of a merely implicit being conscious of something and the difference between the merely intended and the clearly grasped object to which the difference between signitive-symbolic givenness and evident self-givenness corresponds.

The exposition of these and many other essential features of consciousness forms part of an eidetic doctrine of consciousness. If a pure phenomenology is to be a science that deals with nothing but inquiries into essence, this gives us *a first signification of "pure."* Phenomenology would be pure phenomenology insofar as it is not concerned with empirical facts of reality, not even the psychic ones, but rather proceeds on the basis of eidetic reduction and in so doing abstracts from anything factual. It makes statements only about what is purely of the essence of its objects of inquiry. If this object is consciousness, then manifestly it has the field of research of eidetic psychology. As pure (i.e., as eidetically pure) it could supply the apriori basis of empirical psychology or the regional ontology of the psychic that, analogous to the regional ontology of Nature, is already the basis of all empirical inquiry into its field (IX 221 & 224). Eidetic reduction is consequently the mode of approach to such a realm of eidetically pure data.

There are a number of formulations in Husserl that justify such a concept of phenomenology as pure or eidetic psychology, and it makes sense to characterize such an eidetic science of consciousness, according to its claim and eideating method, as a pure (i.e., as an eidetically pure) psychology. Nevertheless, in 1913 Husserl refused to acknowledge a phenomenology pure in that sense. The reason is that such an eidetic science would still be a science of the natural attitude. It is true that the empirical character of data is abstracted from empirical facts (or events), but the essences attained remain essences of realities, are conceived of as such, and retain their relations with such realities in such a way that the latter are represented "through" or "in the light of" the cognition of essences and are taken as exemplary empirical concretions of the essences.

IV.

A purity quite in contrast to the merely eidetic purity from all that is factual is required for the "pure" phenomenology of 1913. This science is to be a science of *transcendentally purified phenomena*. The decisive step is not eidetic reduction but rather transcendental reduction or epoché, which entails a fundamental alteration of the natural attitude. In *Ideas I* Husserl unfortunately characterizes it as a "suspension" or "bracketing" of the world and of all transcendent being. Some later expressions are more appropriate: in the epoché the being of any kind of transcendent thing is left open; we "inhibit" any naive belief in existence; we no longer attach any validity to it, not to doubt its truth but because we make it the object of reflective analysis and aim at finding out which sense might legitimately be attributed to that which we normally regard as being; or we take it merely as something "meant as being." Thus any kind of being is kept within the epoché in a modified form, not as being that is unquestionably already given but as something that claims being and requires, with respect to this claim, phenomenological analysis. This is what Husserl had in mind in demanding that the transcendental reduction be employed to reduce all existence to pure phenomena of being or phenomena in pure consciousness.

But what sort of purity is this and what has it to do with psychology? Without a doubt it was Husserl's intention to conceive pure phenomenology as above all a science of the transcendentally purified phenomena. Such a purity is brought about by a procedure no longer followed within the realm of the natural thinking of the natural attitude. Rather, when the transcendental epoché is universally performed, the world itself becomes a phenomenon whose claim to being must be examined phenomenologically. The world is thus a phenomenon for a consciousness that can no longer be the natural empirical consciousness that is part of the world but rather must be what is disclosed as a transcendental consciousness in and through epoché. That it is a transcendental consciousness means, at the stage of *Ideas I*, nothing more than that it contains all transcendent being intentionally. How and in which way it "contains" the world as a phenomenon—namely, through sense-producing achievements and manifold syntheses of sense-constitution—is only to be shown later by the more refined procedures of intentional analysis or constitutive analysis in the narrower sense.

This sense-constitution and its genuine transcendental function remained a secret to the consciousness called "transcendental" in *Ideas I*. The predicate "transcendental" appears without its full signification's becoming visible. This is, however, the consciousness that, in 1913, was said to be "pure and transcendental" consciousness. As *transcendental* consciousness it is not yet transparent since it is only concerned with its phenomena as, so to speak, instantaneous products. It is a consciousness that still conceals its proper share in sense-giving performances. Is it at least fully transparent what this consiousness is as a *pure* consciousness? One must realize that, in starting out from the natural and prescientific attitude, the transcendental reduction can lead only to an individual transcendental consciousness. They are my cogitations alone upon which epoché is performed, it is my pure consciousness, as Husserl rightly formulates it, that is aimed at in the epoché. It may well be named "pure" consciousness insofar as all naive reference to transcendence is purged by transcendental reduction. This would include the transcendence of my own body, which then also becomes a "phenomenon," something experienced by me as a correlate of the noetico-noematic situation under the epoché.

It would take us too far afield here to discuss whether Husserl's conception of 1913 was still valid when, as a result, he considered the transcendentally pure consciousness to be a special and totally isolated region of being (III 110ff) or whether he may have fallen prey to his own metaphor of the "suspension" of the world. In any case, however, the purity of consciousness was meant even here to express its inner seclusion and this, quite plainly, is quite another signification of "purity" than pureness of essence expresses.

One must not overlook, however, that for this transcendentally pure consciousness there is no psychology brought into consideration, not even phenomenological psychology. For if psychology is to be a science it cannot be concerned merely with my individual con-

sciousness but rather must make general statements about consciousness. This was, however, already being done de facto in *Ideas I*,
because actually this "pure and transcendental" phenomenology
conceived my individual consciousness from the outset merely as a
potential, exemplary individualization of consciousness in general.
The noetico-noematic analysis of it leads to exemplary results for the
general structures of the *eidos* transcendental consciousness, although, it is true, this was not made very explicit. This signifies,
however, that the statements made in this "pure and transcendental" phenomenology are eidetic statements (*Wesensaussagen*), propositions about eidetic data, for which my consciousness serves only as
an exemplification.

To put this all more precisely, the "pure" phenomenology of 1913
is pure in a double sense. It is concerned not only with transcendentally
purified singular phenomena but also with eidetically pure data. In
other words, this phenomenology as transcendental phenomenology already implies the pure phenomenology of essence either in
being preceded by essential analysis of consciousness or through
having eidetic abstraction performed on the already transcendentally purified *singulum* (i.e., my own consciousness). Thus the proper
field of this "pure and transcendental" phenomenology is by no
means merely the transcendentally reduced fact of my consciousness but is instead the *eidos* of transcendental consciousness. There
are two ways to reach it from the natural and empirical attitude of
psychology—through eideation from transcendentally reduced
single facts or through transcendental reduction performed on the
previously eideated essence, of which my individual consciousness is
but an example.

V.

The inconsistencies that obviously arise in Husserl's work, where
the relationship between phenomenology and psychology is concerned, can now be explained in relation to two different ways of
phenomenological procedure. In *Ideas I* Husserl first tries the way
from the prescientific natural attitude toward a phenomenology of
essence but does not follow it immediately through to transcendental phenomenology, instead breaking off and returning to the natural attitude in order to show the way, in another direction, to the
transcendental phenomenology, which indeed is the main issue of
that text. With regard to this latter way, psychology as a transcendentally unreduced doctrine of the essence of consciousness does not

belong to phenomenology; thus it could not appear as phenomenological "psychology" in 1913.

The case is quite different in the lectures on phenomenological psychology of 1925. There Husserl at once (IX 44) distinguishes eidetic psychology from transcendental phenomenology as, however, he had already done implicitly in *Ideas I*. Only now he deliberately chooses the way from the prescientific natural attitude to the eidetic attitude and from there points the way to a transcendental and eidetic phenomenology (i.e., to "phenomenology" in the full signification of Husserl's term). Actually he never tried to follow this way in detailed steps in those lectures. But the intention to do so leads Husserl from the very beginning to regard eidetic psychology as phenomenology. Once acknowledged as phenomenological psychology, it is a starting point for the rise toward transcendental phenomenology. This is why in 1925 Husserl also pays particular attention to analyzing thoroughly the eidetic procedure, which still appeared somewhat mysterious in *Ideas I*, modifying the account of the method to include eidetic variation and thus to make the cognition of essences as certain as possible for further application in transcendental phenomenology.[4] Thus phenomenological psychology is not even now identical with phenomenology. Nevertheless phenomenological psychology now belongs to phenomenology.

We can at this point finally ask about the genuine nature of the mutual relationship of phenomenology and phenomenological psychology. Is it a matter of whole and part or could it be that one is the reason for or basis of the other? Again Husserl makes statements that at first seem paradoxical. On the one hand he says that phenomenological psychology should be the "natural point of departure" (IX 47) for the way toward transcendental phenomenology and on the other hand we are given to understand that phenomenological psychology is properly grounded through transcendental phenomenology (IX 222). Along with these statements come several remarks to the effect that epistemology must be founded on eidetic psychology. If we assume that one of the goals of transcendental phenomenology is a phenomenologically founded theory of knowledge, the latter statement may be interpreted in such a way that transcendental phenomenology is based on eidetic psychology.

---

[4]The most detailed analysis of eidetic method is to be found in § 9 of *Phenomenological Psychology* (IX 72ff). For a short sketch, cf. *Formal and Transcendental Logic*, § 98 (XVII 254f). *Experience and Judgment*, to which most references are made, contains only an abbreviated version of the analysis in *Husserliana IX*.

This contradiction is also merely apparent. When Husserl speaks of transcendental phenomenology as being the foundation of the eidetic or phenomenological psychology, he does so in precisely the sense in which transcendental phenomenology can perform a grounding role for all science in the natural attitude, namely, insofar as a transcendental regression is needed to explore the conditions of the possibility of worldy science in the sense-constituting functions of transcendental subjectivity. The former claim (i.e., that transcendental phenomenology must have its basis in eidetic psychology) can also be resolved since it implies a different explication of the term "basis (*Boden*)" (i.e., as starting point for phenomenological procedure. The foundational relationship is consequently a strictly one-sided relationship. Phenomenological psychology, which is not yet transcendental phenomenology, should be the "base camp," as it were, for ascending toward the latter (IX 293). Through the transcendental reduction of this psychology, the knowledge of essence can be deepened by being elucidated in its own constituting achievements, which, incidentally keeps Husserl's doctrine of essence from an untenable Platonism. Hence Husserl even speaks— and logically so—of transcendental phenomenology as "transcendental psychology" (IX 44 & 222).

VI.

The choice of the term "transcendental psychology" may be yet another proof of Husserl's profound interest in psychological problems, problems of a psychology, however, that is not empirical psychological science but its phenomenological basis. These are not problems concerning empirical laws or empirical applications. As far as eidetic psychology is concerned, it deals exclusively with eidetic laws of consciousness, especially its intentionality, which is the basic form of any kind of psychic life. These laws are to include all forms that may hold in principle for consciousness in pure ideality. Where empirical consciousness is concerned, the laws show themselves to be the structures that have always already been their fundament, their unbreakable apriori frame (IX 49), a form whose empirical filling can never occur except according to these structures, so that empirical psychology remains once again essentially and necessarily referred to them. As apriori necessary structures, they are not immediately concerned with empirical psychology. However, the fact that phenomenology thematizes and analyzes them is likely to have a certain impact on empirical psychology to the degree that it is important for the self-understanding of a positive science to clarify its basic terms and what is referred to by them. After all, nothing but this clarity in the usage of our terms was sought by Husserl in his phenomenological psychology.

The notion of *"transcendental* psychology," which is expressed only occasionally in Husserl's lectures of 1925, receives its full clarification only in his last work, *The Crisis of the European Sciences and Transcendental Phenomenology* of 1936. It may be a disadvantage to the reader that this paper has failed to deal with the *Crisis*, especially since Husserl, at the very end of this work, speaks of a possible "way" psychology may go toward transcendental phenomenology. This metaphor, often used in the development of Husserl's phenomenological method, has a peculiar signification in this last work, which can be seen in the fact that he no longer looks on psychology as in a specific relationship with transcendental phenomenology but finally identifies them. That identification, which involves some subtle questions about Husserl's concept of "phenomenological reduction," must, however, be made the subject of a separate paper.

RICHARD COBB-STEVENS

TWO

TRANSCENDENTAL AND EMPIRICAL
DIMENSIONS IN HUSSERL'S PHENOMENOLOGY

> If I imagined two kingdoms adjoining one another, with one of
> which I was fairly well acquainted, and altogether unfamiliar with
> the other, and I was not allowed to enter the unknown realm,
> however much I desired to do so, I should still be able to form some
> conception of its nature. I could go to the limits of the kingdom
> with which I was acquainted and follow its boundaries, and as I did
> so I should in this way describe the boundaries of this unknown
> country, and thus without ever having set foot in it, obtain a gen-
> eral conception of it. And if this was a task that engrossed my
> energies, and if I was indefatigable in my desire to be accurate, it
> would doubtless sometimes happen that, as I stood sadly at my
> country's boundary and looked longingly into the unknown coun-
> try which was so near me and yet so far away, some little revelation
> might be vouchsafed me.[1]

THIS PASSAGE FROM Kierkegaard's *Either/Or* may serve as a guide
for some reflections on the most enigmatic issue of Husserl's philosophy, the relationship between transcendental and empirical
spheres. The imagery of adjacent countries with closed frontiers
would at first seem to offer an inappropriate model because it invites
us to picture transcendental consciousness as an uncharted region
alongside the more familiar region of empirical things, events, and
persons. Moreover, it suggests that the two parallel regions can be
located within a broader map of reality as a whole. We know that
Husserl made a decisive break with any such view of consciousness as
a part of the world or as a region within an encompassing whole.
The text of *Ideas I* is most instructive in this regard because it begins
by considering consciousness as a psychic region opposed to the
region of things; it advances to a perspective that describes the
transcendence of things as a mode of givenness within immanence;
finally it recognizes that this new dimension of immanence ought
not to be understood as being situated within the coordinates of a

---

[1]Søren Kierkegaard, *Either/Or*, Vol. I, trans. David and Lilian Swenson (Princeton,
N.J.: Princeton University Press, 1944), p. 64.

pregiven world horizon.[2] There is an intriguing progression of spatial images involved in this succession of perspectives: consciousness is first a limited mundane region, then a broader zone of givenness for both immanent and transcendent objects, and finally an absolute dimension within which even the world horizon is constituted. Thus Husserl takes the metaphor of "region" to its limits by inviting us to think of transcendental consciousness as an enclosure or a zone which "has no spatio-temporal exterior and can be inside no spatio-temporal system."[3] If we are to understand what Husserl meant by the transcendental dimension, we must explore the implications of its description as a zone that has no outside, or as a "space" of manifestation that cannot be located within the context of the world horizon.

Nevertheless, even the most philosophically sophisticated reader of Husserl naturally tends to construe the sphere of immanence as a mundane region. Husserl notes that this same tendency prevented Descartes, Berkeley, and Hume from appreciating the transcendental breakthrough that they had intitiated.[4] These brilliant precursors of transcendental thought all conceived of consciousness as being situated within an unthematized zone of objectivity even while doubting or questioning the validity of every transcendent object. Each of these otherwise truly radical thinkers thus interprets consciousness as an objective reality, although each understood that every form of objectivity is given in and through the life of consciousness. The reason for this error is twofold: (a) our natural uncritical acceptance of the world horizon as the zone of all manifestation, and (b) the confirmation of this conviction by all ordinary scientific thinking. This presupposition, warranted in natural science, becomes an objectivist prejudice when it remains unnoticed in a fundamental reflection that claims to be a first philosophy.

Husserl stresses both the difficulty of arriving at a proper under-

---

[2]Edmund Husserl, *Ideas: General Introduction to Pure Phenomenology,* trans. W. R. Boyce-Gibson (New York: Collier, 1962). This progression is described in the 'Nachwort' (1930) written well after the original publication of *Ideas I* (1913) and included in Boyce-Gibson's translation as the "Author's Preface to the English Edition"; cf. pp. 8–12.

[3]Ibid., p. 139 (sec. 49); see also p. 138 (sec. 49) and p. 142 (sec. 51), where Husserl says that the absolute realm "has no boundaries which might separate it from other regions."

[4]Edmund Husserl, *Erste Philosophie*, Vol. I (Husserliana VII), ed. R. Boehm (The Hague: Nijhoff, 1956), pp. 60–70 and 148–182; see also Edmund Husserl, *The Crisis of European Sciences and Transcendental Phenomenology*, trans. D. Carr (Evanston: Northwestern University Press, 1970), pp. 73–90 (secs. 16–24).

standing of the transcendental sphere and the subsequent danger of losing the initial insight. This may explain the repetitive quality of his texts on the topic—the constant effort to clarify his position by renewed contrasts with the views of earlier philosophers of immanence and the frequent warnings that the transcendental attitude remains threatened by misunderstandings.[5] We may conclude that incessant struggle with the objectivist prejudice, along with the paradoxes that it generates, provides a privileged point of access to the deepest levels of Husserl's thought. We must first contend with the image of the transcendental as a mundane region if we are later to grasp how transcendental consciousness grounds all regionality. It is as though our understanding of Husserl's thought must pass through programmed stages: partial insight, subsequent regression to the natural attitude, analysis of the reasons for this relapse, and final clarity. The force of the natural attitude is such that it must be twice vanquished, once by the initial epoché and reductions and then again by a reinforcement of these procedures in conjunction with a critique of that which Husserl calls transcendental psychologism. Our tendency to depict the transcendental as something worldly, even after the reductions, must be recognized, explained, and surpassed. Kierkegaard's imagery of parallel kingdoms will help us to focus on this persistent error. Moreover, his theme of using the limits of the known as a clue to the bordering unknown will serve, on a different level, as a guide to further exploration of transcendental life.

There are three apparent difficulties that seem to weaken Husserl's conviction that transcendental subjectivity is the final source of the sense and validity of whatever is or can be: (a) the problem of intersubjectivity, (b) the priority of the lifeworld, and (c) the paradoxical relationship between the transcendental ego and its mundane correlate. This paper shall attempt to show that these issues appear as insoluable only when the transcendental is construed as a mundane region and that the point of Husserl's repeated elaboration of these problems is to dissipate this false view. When it seems that transcendental philosophy ends in factual solipsism or that the lifeworld resists reduction or that the transcendental ego must be part of the world it constitutes, then we have slipped back into the natural attitude. Husserl always takes the emergence of

[5] Edmund Husserl, *Erste Philosophie*, Vol. II (Husserliana VIII), ed. R. Boehm (The Hague: Nijhoff, 1959), pp. 120–123, and *Crisis*, p. 180 (sec. 53); see also Edmund Husserl, *Formal and Transcendental Logic*, trans. D. Cairns (The Hague: Nijhoff, 1969), pp. 241–242 (sec. 96b).

these paradoxes as signs of a relapse into natural reflection and as an occasion for explaining the necessity of a return to transcendental reflection. Three questions must be distinguished, if we are to justify this reading of Husserl in a coherent fashion:

1. What is the relationship between natural and transcendental reflection?
2. Within the transcendental perspective, in what manner does the transcendental ego "appear" to a phenomenological seeing?
3. What are the limits of transcendental reflection and of its linguistic expression?

The response to each of these questions will provoke a shift in perspective with regard to our original problematic, the project of coordinating transcendental and natural experience, so that at the end we shall both have discovered the inadequacy of the original formulation of the problem and have acquired "some little revelation" concerning its solution. This approach is consistent with Husserl's claim that progress in phenomenological insight is linked with reflection on method. In successive stages, therefore, this paper shall contend that (a) the relationship between transcendental and empirical can be grasped only within the transcendental perspective; (b) the primal life of the ego does show itself, but it does so in a mode of givenness that resists full thematization; and (c) an assessment of the limits of transcendental reflection and of its linguistic expression is intimately linked with insight into the ultimate ground of transcendental life. It shall be concluded that the locus of Husserl's most profound discovery is the "space" that transcendental reflection opens up between its own unthematic life and its thematic appropriation of that life. The interplay of anonymously lived and thematically reflected transcendental life yields an oblique or indirect seeing of the "being-for-itself" of the ultimate source.

I. THE NECESSITY OF MAINTAINING THE TRANSCENDENTAL PERSPECTIVE

Everyday natural reflection invariably grasps conscious acts as mundane events occurring within the space and time of nature. A brief analysis of typical acts of memory and imagination explains how and why this objectification occurs. When I remember an experience of seeing some object (e.g., a house) I *re*-present the object

along with the "I" of the original seeing, which, says Husserl, "is part
of the intentional essence proper to the remembered house as the 'I'
for whom it was there."[6] Moreover I reconstruct this event as occurring at a definite time and place. In an analogous manner, when I
imagine some fictive scenario, I either posit an imaginary version of
myself as participant in the fictive events or as pure spectator. In the
latter case, I am aware that the fictive scene appears to me "as if" I
were perceiving it, and hence I posit myself as a fictive perceptual
observer. In each of these instances, the original perceiving or imagining acts are easily confused with the acts that are represented as
belonging to the remembered or imagined zones of objectivity. In
the natural attitude, we tend not to notice the difference between
originally lived acts and their objective representations. It is as
though the original acts are pulled into the orbit of their objects. In
this attitude, every new object presents itself as belonging to a horizon of pregiven realities. This situation is not changed when the ego
reflects on its earlier consciousness of an object. It is true that consciousness now becomes a theme, but it does so in the context of the
pregiven world, which has validity at the same time. The now
thematized consciousness appears, in the same way as does any other
object, as belonging to the horizon of the world. The ego thus discovers itself within the world and then readily misunderstands itself
as a special kind of thing alongside other things. Our experience of
the stable and resistant character of things leads us to interpret them
as independently existing beings, situated "outside" the sphere of
consciousness. We next naturally interpret the "late" arrival of our
consciousness on the scene as the intrusion of a unique knowing
entity, whose nature is then described in metaphors borrowed from
the experience of things. The reification of consciousness is complete.

The purpose of the epoché and the reductions is to recognize this
interpretation precisely as an interpretation and as one that inaccu-
rately describes both the manner in which things are given to consciousness and the consciousness to which they are given. Thus the
celebrated bracketing of being is not an exclusion of something
given but an effort to reappropriate an original mode of givenness
that has been obscured. Husserl contends that, in fact, transcendent
things present themselves in a particular style of givenness within an
englobing zone of immanence. A careful description of this man-

---

[6]*Erste Philosophie*, I, p. 264. "Ich, das zu dem eigenen intentionalen Wesen des
erinnerten Hauses gehört, als das, für das es dawar. . . ."

ner of appearing also reveals the structural characteristics of the conscious life in which it appears. In similar fashion, the styles of appearing that characterize mathematical objects, images, signs, the psychophysical self, and other persons can also be brought to intuitive givenness. In correlation with each of these appearances, the processes in which they are achieved (i.e., the hierarchically ordered synthetic acts of consciousness) can also be made to appear. According to Husserl, therefore, many of the synthetic operations, which Kant thought could only be deduced as conditions of possibility, can actually be intuited with ever-increasing clarity. This approach isolates the concrete life of consciousness in its purity (i.e., as uncontaminated by the prejudice that interprets it as a mundane occurrence). Husserl mentions the theme of purification whenever he speaks of the relationship between natural and phenomenological reflection.[7] If we bracket the mundane status of each natural reflection, we reduce it to its pure givenness. It would seem that if we then applied this same procedure to the remembered and anticipated totality of our experience, we might arrive at a purified version of conscious life as a whole. Moreover, by bracketing the contingent aspects of any particular conscious life, we might grasp the eidetic structures of pure consciousness in general. Such was Husserl's method in his earlier works, but he later recognized that this step-by-step treatment, first of individual acts and then of my whole life or of any imaginable life, does not necessarily call into question the general context of objectivity, which remains the unthematized horizon of natural reflection.[8] Unless every reference to the "footing of the world already given as existing" is bracketed, we may still be tempted to look upon the pure concrete life of consciousness as somehow situated within an objective context, even though it is clearly distinguished from the life of the psychophysical organism in the midst of the world.[9] This last vestige of objectivism must be removed by a new epoché and a truly transcendental reduction that reduces the world horizon to its sense for consciousness.[10] Even the horizon of the

---

[7] Ibid., p. 268; see also Edmund Husserl, *Cartesian Meditations*, trans. D. Cairns (The Hague: Nijhoff, 1973), pp. 20–21 (sec. 8), and *Ideas*, p. 40.

[8] *Erste Philosophie*, I, pp. 269–276, and *Ideas*, pp. 8–12.

[9] *Cartesian Meditations*, p. 34 (sec. 15).

[10] *Crisis*, pp. 146–147 (sec. 38); see also p. 150 (sec. 40), where Husserl describes this transcendental reduction as the achievement of an attitude which places the philosopher "*above* the pregivenness of the world"; p. 151 (sec. 41) "It is through this abstention that the gaze of the philosopher first becomes fully free: above all, free of the strongest and most universal, and at the same time most hidden, internal bond, namely, of the pregivenness of the world"; see also *Crisis*, pp. 186–187 (sec. 55), *Cartesian Meditations*, p. 136 (sec. 58), and *Erste Philosophie*, I, pp. 271–272.

lifeworld is constituted in absolute transcendental subjectivity. Thus Husserl's "return" to the lifeworld does not involve a rejection of some form of metaphysical idealism in favor of realism but rather the incorporation of a final heretofore unnoticed sense within the zone of manifestation of every conceivable sense.

In the light of this analysis, we are now in a position to interpret Husserl's sometimes confusing references to the paradox of human subjectivity as subject for the world and object in the world. In the *Cartesian Meditations* Husserl unravels the constitutional levels involved in the appearance of a world that is experienced as continually there for all of us. He demonstrates that the sense of the common world is an achievement of transcendental intersubjectivity, which in turn is an achievement of my subjectivity.[11] This priority given to the Other does not indicate a break with the transcendental perspective but merely a recognition that the constitution of the Other is a necessary condition for the constitution of a common world. Obviously, as a human being, I am part of this intersubjective community and common world. In the *Crisis*, Husserl notes that this situation suggests the following paradox: "The ego . . . constitutes transcendental intersubjectivity, to which it then adds itself as a merely privileged member."[12] This "self-objectification" of the ego seems paradoxical, however, only when we misunderstand the philosophical solitude created by the epoché. The transcendental ego is not an objective individual who, having somehow cut himself off from the human community, generates, from his private experience, a sense of community and of the public character of the world. Husserl insists that the transcendental ego is "nothing mundane" and that all mundane realities (private world, public world, my soul, my psychic life, all of mankind, even "the whole ordering of personal pronouns") are phenomena for transcendental consciousness.[13] The transcendental ego "stands above" all natural existence as the "center of function" for the manifestation of everything objective. Husserl notes that this primal ego is so radically other than an objective individual that it "is actually called 'I' only by equivocation."[14] We must consider the mode of givenness of the transcendental sphere before we can pass judgment on the appropriateness of referring to this nonobjective locus of all manifestation as an ego. It is already clear, however, that terms like "ego" and "subjectivity",

[11]*Cartesian Meditations*, p. 84 (sec. 41), p. 100 (sec. 45), p. 107 (sec. 49), p. 136 (sec. 58).
[12]*Crisis*, p. 185 (sec. 54b).
[13]Ibid., pp. 183–184 (secs. 54a and 54b).
[14]Ibid., p. 184 (sec. 54b).

when applied to the transcendental, may no longer be understood in their ordinary senses. We shall see that the structures of psychic life serve as a guide to the structures of transcendental subjectivity. Husserl recognizes that this "parallelism" makes it easy to confuse the psychic and the transcendental. This is the temptation of transcendental psychologism, which can be avoided only by an "undeviating observance of the transcendental reduction".[15] Husserl is rigorously consistent on this point: after the transcendental reduction it is illegitimate to preserve some aspect of the natural attitude within the transcendental perspective. The most common error is to reduce individual objects to their transcendental sense, while still considering the transcendental ego itself and the lifeworld from an objectivist perspective. Every such mitigated version of transcendental philosophy tends to involve itself in insoluable paradoxes. Neither the transcendental ego nor its constitutive performances nor its objective correlates (human ego, Others, immanent and transcendent objects, lifeworld) may stand outside the transcendental perspective, either collectively or individually.

We may conclude that the transcendental-empirical relationship is meaningful only from the transcendental perspective. The appearance of the ego's life as a mundane event can be explained from the transcendental perspective, but the transcendental ego is always misunderstood from the empirical perspective. This discovery calls for a reformulation of our original problem. We may no longer speak of the juxtaposition of transcendental and empirical regions within a pregiven objective context. Since the world horizon manifests itself within the absolute zone of immanence, we must think of this zone as being situated literally nowhere, against no contextual backdrop. This is why it is not a "little fragment of the objective world," an expression Husserl used to describe Descartes' *res cogitans*.[16] Having arrived at this extraordinary notion of a contextless zone of all manifestation, Husserl was convinced that it had been his good fortune to have discovered "a completely new domain of knowledge, an absolutely self-enclosed domain, in which it was given to us to see what had never before been seen, and to think what had never before been thought."[17] We must ask whether or not this thought can really be had, or better, whether or not such a context-

---

[15]*Cartesian Meditations*, p. 32 (sec. 14); see also *Ideas I*, pp. 7–11.

[16]*Erste Philosophie*, I, p. 73, "Stückchen der objektiven Welt"; see also *Cartesian Meditations*, p. 25 (sec. 11).

[17]*Erste Philosophie*, I, p. 283, "ein völlig neuartiges, in sich absolut geschlossenes Erkenntnisreich sich erschloss, in dem nie Geschautes zu schauen, nie Gedachtes zu denken war. . . ."

less zone can be phenomenologically exhibited. Moreover, although we now understand that the transcendental ego is not a psychic entity in the midst of the world, we may still wonder about its status. The ego is clearly more than a mere formal principle or a bare condition of possibility. We are compelled to ask once again, What *is* the transcendental ego? If these new questions are to be addressed without relapse into the natural attitude, we must clarify the manner in which the transcendental ego "appears."

II. THE MODE OF GIVENNESS
OF THE TRANSCENDENTAL EGO

Husserl was convinced that it is possible to bring the life of the transcendental ego to an appropriate form of intuitive givenness. In this regard, he remarks that Kant's "mythically constructively inferring method" must be supplanted by a "thoroughly intuitively disclosing method."[18] Although lived acts of consciousness are directed toward their intentional objects, Husserl claims that it is always possible for subsequent reflective acts to focus on these originally conscious, but unnoticed, *cogitationes.*[19] The whole enterprise of phenomenology rests on the validity of this claim. The eidetic structures of consciousness cannot be investigated unless originally unreflective acts are subsequently accessible to reflection. We shall eventually take up Husserl's justification of this claim, but for the moment let us consider the series of images that he employs to describe the appearance of the pure ego in and through reflectively apprehended acts. *Ideas I* tells us that the ego "radiates" through its acts, that it is like a light source from which "beams" or "shafts" emanate.[20] Husserl notes that, although each visible ray is perishable, it seems nonetheless to proceed from a self-identical source. He concludes that we must regard the pure ego as a phenomenological datum. The false transcendence of the empirical self is bracketed by the phenomenological suspension, but the pure ego remains irreducible because it is characterized by a unique type of transcendence: "a non-constituted transcendence,—a transcendence in im-

[18]*Crisis,* p. 115 (sec. 30).
[19]"The unthematic, so to speak anonymous, but co-conscious life of consciousness is accessible at any moment in the form of reflection," ("Das unthematische, gewissermassen anonyme, aber mitbewusste Bewusstseinsleben ist jederzeit zugänglich in Form der Reflexion.") *Erste Philosophie,* I, pp. 261–262; see also *Ideas I,* p. 111 (sec. 38), and *Formal and Transcendental Logic,* p. 273 (sec. 103).
[20]*Ideas I,* p. 109 (sec. 37), p. 156 (sec. 57), p. 315 (sec. 122).

manence."[21] This last description is ambiguous, however, since *Ideas I* also makes vague allusions to the constitution of the ego in imma-nent time.[22] Another ambiguity emerges in *Ideas II*, which describes the self-identity of the pure ego in apparently contradictory sets of images. On the one hand Husserl describes the ego in the spatial imagery of a point: the ego's identity is that of an "I-pole," a "func-tional center," a pure point of departure; on the other hand the ego is a perduring life, structured by "habitualities," attitudinal stances that are retained in a cumulative fashion.[23]

How is it that the pure ego can be described both as constituted and nonconstituted, as a point-like pole and a perduring substrate of habitualities? *Ideas II* makes a preliminary attempt to make sense out of these complex and conflicting descriptions. The self-identity of the ego amidst the flux of *cogitationes* (its transcendence in imma-nence) should not be confused with the identity of a perceptual object through a series of profiles. The pure ego offers no such profiles; hence it has no objective content that might be described.[24] For this reason it is not constituted in the ordinary sense (i.e., as the object of a multiplicity of acts). However, the ego remains one single perduring life, whose permanence is other than that of the con-tinuity of its acts. At this point Husserl only hints at an explanation of this unique identity in multiplicity. The permanence of the pure ego, he says, derives from the deepest level of immanent time. The ego is constituted in immanent time as its unity or identity.[25] As a unity, it may be depicted as a stable point of reference, and yet as a temporal continuity it is most appropriately described as a perdur-ing style of living, with permanence of attitude and manner rather than of content. Finally Husserl insists that, although the ego is not an object in the ordinary sense, it can nevertheless be "grasped in reflection as a functional center in adequate insight."[26]

In his retractions to *Ideas I* Husserl explains that he had not dealt explicitly enough in this text with the problem of the world horizon. The bracketing of every object in the world leaves intact our un-thematized belief in the world itself as horizon of objectivity. This

[21]Ibid., p. 157 (sec. 57).
[22]Ibid., p. 216 (sec. 81) and pp. 307–308 (sec. 118).
[23]Edmund Husserl, *Ideen zu einer reinen Phänomenologie und phänomenologischen Philosophie*, Vol. II (*Husserliana IV*), ed. Marly Biemel (The Hague: Nijhoff, 1952), pp. 104–105 and pp. 113–119.
[24]Ibid., p. 105.
[25]Ibid., p. 102.
[26]Ibid., p. 105, "ist in der reflektiven, auf es als Funktionszentrum zurückgehenden Blickwendung adäquat zu erfassen."

omission was not prejudicial to the validity of eidetic analyses of subjectivity, taken in the sense of a pure phenomenological psychology. But, as we have seen, Husserl's thematization of the constitution of the lifeworld leads to a clear distinction between psychological and transcendental subjectivity. In his later works Husserl uses the expression "transcendental ego" to underline this all-important "nuance."[27] We must determine what effect this more explicitly transcendental perspective had on his subsequent analyses of the ego's givenness.

Cartesian Meditations repeats the themes of ego as identical pole and substrate of habitualities but distinguishes this polar-perduring sense of the ego from the transcendental ego taken in its fullness. The complete "concretion of the ego" includes the "I" as identical pole and basis of permanent style along with all of its *cogitationes*, their objects, and the world horizon. This complete and concrete ego Husserl calls "monad" (i.e., my factual all-embracing transcendental life in which every form of objectivity finds its sense). An eidetic reflection on this monadic ego brackets its particular and contingent features, thus revealing the *eidos*, the transcendental ego as such.[28] However paradoxical it may seem, transcendental reflection thus arrives at an *eidos* of a singular and unique ego; the essence is the sense of my ego, which resists the imagined variations of my factual transcendental life. It should be emphasized that this monad, unlike that of Leibniz, includes within its compass both the intersubjective sphere and the ordinarily unnoticed world horizon. As a thematic object of reflection, the *eidos* transcendental ego is clearly constituted and thus can serve as a transcendental guide to an ultimate constituting source.[29] The elucidation of this source and of its relationship

[27]*Ideas I* pp. 9ff. Husserl adds that "it must be felt at first as a most unreasonable demand that such a 'nuance' springing from a mere change of standpoint should possess such great, and indeed, for all genuine philosophy, such decisive significance" (p. 9).

[28]*Cartesian Meditations*, pp. 66–72 (secs. 31–34); for a more detailed analysis of Husserl's conception of the ego, see Joseph J. Kockelmans, "Husserl and Kant on the Pure Ego"; in *Husserl: Expositions and Appraisals*, ed. Frederick A. Elliston and Peter McCormack (Notre Dame: Notre Dame University Press, 1977), pp. 269–285.

[29]*Cartesian Meditations*, pp. 28–29 (sec. 12), and p. 53 (sec. 21); see also the unpublished manuscript Ms C 21 s. 11 (1931), which states that the transcendental ego as substrate of habitualities and monad is constituted: "dieses trans. Ich ist schon ein konstituertes Gebilde und als das einzuklammern. . . ." This reference was given to me by William Vallicella, who also made many helpful comments on an original version of this paper. For an analysis of many of Husserl's unpublished manuscripts on the primal ego, see Klaus Held, *Lebendige Gegenwart: Die Frage nach der Seinsweise des transzendentalen Ich bei Edmund Husserl entwickelt am Leitfaden der Zeitproblematik* (The Hague: Nijhoff, 1966).

with its constituted correlate becomes the task of a final stage of reflection, which Husserl calls "genetic phenomenology."[30] In *Cartesian Meditations* Husserl refers back to his earlier analyses of the structure of immanent time to explain both the possibility of transcendental reflection and the peculiar self-manifestation of the ego's life in that reflection. The "auto-constitution" of the ego in immanent time, a theme merely alluded to in *Ideas II*, now becomes the principal consideration. We have seen that the temporal flux of the ego's life can be constituted in its entirety as an object of reflection. Husserl struggles with the paradox that this possibility engenders: how can the unity of immanent time be thematized, since the condition of its thematization is the unity of temporality itself?[31] The flux that makes it possible for the form of time to appear to immanent reflection cannot itself be within the form of time. So we must clarify the relationship between reflecting transcendental life and the object of its reflection, the *eidos* transcendental ego.

Every form of reflection involves a "splitting of the ego": a presently reflective ego "looks down upon" a past ego, whose focus of attention was directed not to itself but to some object. In ordinary unreflective living, consciousness is so absorbed in its objects that Husserl describes its life as anonymous. How is it possible, therefore, that reflective consciousness can recognize an originally anonymous act as its own? Husserl answers that the "anonymity" of unreflective life refers not to some literally unconscious process but to an unthematic consciousness.[32] Intentional life is always operative before it is thematic, but this does not mean that the ego's self-awareness is the product of some agency or process other than itself. How shall we explain the unity of the ego's unthematic and thematic life, and yet account for the "gap" between the two, a gap made manifest by the fact that reflective consciousness can take its life as a theme only retroactively?

In *Ideas I* Husserl observes that a reflective grasp of originally unreflective experience is possible because of a structural unity that holds reflecting and reflected together, the flux of experience itself: "in the case of immanently directed . . . perception, perception and perceived essentially constitute an unmediated unity."[33] An immanently directed act is so constituted that its intentional object is given

---

[30]*Cartesian Meditations*, pp. 69–81 (secs. 34–39). I am indebted to a colleague, Richard T. Murphy, for a lucid analysis of Husserl's genetic turn.
[31]Ibid., p. 43 (sec. 18).
[32]*Erste Philosophie*, I, pp. 261–262, and *Crisis*, p. 109 (sec. 28).
[33]*Ideas I*, p. 112 (sec. 38).

as belonging to the same stream as itself. We must look to Husserl's analysis of immanent time for a fuller explanation of this unmediated unity. We experience the temporal modes ("now," "just-past," and "about-to-be") as phases of some temporal object. Since they are modes of the experienced temporal object, we must distinguish their flux from the flux in which they are experienced.[34] This is why Husserl distinguishes a constituting primal flux from a constituted immanent flux. The constituting flux, which he calls the "living present," is composed of a primal impression, along with retentions and protentions. The constituted flux is made up of the chain of immanent objects, interrelated according to the temporal modes. The central impression of the constituting flux is always correlated with a constituted now-phase; retention holds onto a former now-phase as just-past; and protention anticipates a forthcoming now-phase. Retention is not a separate act but an intentionality of a special kind, whose function is to preserve an elapsing experience within the purview of the living present, thus permitting it to become the object of a reflective act. While I am conscious of a now-phase, an earlier phase is included within the perspective of my present consciousness (i.e., as just-past). While I am conscious of the next phase, the former now-phase, along with my consciousness of it and the retentional consciousness of the earlier phase, is presented as just-past in a new retention. Thus each retentional modification and its corresponding retentional consciousness is assimilated by a subsequent retentional consciousness. Retentional consciousness must not be confused with reflection. Reflection takes an earlier unreflective act as an object; retention assimilates a receding unreflective act as an integral part of the "perspective" of a subsequent unreflective act.[35] The perspective of the receding act is contained within the subsequent act in a modification that makes the temporal sense of "subsequent" possible. Properly speaking, terms like "past" and "present" should not be applied to this level since retention refers to the assimilative "holding" process that makes the distinc-

[34]*Cartesian Meditations*, p. 43 (sec. 18); for a full justification of this distinction in Husserl's texts, see John Brough, "The Emergence of an Absolute Consciousness in Husserl's Early Writings on Time-Consciousness," *Man and World*, V (1972), 298–326.

[35]Edmund Husserl, *Zur Phänomenologie des Inneren Zeitbewusstzeins (Husserliana X)*, ed. R. Boehm (The Hague: Nijhoff, 1966), p. 118. Robert Sokolowski calls this cumulative effect a temporal profiling, and distinguishes it from the structure of spatial profiles in which transcendent objects are presented: "The profiles of spatial wholes are disjunctive and exclusive, the profiles of temporal wholes are assimilative." (Robert Sokolowski, *Husserlian Meditations: How Words Present Things* [Evanston: Northwestern University Press, 1974], p. 163.)

tion between past and present possible.[36] Consciousness can grasp itself reflectively in an immanently directed look because it originally holds itself together in an unmediated retentional continuity.

Husserl ascribes to the primal flux two different intentionalities.[37] In a "vertical" direction, the flux intends its objects in the various temporal modes and thus constitutes the stream of immanent time in which all objects appear. Of course, as we have seen, immanent objects appear as components of the flux, whereas transcendent objects appear as other than the flux. Brough points out that the metaphor of verticality serves to indicate that the primal flux grounds the constituted life of consciousness. In a horizontal direction, the primal flux retains its own elapsing phases; in other words, it retains its retentions of the constituted now-phases. Brough summarizes as follows: "The retention of retention is, in effect, the flow's self-retention and thus is at the core of the constitution of the flow's self-appearance."[38] The primary focus of the flow's intentionality is in the vertical direction, toward its intentional objects. Hence the horizontal intentionality is best described as an oblique or indirect form of consciousness. This oblique intentionality is the key to the auto-constitution of the ego. In constituting the temporal unity of immanent objects, the primal flux constitutes its own unity through an oblique awareness of itself. We must be careful not to imagine the primal flux as a mundane process. As the "presencing" of everything mundane, it cannot itself appear as a mundane object.[39] The image of horizontal intentionality says that this presencing shows itself obliquely in the process of displaying objects. Thus, although vertical and horizontal intentionalities may be distinguished, they cannot really be separated since they are two aspects of the same transcendental life. This life manifests itself in two different but interwoven dimensions: (a) as a reflectively constituted immanent object, the *eidos* ego or monadic complex (including polar ego, *cogitationes*, objects, lifeworld), and (b) in an oblique unthematic self-awareness. Neither of these manifestations can occur independently of the other, and their relationship is structurally determined. The oblique

[36]Edmund Husserl, *The Phenomenology of Internal Time-Consciousness*, trans. J.S. Churchill (Bloomington: Indiana University Press, 1966), p. 100 (sec. 36).

[37]Ibid., pp. 105–110 (sec. 39).

[38]Brough, "The Emergence of an Absolute Consciousness in Husserl's Early Writings on Time-Consciousness," p. 319.

[39]The term "presencing" is taken from Thomas Prufer, "An Outline of Some Husserlian Distinctions and Strategies, Especially in the *Crisis*"; in *Phänomenologie Heute*, ed. E. W. Orth (Munich: Verlag Karl Alber, 1975), pp. 89–104. Prufer describes retention as "the presencing of the absenced presencing." p. 95.

manifestation of constituting life shows itself only in the background of, and in inseparable unity with, the appearance of the constituted flux. On the other hand, the constituted flux (the unity of immanent time) shows itself in the constituting flux, which in turn is obliquely exhibited as a kind of temporality. In the following text Husserl brings the complex strands of this analysis together:

> . . . like two aspects of one and the same thing, there are in the unique flux of consciousness *two* inseparable homogeneous *intentionalities* which require one another and are interwoven with one another. By means of the one immanent time is constituted. . . . In the other is constituted the quasi-temporal disposition of the phases of the flux. . . . This pre-phenomenal, pre-immanent temporality is constituted intentionally as the form of temporally constitutive consciousness and in the latter itself. The flux of the immanent temporally constitutive consciousness not only *is*, but is so remarkably and yet so intelligibly constituted that a self-appearance of the flux necessarily subsists in it, and hence the flux itself must necessarily be comprehensible in the flowing.[40]

Although the life that thus shows itself in two dimensions is ultimately one life, we must be careful not to describe its quasi-temporal phases as a process occurring within the constituted time-frame. Sokolowski points out that we cannot legitimately say that the primal impression occurs at the same time as its constituted now-phase, or that retentional consciousness is simultaneous with the now-consciousness.[41] Simultaneity refers to the sharing by two events of an identical moment within an established time frame. Hence description of transcendental life in terms of simultaneity would subtly reintroduce an objective context within which that life might be thought to appear. There are no objective horizons, spatial or temporal, within which transcendental life may be situated. Once again we see that on every level phenomenology must constantly struggle with the objectivist prejudice.

Husserl is well aware that a drift toward objectivism is encouraged by the use of spatial and even temporal metaphors. For this reason he frequently makes corrective remarks designed to indicate the limits of their applicability. We have seen how he qualifies the spatial images used to describe the transcendental "zone." In the same vein he adds this cautionary note with regard to the use of temporal expressions: "We can only say that this flux is something we name in conformity with what is constituted, but it is nothing temporally objective."[42] Moreover, we may recall his remark that even the term

[40] Husserl, *Time-Consciousness*, p. 109 (sec. 39).
[41] Sokolowski, *Husserlian Meditations*, pp. 134 and 158.
[42] *Time-Consciousness*, p. 100 (sec. 36).

"ego" is used equivocally when applied to transcendental life. All of this indicates that the basic structure of the transcendental can be expressed only by approximation. Thus the clarification of the transcendental ego's mode of givenness culminates in a meditation on the limits of phenomenology. Husserl's claim that the auto-constitution of the ego cannot be thematically displayed but only obliquely disclosed testifies to his recognition of the limits to transcendental reflection. We must ask what effect this encounter with limit has on the original goal of phenomenology, the ideal of philosophy as a rigorous science based on foundational clarity. We must also ask whether a final objectivist presupposition escaped Husserl's vigilance. Many commentators have pointed out that the metaphor of "life" plays a largely unthematized role in Husserl's thought and tends to keep the transcendental excessively tied to the model of the psychic. Derrida explores the ramifications of this hidden commitment, noting that even Husserl's disassociation of transcendental subjectivity from mundane consciousness takes place within the context of a constant parallelism between the transcendental and the psychic.[43] We must determine to what extent this parallelism keeps Husserl's understanding of the transcendental within the matrix of traditional metaphysics: truth as disclosedness and being as present-at-hand.

III. THE LIMITS OF TRANSCENDENTAL REFLECTION AND OF ITS EXPRESSION.

It seems that the main function of the final genetic stage of phenomenology is to exhibit the oblique, unthematic givenness of the primal flux, and thereby to display the impossibility of bringing that flux to total reflective clarity. This is a strange conclusion for a philosophy committed to the ideal of securing an apodictically evident foundation. Let us recall an earlier formulation of the goal of phenomenology:

> Profundity is the mark of the chaos that genuine science wants to transform into a cosmos, into a simple, completely clear, lucid order. . . . Profundity is an affair of wisdom; conceptual distinctness and clarity is an affair of rigorous theory. . . . I dare to hope [that] philosophy [will] fight through from the level of profundity to that of scientific clarity.[44]

[43] Jacques Derrida, *Speech and Phenomena, and Others Essays on Husserl's Theory of Signs*, trans. David B. Allison and Newton Garver (Evanston: Northwestern University Press, 1973), pp. 10–15.

[44] Edmund Husserl, "Philosophy as a Rigorous Science," trans. Quentin Lauer; in *Phenomenology and the Crisis of Philosophy* (New York: Harper & Row, 1965), p. 144.

If the absolute foundation, the primal transcendental flux, cannot be thematized and hence described with "conceptual clarify and distinctness," then it would seem that the ideal of a rigorously scientific philosophy cannot be attained. Since Husserl clearly did not consider phenomenology a failure, how shall we interpret this disparity between the declared goal and the admitted result? One possibility is that Husserl maintained the aim of total objective clarity as an ideal situated in infinity on the grounds that pursuit of this impossible ideal might generate a progressively more adequate, but never perfect, disclosure of the founding level. If this interpretation is correct, then Husserl would have recognized the impossibility of absolute self-presence, while preserving the notion of truth implied in that infinite regulative idea. From a Heideggerian point of view, such a commitment to the Cartesian ideal of truth would have prevented Husserl from recognizing the concealment that makes possible the disclosure of everything that appears, the difference between Being and beings.[45]

It is certain that the discovery of the primal ego's mode of givenness was for Husserl an encounter with limit. However, I should like to suggest a different interpretation of Husserl's appreciation of that limit. It is true that he endeavored untiringly to disclose more fully the structure of the primal flux, while recognizing that such further disclosure could never be transformed into a totally thematic display. But the task of progressively more adequate disclosure could be achieved without maintaining the goal of total reflective clarity. I submit that his reason for this apparently fruitless methodological obstinacy was not an unnoticed commitment to some preconceived ideal of truth but a realization that only an unflinching effort to attain reflective clarity reveals its impossibility. Every major discovery of phenomenology has come as the result of a rigorous adherence to the method of eidetic disclosure and constant resistance to every attempt to limit the scope of the transcendental reduction. This procedure has permitted both the discovery of the living present and the analysis of its structure. The structural arrangement of horizontal and vertical intentionalities explains the essentially unthematic manner of the primal flow's mode of disclosure. Husserl was convinced that he had disclosed the "being-for-itself" of the primal ego in the only manner appropriate.[46] He had brought to scientific clarity the fact that the primal flux itself cannot

[45]See Hans-Georg Gadamer, "The Phenomological Movement"; in *Philosophical Hermeneutics*, trans. and ed. David Linge (Berkeley: University of California Press, 1976), pp. 170–171.
[46]*Cartesian Meditations*, p. 43 (sec. 18).

be brought to scientific clarity. There is no reason to suppose that this discovery brought a sense of frustration rather than one of achievement. Scientific clarity is perfectly compatible with the discovery of limit when the limit derives from a structural aspect of that which is being investigated, rather than from the obscurity of explanatory concepts. Husserl maintained the goal of reflective clarity because he recognized that only in the failure to attain that goal does reflective consciousness unveil its own life. Recognition of limit is an integral part of the disclosure of the primal flux. It is not as though some privileged, direct glimpse at the true nature of the primal source reveals by comparison the inadequacy of reflective descriptions. The structure of intentionality makes impossible any direct look at the primal source. The only access to that source is provided by the interplay of anonymous and thematic consciousness. We have seen that every attempt to focus reflectively on anonymous or unthematic life preserves the priority of the unthematic. For the reflective act, which takes an originally unthematic act as its object, necessarily has only an unthematic consciousness of itself. Thus reflective consciousness can never thematize its own constituting life. However, a second-order reflection may direct its focus on this interplay between thematic and unthematic and recognize the structural necessity of an irreducible gap between the two. When the life of consciousness is considered in its entirety the gap manifests itself as the difference between the thematized constituted flux and the anonymous constituting flux. If we attempt to collapse the difference between the two, we inevitably lose sight of the unthematic dimension. We might say, therefore, that the difference between thematic and unthematic is the "space" within which the primal source is disclosed. But we must not think of this space of disclosure as a context that precedes the transcendental source, as a pregiven horizon for its appearance. Rather the transcendental provides its own context since the difference between unthematic and thematic consciousness is both the locus of disclosure and the essence of the disclosed.

Emphasis on this difference preserves the transcendental context and thus enhances our oblique awareness of the primal flux. Understanding of the necessary thematic absence of the primal flux serves to make us notice its unthematic presence.[47] This more explicit manifestation of our unthematic awareness remains an oblique form of

---

[47]This is only one of the ways in which presence and absence interrelate. For a detailed analysis of the play of presence and absence as a philosophical motif, see Robert Sokolowski, *Presence and Absence: A Philosophical Investigation of Language and Being* (Bloomington: Indiana University Press, 1978). For example, Sokolowski notes

seeing, but becomes intensified by the critique of direct thematic seeing. We know that reflection always objectifies and therefore that thematized transcendental life necessarily appears as a constituted object. Our recognition of the imperfection of this thematic seeing converts it into a foil for displaying a heretofore unnoticed, but always present, oblique, unthematic seeing. Thus, a critical appraisal of the objectifying tendency of thematic reflection is integral to this indirect form of phenomenological exhibition.

The theme of a transcendental context for the display of transcendental life dispels a misunderstanding that may arise from one of Husserl's less fortunate metaphors—his description of the transcendental perspective as an Archimedean point of view.[48] This image suggests an observation platform above the earth but within the universe. There could be no more perfect imaginative representation of the way transcendental psychologism understands the transcendental (i.e., as a region other than the empirical but nonetheless situated within an objective horizon). In fact, the locus of transcendental viewing is neither within the world nor outside of the world (some godlike or other-worldly point of view); it is rather that unique but verifiable space provided by the reflective structure of consciousness. As the space for the presencing of all objects, it is not contained within the horizon of objective presence. Hence it cannot appear to an empirical point of view. That is why preservation of the transcendental context is the only way to disclose transcendental life. The temptation to look at the transcendental domain from the "outside" or from "above" must be overcome in the same manner as every other temptation to return to the natural attitude. The lure of naturalism appears at this deepest level of phenomenology as the seduction of a posttranscendental empiricism. Preservation of the transcendental context and of its oblique display of the primal source guards against such speculative excess.

Our acknowledgment of the objectifying tendency of some of Husserl's metaphors leads to a broader consideration of his failure to reflect on the influence of the linguistic matrix in which phenomenology was developed. We have noted that he often points

---

that the ordinary naming of something as present implies a "dimension of possible but excluded absence" (p. 28). Thus the possible absence of an object serves as a foil for highlighting its presence. When we attempt to thematize this play of presence and absence we engage in philosophical discourse, which in turn requires a kind of absence as a foil for philosophical presence: "The absence that works as a foil in philosophical naming is the unthematic anonymous awareness we have of presencing before we turn to it philosophically" (pp. 154–155).

[48]*Erste Philosophie*, I, p. 62, and *Crisis*, p. 80 (sec. 18).

out the inadequacy of spatial and temporal expressions but he never conducts a comprehensive inquiry into the implications hidden in the network of basic philosophemes. We have seen, for example, how his uncritical attachment to the metaphor of "life" may have lent an excessively "subjective" tone to his interpretation of the transcendental. Gadamer observes that Husserl's stress on the "anonymous" performances of transcendental life shows that he eventually interpreted the transcendental less exclusively in terms of the model of a self-present subject in the presence of objects and more according to the model of a more primitive form of life. Some passages seem to employ the metaphor of the living organism to suggest a prior organic unity, which grounds the subsequent polarity of subject and object.[49] Nevertheless the fact that Husserl does not make this nuance a central theme is revealing. As Taminiaux points out, the privilege given to the psychic region as transcendental guide always tends to keep Husserl's study of the transcendental within the confines of a theory of knowledge.[50] Heidegger's deconstruction of basic philosophical terms permits him to displace the theme of the transcendental, to loosen its moorings in the theme of subjectivity. The locus of the transcendental becomes a "there," a clearing in being. A comparison with this analysis highlights the limits of Husserl's problematic and of its linguistic matrix.

As we have seen, however, these limits do not prevent Husserl from discovering both the difference between nonobjectifying disclosure and objective manifestation and their necessary interinvolvement. The transcendental is the difference between oblique unthematic and direct thematic disclosures, a difference that does not show itself within the objective zone, although it grounds the possibility of every objective manifestation. Moreover, the "space" opened up by this difference gives the only access to the difference. We may conclude, therefore, that the confines of Husserl's prob-

---

[49] Hans-Georg Gadamer, *Truth and Method* (New York: Seabury Press, 1975), pp. 217–220. Gadamer cites a text from the *Crisis*, pp. 113–114 (sec. 29), in which Husserl, speaking of the subjectivity that functions at the ultimate or deepest level, describes its transcendental status as follows: "It belongs essentially to this world-constituting accomplishment that subjectivity objectifies itself as human subjectivity, as an element of the world. All objective consideration of the world is consideration of the 'exterior.' . . . The radical consideration of the world is the systematic and purely internal consideration of the subjectivity, which 'expresses' [or 'externalizes'] itself in the exterior. It is like the unity of a living organism, which one can certainly consider and dissect from the outside but which one can understand only if one goes back to its hidden roots. . . ."

[50] Jacques Taminiaux, *Le regard et l'excédent* (The Hague: Nijhoff, 1977), p. 180; see also the introduction (ix) and pp. 93–95.

lematic and of its unexplored linguistic matrix tend to obscure the breadth of his final discovery. Although he does explicitly disassociate the transcendental from every mundane region, its parallelism with the psychic region generates the distressing paradoxes of transcendental psychologism. His critique of this fallacy and of the confusion that it brought about in earlier philosophies of immanence shows that he intended to give to the traditional themes of immanence and subjectivity a radically new sense, "a thought never before thought" in the history of philosophy. But the long history of these terms exercises a kind of gravitational pull on Husserl's thought. This accounts for the sense of the need for constant restatement and clarification, communicated by his texts. There is much to be said, however, for this struggle to imbue traditional philosophic expressions with new meanings. It is easier to filter out inappropriate senses attached to traditional words than to control the multiple connotations of imperfectly defined neologisms and radically new metaphors. At any rate, Husserl was convinced that confrontation with traditional philosophic language and a careful mapping of its limits would most appropriately disclose the uniqueness of transcendental subjectivity.

This conviction recalls a theme enunciated in Kierkegaard's text: the indefatigable desire to be accurate in tracing the limits of the known kingdom—a phrase that perfectly describes Husserl's methodological caution—is rewarded with some insight into the unknown kingdom. We have already commented amply on the ambiguities of the imagery of adjacent regions as applied to the relationship between empirical and transcendental. But if we bracket the spatial connotations of Kierkegaard's analogy, we find that the theme of the limits of the known as revealer of the unknown is more instructive. We appreciate the status of the transcendental only by approaching it in this oblique fashion. This is the lesson of Husserl's untiring exploration of the limits of transcendental reflection and of its philosophical expression.

THREE

THE ORIGIN OF OTHERNESS AND OWNNESS IN THE LIVING PRESENT:
TOWARDS A PHENOMENOLOGICAL DESCRIPTION OF THE GENETIC CONSTITUTION OF THE OTHER

I. INTRODUCTORY: ON PHILOSOPHIZING IN THE CARTESIAN MODE

THE ACHILLES' HEEL OF THE CARTESIAN APPROACH in philosophy is the charge of solipsism from which it must defend itself if it is to maintain any credibility. How do I know that the world I live is not quixotically my own? It is built, to be sure, upon the indubitable certainty of my cogito; but it is also moored to it, limited by it, in ways that make of discourse among agents an impossible task—bridging the chasm of their reciprocal dubitability. The ones dissolve in front of the other who, singly anchored upon the apodicticity of his own existence, views them through an unreliable mesh of analogies and inferences, or so the traditional position has it. The resort to God as *fundamentum tremendum et inconcussum* falls short of the task, undermined by the very ingeniosity of its inventor. The magnitude of the problem reveals the flimsiness of the solution for it shows far too emphatically the discrepancy between the means used and the rich prize that a solution would secure—namely, a genuinely founded intersubjective world where the truth is one for all, and each may know it in and for itself. Doubting bears only the negative imprint of my knowledge of what truth, ideally, may be. It cannot be surreptitiously turned inside out and transformed into the direct, *ontologically founded*, acquaintance with a truth that is "wholly other," as Descartes thought it might. Hence the resort to the ontic "cause" of *my* ideas, where that cause is taken to be "wholly other," remains beyond what methodical doubt can allow. The encounter with the truth has to be limited to the meeting of intention and occasion, of form and actually lived experience.

The only certainty I have *qua* living and lived experience of doubting is the certainty of the *cogito, sum*. It is *actually* apodictic and, because of that, the *only* proper foundation for whatever other truths there are. Hence it is strictly *and solely* within the confines of what *cogito, sum* bespeaks and "contains" in each "living now" that certainties can be recognized. From this thick "living now" with its structurations, the apodicticity of the *cogito sum* may be traced back to an actual founding layer and *its* form. Thus, abandoning any ontological thesis concerning the "wholly other," I can trace my doubting, my *cogito* in the form of *dubito*, back to the intentional structure of my *cogitatio* (what I enacted *qua res cogitans*), and show how doubt means nonfulfillment of that intentional structure: *is* the *act* of nonfulfillment my *cogitatio becomes* "now." The "nonfulfillment" contains both the intentional structure which is unfulfilled by whatever upsurges in the present "now," and that upsurge thematically apprehended as nonfulfilling — not by inference, but by direct perception. Doubt can therefore be analyzed into separate moments: (a) the neutral presentation of nonfulfillment with its empty intentional structure; and (b) the thematic and thetic judgment "I doubt that . . ." with which the neutral presentation of nonfulfillment of an intended instance of "it is the case that . . ." can be represented with apodictic congruence.

Making the singular event "awareness of this nonfulfillment" thematic by means of bracketing and suspension (the phenomenological "reduction," which places out of consideration the question of the ontologically "wholly other"), reveals with evidence the intentional structure (which remains empty) *and* its emptiness. Making the event of nonfulfillment thematic transforms this event into the presentational referent to the intentional structure, subtending the later judgmental awareness "*It is the case that* my previous intention was unfulfilled" (the neutral presentation of fulfillment is "now" present, and what is fulfilled is the intentional structure governing all awareness of the type "It is the case that. . . .") The intention to knowledge has thereby been fulfilled in the reflexive move that made thematic the previous unfulfillment, and the neutral presentation of fulfillment can be converted through a judgmental awareness into a *positing* awareness with a full guarantee of apodicticity.

The phenomenological description of the Cartesian *cogito* thus results in the same "constat" of apodicticity, the same lived awareness of truth in a *de facto* instance of knowing, which, under further phenomenological probing (i.e., the transcendental reduction) reveals its *formal* and *legitimizing structure* (the *act-form* "knowing"). This structure shapes *both* the unfulfilled "now" in its unfulfillment (though it is now bracketed, and the act shaped by the structure is suspended) and the fulfilled "now" for which the previous, suspended and bracketed living-present is the fulfilling content. The structure is therefore *of* neither lived moment but, almost in a Kantian sense, occurs *with* both, *transcending* them both. The self-identity *is* independent of *my* volition, though the enactment of the act of awareness it prescribes is not. As formal structure, its self-identity and its presence are the sole source of de jure legitimation the contents of the awareness so-structured have insofar as they present themselves as "fulfilling." Correlatively, such contents as announce themselves as nonfulfilling derive whatever de jure legitimation they have for presenting themselves as such from this overarching operational structure as well.

The transcendental reduction enables me to recognize the proper ground for de jure legitimation in the structures of intentionality, which subtend (transcend) whatever lived-now they shape. This ground, after a suitable generalization formally presented from *one* intentional operational structure to *any*, Husserl named "the transcendental ego." It is purely formal, devoid of lived content and "does not act," albeit, insofar as the Husserlian phenomenologist faces himself within its pure perspective, a "transcendental mental life" makes itself manifest within *his* stream of lived experiences, and its actual description involves either cumbersome paraphrases or grievous ambiguities. The small point that has been gained over the Cartesian description is that the phenomenological description has revealed the source of apodicticity to be purely formal and purely within the structures of *cogitatio* without any recourse to some "exterior" ontological source. The "transcendence" of the transcendental realm is "immanent," as Husserl remarks in the last of the *Fünf Vorlesungen*. Again, the transcendental realm is not *of* mental life but it appears *with* and *through* it.

The phenomenological "principle of principles" forces me to take this appearing on its own terms and without recourse to any ontological explanation of it. In so doing, however, I remain ontologically moored to my own existence and can be accused of solipsism. Still, somehow the very apodicticity of the foundational truth I have encountered — *cogito, sum* — argues against solipsism. It is not my whim; nor is it subject to appear and disappear at *my* whim. Precisely, it is *independent of my imaginings and of my desires*. I *have to* believe it *whether I want to or not*. And this is not some contingent, psychological necessity; it is a *formal* necessity that *announces itself to me as independent of me*.

The grounding of whatever objectivities I observe and experience in formal structures traceable to this transcendental realm suffices to guarantee their *de jure* legitimacy. Yet, until such time as I have shown in what way this realm *is* formally independent *of* me — until such time as I have grounded in its structures the appearing of otherness, the intra- and the extra-subjective, the other, the inter-subjective and the apodictic uniqueness of transcendental subjectivity as the proper locus of the epistemically intersubjective — all I have is a slight improvement on the Cartesian description. I have not answered the unavoidable challenge to the Cartesian position which, equally unavoidably, opens the door to all philosophic realativisms. "Philosophy as a strict science" appears as a chimaera, a quixotic quest in which Cartesian knights tilt at their ordinary windmills while other philosophers grind ordinary millet within the limited but pragmatically efficient confines of empiricistic common sense.

The present essay is a rough sketch of what such a grounding might entail. It is what the Spanish would call a series of "Apuntes," a word covering anything from "notes" to "prompting cues." Here it shall be used to denote that I am going to reconnoitre the terrain with seven league boots, well aware that I shall stride over many dark valleys, hopeful nonetheless that the path I think I have found is practical for all.

II. THE STARTING POINT: *MY* LIVING PRESENT

1. THE HUSSERLIAN BASE.

Every Cartesian philosopher must begin with his own solipistic *presence*. The dimension of that "living now," its structures, were for the first time described as part of the phenomenology of the operation of constitution by Husserl in the texts assembled under the title: *Vorlesungen Zur Phänomenologie des inneren Zeitbewusstseins*. In these texts a new phenomenological "psychology" appears: the a priori description of the prerequisite for the operation of performance by any awareness whatsoever. These are not *ontological* prerequisites. Whether or not there are or can be awarenesses that are so equipped as to perform all, part, or none of these operations is beyond the purview of the descriptions of the prerequisites themselves. What the descriptions give is strictly and solely the operational structure "performance" (albeit in the text the performance described is that of selected operations), complete with the minimum ontological requirements a *purported* performer would have to meet.

An awareness thus attempting a particular constitution of sense would have the following fundamental features:

1. A living "now" polarized into
2. A primal perceived upsurge, and
3. A primal perceiving presence, neither of which can be *actually* separated one from the other.

The living "present" is thus a *continuum* — "upsurging presence to" and "passively receptive aware-living." Analysis may emphasize one pole rather than the other, but their intrinsic mutual reference and interconnectedness is as indissolubly fused as that of the actual basis for an optical illusion involving the alternative possibility of two mutually exclusive perceptual patterns (the Vase or the Rabbit illusions come to mind as possible examples here).

"Worlded awareness" and "lived world," the two fused aspects of the living present, are the minimum required ontological basis upon which every other "sense," whether emotional and preverbal or doxic or even epistemic, is "constituted." This continuum of sentience — "perceiving-being perceived" — is eidetically the *actual* possibility of every sense whatever including whatever sense one makes eventually of the "Being" or "beings" thus manifested. Every awareness of any kind whatsoever is thus eidetically and originally such a possiblity, although in point of fact the contingencies of embodiment may place *noneidetic limitations* on what a particular awareness can accomplish. Such noneidetic limitations involve contingencies governed by causal laws having to do with the context within which the awareness is born (and by which it is borne) and not with the *formal* possibilities eidetically open to the awareness *qua* awareness; traditional psychology of whatever kind concerns itself with these causal laws, which have no place in eidetic phenomenological psychology.

Nor is there room in eidetic phenomenological psychology for "fundamental ontology" and its existentialist analogues. Moreover, their purported solution to the question of solipsism — the opening to Being in its immediate and pristine manifestation — can be shown to be an apparent solution only. It may be well to dwell on this in order to dispose of the tempting misunderstanding according to which Husserlian phenomenology finds the foundation its initiator sought in vain, in a return to ontology by way of Heidegger's reinterpretation of phenomenology, or by way of the Sartre-Kojève resort to Hegelian-Marxist dialectics.

2. The Paradox of the Ontological Turn: It Affords an Escape from Neither Solipsism nor Eidetic Universality.

Phenomenological psychology focuses on the formal structures of any awareness whatever. It describes *eidetically* the "given" of the problem that *any* aware living confronts "really and actually," that is to say, from within the eidetic limits embodiment per se has placed upon its unique presence. Phenomenological psychology is thus antecedent to any enactment problem stemming from the limitation of actual embodiment and hence prior to any behavioral or experimental psychology since it describes the field within which experimental and behavioral studies will place themselves. Furthermore, any ontological sense, making verbally manifest that which is ontically lived within the contingencies of embodiment, is thus doubly derivative from the eidetic point of view. First, it is based upon the actual preverbal ontic sense (or understanding) which the specific living presence concerned "is" (a particularization, or instantiation, of the eidetic "living awareness lived world" which phenomenological psychology describes); and second, it purports to make manifest in its temporality through authentic expression the *ontological* value of this ontic understanding. Thus it derives from a reflexive questionning of this ontic understanding a "true" characterization of the specific manifestation of "Being" which this one instance "is" within the uniqueness of its actual embodiment. No one will quarrel with the "truth" of the description thus reached, nor with its existential limitations to the "being" of the living-presence involved. Drowned in the contingencies of embodiment (psychological, sociological and historical limitations) this "truth," in its historicity, is, when looked upon somewhat critically, nothing more than the self-manifestation of presence to itself with whatever flavour it may be felt to have. Far from breaking through the dangers of solipsism, it makes of solipsism a virtue since it hypostasizes the actual opacity of living-presence into an eidetic law of its manifestation, and asserts operationally ("non-dogmatically," as Sextus might put it) that such opacity can *never* be dissipated.

3. The Genetic Constitution of the Real; Stasis, Flux, the Law of Partial Actualization; the Origin of Otherness and Ownness.

a) THE GENETIC CONSTITUTION OF THE REAL; STASIS, FLUX, THE LAW OF PARTIAL ACTUALIZATION.

All we have then, as the *actual* starting point, is the "living-awareness lived world" Husserl has recognized and whose main features I have described earlier without any ontological colouring whatever. Husserl's description, in the *Vorlesungen zur Phänomenologie des inneren Zeitbewusstseins*, begins at a high level of conscious life and concerns itself ultimately with the constitution of atemporal objects such as mathematical objectivities. He is thus led to recognize the rather complex features of a complex consciousness at home in both the doxic and the epistemic layers of objectivities. The predoxic, passively receptive layer is barely recognized and not analyzed very searchingly. Later works, such as the studies which formed the basis for *Erfahrung und Urteil*, and those posthumously published in *Analysen zur Passiven Synthesis*, provide more searching forays into the phenomenology of the predoxic. In the *Vorlesungen*, as we have seen, Husserl describes the primal perceptual upsurge and the perceiving aware-living which a *living "now"* "is." Such a living presence Husserl recognizes as the origin of a "stream of lived experiences" and of the unity of such a stream. Thus, he describes the "intentionalities" which constitute objectivities within that stream. "Retention," "protention," both immediately observable in the perception of any temporal object, evidence a "passive synthesis" through which a thickness of sorts inflates the living "now," into a living "present," which, later, in the *Analysen*, will be referred to as a "field of presence." We need not go into the phenomenologically important descriptions of, and distinctions between, primal memory and the more usual kind, or between recollection and presentification; nor do we need to retrace the constitution of essentially temporal objects, that of objects intrinsically moored to my field of presence, or that of completely alocal objects (that is to say, objects essentially and intrinsically separated from, impervious to, my field of presence or my stream of lived experiences). Although these are fundamental phenomenological descriptions which we may find useful later, they belong to levels higher than the one with which we shall be concerned here, namely, the protodoxic or preverbal layer.

At the predoxic layer, Husserl recognizes a passive receptivity passively synthesizing moments of the primal perceptual upsurge into receding continua retentively held.

Observing the living-awareness in the receding thickness of its living presence, Husserl characterizes the "locus" of this recession as a "flow of lived experiences," calls it the "absolute flow of consciousness," adds that it is a flow "only metaphorically." In the context of that description one is no longer sure whether (for Husserl) what is being characterized is the objectivity naively beheld in its ontological presence, or the ultimate structural prerequisite to the action of performance. Husserl's own hesitation is apparent here in his suggestion that the term "flow" be taken only as a metaphor.[1]

What the phenomenological reduction practiced here reveals is a fundamental scission within the living presence. Although the "lived world" and the "worlded awareness" are two fused moments of one and the same presence, and one cannot *really* separate them, a double asymmetry appears once this predoxic reduction is performed. On the pole of awareness, the "protointentionality" (which the awareness is in essence) opens eidetically to *two possible* aspects —*flux* and *stasis*. *A living-awareness, by essence, is receptivity to both stasis and flux.* On the pole of the world, in any one *specific, actual, primal perception,* only *one* such aspect makes itself really manifest as the one aspect the world *is (the Law of Partial Actualization;* cf. the above-mentioned essay). Thus eidetically, the living-awareness is always open to more than what the world makes *actually really* present. And *actually* the world makes *really* manifest *only* one of the aspects to which the living-awareness *qua* living-awareness is open. The preverbal, primal experience of presence is the experience of this discrepancy through which all Berkeleyan illusions disappear. The world announces itself as irreducible to the perceiving activity of consciousness that it fulfills only on its own terms, and only partially.

b) THE ORIGIN OF OTHERNESS

Immediate Resiliency — In the confrontation with living presence, through the disappointment of partial fulfillment, the world announces itself as indifferent to consciousness, resilient in front of it and *immediately* independent. Thus the primal experience is one of lack, dissatisfaction, estrangement. The world announces itself as "all there is" in that it completely fills the perceptual field of living presence, and it announces itself as indifferent to consciousness. Awareness, at the predoxic and direct perceptual level, *is* this dissatisfaction which permeates the whole field of presence. Because

---

[1]As I have remarked in another study (Notes on the genetic constitution of the Real—*Cultural Hermeneutics*, Vol. 1. Nbr. 2, 1973, pp. 225–250), "flow" is an ontologically-weighed metaphor, one that is not intelligible except in contrast with some "permanence" of some kind. Later, Husserl terms the living present: "*Stehend-Strömend*" (remaining-flowing), in an effort to go beyond the confines of the metaphor of the flow. In a still later context, the reference to the living present as a "field of presence" ("*Präsenzfeld*") avails itself of the contrasting "remaining" ("*Stehend*") aspect. In the essay just mentioned I argue for the necessity of a bracketing and a suspension of these ontologically naive characterizations, and I attempt to sketch what predoxic structures (and hence protointentional structures), "constitute" (if one can call it that) either of these ontological colourings in naive mesmerization.

we are dealing here with the preverbal layer, we must be careful not to let the discreteness of words and concepts limit unduly the range and the force of our descriptions. The dissatisfaction permeates all the living present; the indifference is equally total. Any notion of solipsism ends here. At the heart of Cartesian subjectivity properly observed lies the incompatibility of the world with the awareness living it, and the world's *immediate resiliency* to awareness. There can be no later illusion of solipsism: the world announces itself to the awareness as fundamentally impervious to it. This, at the lowest level, is the Gorgon face we know at the doxic level as death.

We have reached here the *origin of otherness*. The world is immediately resilient in its refusal to fulfill the protointentionality in both its objectives. *Immediate resiliency is the first aspect of otherness and the most fundamental one.* It appears to the living-awareness as dissatisfaction; not a dissatisfaction thematized, nor even reflexively intended as the self-presence of the living-awareness to itself. It is apprehended merely as the flavor of the present out-there (objectively) as the aura the world has, the way it feels to the awareness in its naive thematic self-oblivion and pre-reflexive self-presence. The world is apprehended as unsatisfactory, and the present is apprehended as unsatisfactory—the living-presence *is* this dissatisfaction without any ascription of any kind as to either cause or proper origin. The living-awareness as it lives the world in quasi-solipsistic living presence, in effect encounters the *immediate resiliency* of the world and marks this otherness through its immediate dissatisfaction. This is the first appearance of otherness. It *immediately* complicates itself, in a manner which I must now describe briefly before turning to the origin of ownness.

Mediate Resiliency—The living-awareness, as living-presence, in the immediacy of its living presence, experiences the world as unsatisfactory and "at this very same point," simultaneously (this is not chronological and implies no time span) polarizes itself as receptivity to whatever might satisfy it fully, i.e., to the aspect the world has not presented itself as realizing.[2]

When the world has announced itself as *flowing, for instance,* the polarized awareness now filters in passive synthesis all elements of

[2](cf. on all this, the *Cultural Hermeneutics* essay mentioned above). The living presence is no longer the unstructured locus of primal upsurge. Rather it scans what upsurges in primal perception for the missing aspect of reality with which to satisfy itself at last. As I have shown in more detail in that essay, this is the origin of protention and retention, the origin of the passive synthesis Husserl has described.

the primal perceptual upsurge which might represent, however fleetingly, a permanence of some kind. These real elements, experienced really as flowing, are not experienced simply in the momentaneity of their flow. They become the object of a fascinated gaze which selects from the upsurge whatever perdurance it can retain from each of these elements *for as long as the upsurge allows.* The passive association overcomes the instantaneity of the initial encounter with a particular perceptual element by holding unitarily (fusing associatively) with it those moments of the continuing primal perceptual upsurge "akin to it." "Akin," that is to say, not in any deductive or even comparative *process*, but without process, in the direct fulfillment (perfect or partial) of the protention.

In this light, the protention reveals itself to be merely *the inertia of receptivity* turned toward what is upsurging with the configuration of what has just upsurged and—because it is passive receptivity—expecting "no change."

Thus (for example) this *nexus* of perceptual elements (colour, smell, touch), which I shall later be able to identify verbally as a "ball of wax" while I hold it in my hand (another and different nexus) within the full horizonal configuration of what is perceptually present now, *preempts* by dint of inertia what I expect passively from the upsurging perceptual continuum. Should the "ball of wax" explode in my hand, I shall be surprised—not because, knowing it to be a ball of wax, my conceptual expectations have been betrayed; but because, experiencing *passively* my field of presence with this or that perceptual nexus within the perceptual continuum, *any* change is "unexpected" and therefore startling. Nor does the change of the ball of wax held in a spoon over a flame, as Descartes describes it, come any less "startlingly" when viewed strictly from the point of view of first encounter in primal upsurge and for the same reason (the inertia of passive receptivity). In the experiment Descartes describes, the primal perceptual continuum of the field of presence *within which* a perceptual nexus (the ball of wax) changes in all its particulars, *remains itself comparatively constant.* The perceptual continuum as such is primary to the recognition of the different sensory fields (a rather complex set of unitary moves involving the selection of perceptual aspects according to the senses affected, hence involving on the part of the awareness a higher stage than the one considered here, a stage in which abstraction has been made of the very concommitance we are describing here). Thus, the "idea" of wax to which Descartes somewhat mysteriously refers, need only be the perceptual nexus which singles itself out passively through the concommitant variations of colour, smell, and state, while every other aspect of the field remains constant. The inertia of passive synthesis, protended towards this constancy, provides the context within which appears the startling unfulfillment of some of its elements, instantaneously and simultaneously varied in the primal perceptual upsurge. I never have to deduce from an idea the unity of the change (nor does Descartes claim that I do; some of his detractors did, and demonstrably wrongly, it seems to me). This unity, properly described phenomenologically, is the concommitance of variations within the inert context of a passively synthesized primal, perceptual continuum as it occurs in the field of presence of a living "now."

Thus, any change in the perceptual continuum except those the living-awareness *actively* initiates (a different phenomenological region, detailed later with a description of the genetic phenomenology of the "sphere of ownness") appears as another instance of the resiliency of the world, another estranging encounter. Just as the world provides the perceptual elements which lend themselves to passive synthesis, so—and equally wantonly—does it cease to provide them. The living awareness as polarized expectancy may distinguish *through* such elements the aspect of reality it found lacking *in* reality, and thus fulfill by means of these substitutes the other protointentional structure that had been left dissatisfied. This satisfaction will last only so long as the perceptual elements used as substitutes continue to appear. The resiliency with which the world announces itself remains entire though it appears now two-tiered, with some elements in the perceptual continuum lending themselves to passive fusion and others not. In the *Cultural Hermeneutics* essay, I resorted to creating a nomenclature that made possible precision of reference needed to further the investigation. Let me introduce it briefly at this point.

The two mutually exclusive and mutually implicative aspects of the real (*stasis* and *flux*), I call *valences*; the perceptual elements used as substitutes, I call *valence-carriers*; their role as substitute, I define as *protosymbolic*, emphasizing thereby that no intellection has taken place and that we are limited to the immediacy of the preverbal in its singularity uniquely moored to the field of presence and the sequence of lived mental experiences of a conscious life. To use perceptual elements in this manner is to *reclaim* the missing valence *through* the one perceived as real. The elements so used are said to be *haunted* by the missing valence which *hovers behind them* as their unifying principle (when looked upon *naively*, i.e., in pre-reduction ignorance of the role of the protointentional structure). Let us now resume the description of originary otherness.

Thus behind the immediate resiliency of the world in its singular polarization under one valence appearing as real, there hovers the other valence *haunting* specific concatenations of elements which it unifies (or appears to unify). It borrows whatever reality it has from the reality of its protosymbolic valence carriers (and hence partakes of their immediate resiliency) and, because it hovers *behind* these carriers and is apprehensible only *through* them, it achieves a *mediate* resiliency all its own. *Through* the real, *behind* the real, the missing valence appears "naively" as *organizing the real* into unities the real would not have without it. For we must bear in mind that at this stage the living-awareness does not know itself as the structuring agent to which *both* resiliencies provide what answers they can. Without the phenomenological retrospective question, no such self-knowledge can be reached. All that is known is what is received as it gives itself, and it gives itself as "all there is" independently of any subjective structuration. Thus, "naively" (in the technical phenomenological sense of this term) behind the real, a non-real organizing realm appears which introduces the live awareness involved to a *second form of otherness — mediate resiliency.*

Whereas *immediate resiliency* appears as indissolubly fused in living presence with the living-awareness living it, *mediate resiliency* presents itself as visible *through* immediate resiliency *and* as independent of it (or *other* than it, or as belonging to another realm altogether). Whereas the encounter with the *real* takes place within the living presence and hence *within* the sequence of lived experiences, the encounter with the missing valence announces it as non-real ("irreal," ideal) and takes place *through* the sequence of lived experiences and is not *of* it. *At the heart of the Cartesian cogito, and limiting oneself solely to its actual living presence, one finds the opacity of otherness in two related but essentially distinct modes: the immediate resiliency of what announces itself as real under one aspect; and the mediate resiliency of what announces itself as organizing the real under the aspect left haunting it.* Although the haunting aspect is apprehended from the vantage point of a living presence, its mode of givenness is to announce itself as separate from, and not reducible to, the moment of apprehension. It is impervious to the moment of apprehension in a stronger sense than the real for the real does partake of it in the indissoluble fusion "lived world — worlded awareness" and only through its inability to satisfy both aspects of the proto-intentionality does it offer an immediate resistance (i.e., does it establish an immediate otherness). The real is the living-awareness' primal, perceptual experience; one cannot remove part of the tandem without destroying the ultimate phenomenological "given" although, within the bounds of their a-symmetrical relationship, the "world-pole" announces itself as indifferent to awareness, as we have already observed.

Resiliency is the protodoxic experience of otherness. It occurs in the living field of presence *immediately*, and through the living field of presence, *mediately*. It is valenced either in immediate "resonance," or in mediated "haunting" presence-behind the immediately valenced real. To the immediate real corresponds, on the side of the living-awareness, the valenced resonance the real announces itself as having, which the awareness receives and by which it is partially sated. To the mediated non-real corresponds, on the part of awareness, the polarized receptivity it is; to the fusion of real elements in the perceptual continuum, which the missing valence announces itself as governing, corresponds the passive synthesis, the living-awareness "witnesses" as it "actively" concretizes the aspect of the real towards which it thirsts by using real elements as harbingers of its nonreal presence. Thus, both "resonance" and "polarized receptivity" are one and the same aspect of the living-awareness, viewed from the two distinguishable sides of protointentionality corresponding to the two fundamental ontic qualities that govern the manifestation or presence to any awareness whatsoever, of any being whatsoever, or of Being *qua* Being. Here the Husserlian answer to the problem of ontology takes its place in a formal description of the genetic phenomenology of any metaphysics whatsoever.[3]

C. THE ORIGIN OF OWNNESS.

The "Resonance-Polarized Receptivity" as a Pre-Reflexive "Cogito." Perhaps the simplest way to focus upon the part of awareness in any one living present is to proceed by way of the most radical bracketing and suspension of ontical commitment with which this investigation began. The price of formal clarity is a loss of genetic continuity which will have to be made good later. Still, this seems to me the least troublesome way, and with this caveat, let us go on.

Once again we have to bear in mind the phenomenology of living presence as we have observed it so far: in the living present, in the

[3] I have dealt with this question briefly in the *Cultural Hermeneutics* article previously referred to and more pointedly in a lecture given at the inaugural session of the International Metaphysics Society in Varna. We must leave aside this tempting excursus, however, and having described the origin of otherness in living presence, show in what way "resonance polarized receptivity" mark the origin of ownness.

primal perceptual upsurge, the real announces itself now as "all there is" of reality, and its lack of the missing aspect *is* the living-awareness' immediate dissatisfaction in an equally indissoluble tandem. The ominousness of the "all there is" of the real is all the greater that it completely permeates the living now and totally preoccupies the perceiving living-awareness. The effort of reclamation arises immediatley. It is the living-awareness' self-manifestation (albeit as yet non-thematically and pre-reflexively): *a pre-reflexive cogito such as the one Sartre describes occurs at this point.*

"*Cogitare*" is this living of the world in valenced and valencing receptivity. A later phenomenological description such as the one attempted in the preceding section can easily make visible the part of consciousness in all this. By dint of phenomenological reductions carried out at the protodoxic level, one can later (as we have done initially here) pit one naive "thesis" about the ontic qualities of the lowermost layer of presence against another "naive" thesis about the same ("stream" of lived experiences, versus "field of presence") and then trace the origin of this "valencing" to the protointentional structure of awareness, having separated it from the bracketed perceptual context which remains, save for the indexical change in valence, whatever it may have been when naively beheld. There is no inference here, no stepping beyond the bounds of the actually given as it is given to the Cartesian philosopher. Only given the living present in its valencing (that is to say the "*cogitare*," suspending one's fascination with this valencing and bracketing that one living present) can one freely look at it from the point of view of the other valence without changing in it anything other than the valence. Herakleitos' river is *both flowing and static, eidetically*, i.e., when we have performed the epoché and achieved a view of the law of essence of its appearance through free variations. *In point of actual encounter* in naive fascination (i.e., in point of actual *cogitatio*), *it is either* the one *or* other, *but not both.*

At the moment of involvement, in the living present naively lived, awareness is a particular resonance and a polarization, i.e., a naive fascination with a particular reclaiming. Later in the phenomenological attitude, awareness finds itself in its trace, as we have shown, as that part of a living present from which valence (and in the doxic level, sense) originates. Then it recognizes this trace as its own. Through "free variations" it discovers the extent of its already enacted and potentially performable "I can resonate thus and so . . . " in front of the resiliency of the real. But it discovers this on the trace already lived, on the face of a resonance experienced *pre-*

reflexively, nonthematically, though in the fulfillment of performance. Thus this discovery need not be thematically contemporary with the first exercise of this "I can", although it is non-thematically (horizonally, prereflexively) present. The moment of enactment *qua* moment of enactment possesses all the features which the moment of self-knowledge will later distinguish from others and recognize as its own. The moment of enactment *is* distinct from the moment of self-knowledge in the way Sartre and Ryle recognized—enactment does not necessarily mean reflexive self-knowledge, but the enactment of reflexive self-knowledge does presuppose a prior moment of simple enactment. Thus an aware living of some sort "systematically" antedates any self-aware living, and a self-aware "moment" is, as Sartre pointed out, a prereflexive involvement with reflexivity.

In this privileged moment, however, concommitance is apprehended prereflexively between the residue "part of awareness" in the moment reflexively beheld, and the prereflexive "I can" now under enactment. "Apprehended prereflexively," "enacted," and "lived" are all synonymous here. In the face of the valenced "lived world," the "other worldliness" of the resonance (its "non-worldliness") polarized about the prereflexive self-experience I have characterized doxically as "I can," (and therefore misleadingly, but terms are lacking and "it can," though at first glance more correct, is in fact even more misleading), "appears," makes itself manifest, as the epiphenomenon of resonance and polarization. The prereflexive and nonthematic polarization present in the moment of reflexivity, though it may differ from the polarization reflexively beheld in point of actual valence, *remains fused to the polarization beheld in point of their common "otherness" from the lived world,* i.e., from whatever upsurges in primal perception. The "polarization," the "resonance," the "valencing" of receptivity, all those terms designate the "aura" surrounding the contents of primal perception. It is this "aura" which the reflexive cogito thematizes, because any cogitatio exhibits it as the non-thematic color permeating its thematic involvement. At the predoxic level at which we are, the nonthematic color is the resonance that the primal perceptual upsurge *has* in the living-awareness whose living presence it permeates. The phenomenological and reflexive cogitos occur at a much higher level of awareness and abstraction, *but they derive their force,* as I have tried to show, *from the fusion of the moments of resonance in a continuum* which is unitarily experienced nonthematically before it is unitarily beheld, one from which what Husserl termed "the unity of the flux of lived experiences" derives its evidence.

As yet not thematic, at the level of the protodoxic, from the originary

*moment of dissatisfaction on, the continuum of resonance, in its otherness
from the reality of which it is the valence (namely, the reality given in primal
perception), is the origin of the sphere of ownness,* though such a sphere
can only be constituted thematically at a later and higher level of
conscious life.

The Tension Between Stasis and Flux — In reaching the common roots
of ownness and otherness in the living presence "worlded
awareness—lived world" we are able to distinguish on the one hand,
"a continuum of resonances;" on the other, that which upsurges in
primal perception. If we try to isolate more closely the distinctive
feature designated by the terms "continuum of resonances," we find
that it is neither of the ontological qualities to which awareness is
receptive. The continuum of resonances is neither stasis nor flux but
rather a *tension between the realization of either.* What appears in primal
upsurge—the real—does not exhibit this tension. Although it is received and is lived as valenced by the living-awareness, whatever
valence it is naively taken to have—it announces itself as having—*is
extrinsic to it*, as we have seen, and the result of the polarization of the
awareness itself, though in the naive attitude this doesn't appear as
such. How a living-awareness becomes polarized belongs to a later
level of phenomenological description for its general laws, to the
empirical psychology governing the particular kind of awareness
involved for its particular laws. Given whatever valence the real
announces itself as having and is naively taken to have, the tension
towards the other valence which the perceiving awareness immediately becomes is its resonance to the real in this particular living
present. Should the real change valence—for whatever cause—the
living-awareness will immediately become a tension toward the valence now no longer "given."

Thus at its most naive and lowest level, the freedom to receive
either aspects of the real—which, by essence, an awareness is—will
appear as the actual tension between the one aspect realized and the
other, which the awareness lives in its present confrontation with the
real. The awareness itself will perceive itself thematically as this
tension only in the reflexive mode, and at a later level involving
phenomenological reflexivity. But, at the lowest level, *it exhibits this
tension; it is this tension pre-reflexively in pre-reflexive nonthematic
apperception —and, in the continuous fusion of its sequence of lived experiences, this tension underlies the different resonances of the immediately and
the mediately resilient, providing the inner content of the perceptual upsurge
with the live aura of awareness.*

As to the "continuous fusion" mentioned above, we shall see it in more detail when we describe the constitution of the "sphere" of ownness, rather than the mere "point of origin" of ownness. Suffice to say here that it is the originary appearance of a memorizing different from primal memory in Husserl's sense, yet not quite equatable to memory usually so-called or secondary memory in Husserl's terminology. The two types of involuntary memory Bergson recognizes, and Proust's involuntary memory, capture some aspects of this "fusion," as does Husserl's remark that "the stream of lived experiences individualizes" the ego. But all these seem directed at an almost doxic level of remembering, whereas what is apprehended here is the predoxic foundation of all these more particular memorial traces. What is focused upon here is the pedal point of presence as it is prereflexively present to itself, apperceptively and nonthematically, as this continuum of resonances, this tension towards *now* stasis, *now* flux, and its shifting sedimentary trace in the vector-like summation of its polarizations.

The contingent carriers of these valences leave as well a memorial trace which personalizes the aware-living receptive of it by individualizing the sequence of its lived experiences and by structuring its passive receptivity in a way that I shall describe later. Suffice it to say here that the recovery of this memorial trace in its actual sequence and in the discreteness of each of its layered elements, involves a more complete *cogito* than the epistemological one usually associated with Descartes and the Husserl of *Ideen I*.[4]

The full reflexive phenomenological cogito consists, therefore, in successfully making thematic all these structures of awareness and in apprehending them clearly and distinctly in an unbroken fusion with all previous prereflexive nonthematic awarenesses of them as they were enacted.

In the *cogito* carried out strictly at the cognitive level, the mere epistemic or doxic surface is reached; if a precognitive, predoxic layer is reached in transverbal (or even nonverbal) confrontation, a deeper reorganization of the awareness takes place in which its deepest polarization is neutralized, and the awareness *actually* recovers its transcendental freedom towards either valence, thus be-

---

[4]That it is a phenomenological *cogito*, I argue in a study on *Proust and Husserl* published in *The Study of Time*, Vol. II. by J.F. Fraser. (Springer Verlag. N.Y.: 1976). In it, I attempt to show in what way Proust's narrator can be said to be involved throughout the novel with a phenomenology of his concrete existence on the basis of the bracketing and suspension of it that the resort to involuntary memory allows. A follow-up on the results obtained in the published essay points to the deeper lesson of the novel relevant at this point, namely, that the concrete, emotional *cogito* (which reaches through to the lowermost constitutive layer we are describing here) results in the actual recovery of transcendental freedom from all primal memorial sedimentation and naive polarizations.

coming able to receive a primal upsurge in whatever polarity it chooses. This is the *point of balance* at which either stasis or flux are emotionally actually co-possible. Some Zen Koans seem to indicate that those who have reached *satori* have achieved this fundamental reorganization. We cannot go into this here. Suffice it to note that the *tension between stasis and flux*, which is the actualized awareness, can be lived at the neutrality of the point of balance, or through all manners of graduation, in complete enslavement to the momentary fascinations of the living present.

Finally, in concluding this section, let us note that, as *tension between stasis and flux* the awareness is always *totalization in progress*, that is to say, effort to achieve a satisfactory equilibrium between stasis and flux, effort to achieve a complete realization of possibility in the pregnant sense and correspondingly, a complete actualization of transcendental freedom. Whether this equilibrium be achieved "naively," or in full recovery of the "point of balance" is the fundamental phenomenological difference, the one upon which depends the success or failure of the phenomenological "Enlightenment" launched by Husserl in the *Krisis*. Although Sartre, following Hegel and Marx, views consciousness (the "for itself") as totalization in progress, he does so from the passionate point of view of his enacted reclamations which he does not believe he can escape, and those of the individuals and groups he describes, which he does not think they can escape either. As against these naive totalizations in moored fascination with the given taken, eventually, as an inescapable objectivity (whether dialectical or not, materialist or not, it is still the result of a refusal to carry out the phenomenological reflexion to its roots in transcendental subjectivity) there we have reached in this study the theoretical bases for totalizations fully grounded in transcendental freedom, both epistemologically and emotionally. Thus the Cartesian critique of our inherited mores could be launched anew, this time on the strictest and most thoroughgoing phenomenological bases, once we have won our way to the vantage point of the emotional recovery of transcendental freedom in our living present. But first the path from the initial Cartesian isolation to the universality of transcendental subjectivity must be shown clearly and unambiguously as practicable for all.

Having shown the origin of ownness and otherness in the solipsistic living presence, I have marked clearly the ultimate foundation upon which to base the renewed Cartesian critique of what we have achieved thus far culturally, societally and psychologically. Before proceeding with the formal description of the wider framework of that critique, namely, the constitution of the sphere of ownness, of the extrasubjective, of the other as alter ego and of transcendental subjectivity, it may be well to dwell upon this foundation in order to ascertain the grasp of its essential features.

4. Critical Remarks on Developments Visible from the Results Obtained Thus Far.

a) THE GENETIC ORIGIN OF TEMPORALITY AND ATEMPORALITY.

The living-awareness always strives to complement the real it apprehends with the aspect that guarantees its freedom. It may do so in full cognitive and emotional possession of its power to valence or in complete ignorance of it. In either case, its effort is to bring into presence both aspects of the real. Thus all living presence is *totalization in progress* in a stricter sense than the one Sartre saw along with the Marxists. This is observable even at the lowest level of aware living, as we have seen. Even there, as I have described earlier, a confused encounter with otherness takes place. Ownness and otherness are indissolubly commingled: the real appears as indissolubly fused with the living presence. Using a terminology borrowed from a higher level, one might say that the real is subjective. It is limited to the present encounter at the very instant of encounter. Primal contact, primal upsurge, it is no more than this now in its instantaneity, without any thickness whatever, quite passively met. If one could talk about the passive encounters of material particles in their impersonal discreetness and mindless momentaneity, one would have here a good analogy for what the "now" of primal encounter might reduce to, were there not, as one of the elements, a living presence, threatened and unsated by the immediacy of momentaneity. Mindless material encounters are atemporal, in the sense that no living-awareness thickens the "now" into retentive and protentive projections. Hence the instantaneity of material encounters is not even that.

Temporality, lived time, originates in the living "now" of the primal perceptual upsurge, as Husserl saw, in the dissatisfaction of the living-awareness who then immediately thickens with its dissatisfaction both the real and its own presence, as we have seen. The polarized awareness now searching for the other aspect of reality to which it is receptive, passively fuses in anguished protention what retention allows to recede as real representatives of the missing ontological aspect. Lived time is this continually extending and receding "unity of the stream of lived experiences" Husserl talks about (I would prefer the ontologically neutral "sequence" of lived experiences), and whatever times there *are* originate phenomenologically from this one. Time as the dimension of life and of action, the "practical" dimension, is the opening of the atemporal instantaneity of the real upon the mediately resilient (the haunting, the missing aspect of reality) by the living-awareness as polarized receptivity and locus of valenced resonances in continuous fusion.

Thus time originates in an atemporal now and is the opening through which a mediated resiliency announces itself as "wholly other" than, wholly impervious to, the locus of its appearing— namely, the polarized receptivity and the protosymbolic valence-carriers which make up both its field of presence and the fused comet's tail of its sequence of lived experiences. The mediated resiliency announces itself through time, through the unified, extended, sequence of lived experiences; it appears as the wider unifying frame of this sequence; but it appears as well as "other than" and totally detached from this sequence, and hence as atemporal. *Lived time thus occurs between two atemporal moorings, one of which appears as the origin of it, the other of which appears as transcending and encompassing it.* Real permanence is the instantaneity of a transcending flow; real flow is the instantaneity of a transcending permanence.

The immediately resilient, the real, appears indissolubly moored to the moments of its appearance to the living-awareness who lives it; time is the subjective face of the search for the missing ontological aspect; the missing ontological aspect reveals itself as beyond both the encountered reality and time, visible through the former while the later accumulates, and *essentially* independent of both. The missing aspect, in its mediated resiliency appears as "wholly other," totally objective, totally impervious to the contingencies of encounter and the metaphysics of presence. Nor should one mistake the fact that it reveals itself through time (as the retentive-protentive thickness of the living present) for an evidence of its own intrinsic temporality. The mediate resiliency of the other ontological aspect may be apprehended by the living-awarenessthrough its accumulation of *time: that is only the way of living-awareness apprehends it. What is temporal, is the apprehension by the living-awareness,* its contingent characteristics both as performance and in the accidental materials used in this performance (the contingent valence-carriers). *What is seen through this temporally moored screen, in this temporally-moored fashion, is itself beyond and reveals itself as atemporal.*

b) THE METAPHYSICAL LESSON TO BE DERIVED FROM THE FOREGOING
  DESCRIPTIONS

The Eidetic Ontological Matrix. Neither stasis nor flux are intrinsic
qualities of either the real or the nonreal; rather, the real and the
nonreal are the possibility of either stasis or flux, though only one
can be actualized as "really there" in any one living present by the
Law of Partial Actualization. The valencing of the real can ultimately
be traced back through the phenomenological reflexion to the polarity of the receptivity in the same way that the valencing of the
nonreal can be so traced. As to how and why an actual living-
awareness in its first manifestation is already polarized about one
valence rather than the other, this is a question which can only be
answered through particular, concrete, contextual analyses. The
phenomenology of the predoxic will have to be further developed so
as to allow the elaboration of a concrete "psychology" based upon its
findings. Initially, what one has as originally given is the "live
awareness—lived world" as already actually here and already actually polarized. Phenomenology, just as philosophy, occurs *"nell mezzo
del camin di nostra vita"*; it is always a later move performed when one
finds oneself in the obscure woods of naive involvements and by dint
of dissatisfaction is led to phenomenological reflexion. This too is a
matter for a later genetic phenomenological description, when the
phenomenology of the sphere of ownness and of the concrete ego
have been sketched sharply enough to lay the ground work for the
"phenomenology of phenomenology."

  *At this point, the recovery of transcendental freedom from the naive fasci-
nation with the given at all levels would enable one to see in both the real and
nonreal the possibility of either stasis or flow.*

  One will have reached then the "point of balance" between valencing involvements, being free to "play the world," as it were, under
either tandem: real stasis—nonreal flux; real flux—nonreal stasis;
and being free from being so caught in either tandem as not to be
able to switch immediately and at will to the other one. *Hence Being,
as it reveals itself at the point of balance, will appear as the eidetic possibility
of either tandem, thus answering fully the eidetic possibility that consciousness, as protointentionality, eidetically is. It will appear then that no genuine
eidetic ontology is complete which does not countenance two concommitant,
and mutually exclusive, descriptions.* For example, to a science of the
really flowing ruled by an ideal, or nonreal permanence, will have to
be added a science of the really permanent ruled by an ideal, or

nonreal, flow (quantum physics' unholy marriage of the electron as particle to the electron as undular phenomenon would appear here as prototype of the kind of contradictory descriptions one would have to accept as the only truly complete scientific ones).

The Hermeneutic "Index of Realization". Although such descriptions as the ones advocated above would be eidetic, they would still remain moored in a noneidetic actual appearing which perforce would be polarized according to the Law of Partial Actualization. Thus the living-awareness recovering its transcendental freedom does so through the "screen" of a particular "realization," and though it may really view from a fleeting living presence the *moiré* patterns of stasis and flux as co-possible both really and eidetically, it does so either from within a permanence-reclaiming apprehension of the eidetic law governing the manifestation of Being to living-awarenesses of whatever sort, or from within a flux-reclaiming recovery of trans-cendental freedom: namely discovering itself as the real (actual) possibility of either aspect.

In the indexical value of the "screen of realization" (i.e., whether it belongs to a flux-reclaiming or to a stasis-reclaiming project) lies the hermeneutical key to scientific discourses of whatever sort and the key to the "episteme" governing their generation, to borrow a term from Michel Foucault. *Ultimately, all "epistemes" reduce to stasis-reclaiming or flux-reclaiming,* and all preselect the data they retain according as it furthers the reclamation they seek. Those who have abandoned the ideal of the "detached observer," the ideal of the vision of essence and of transcendental purity Husserl still main-tained, have in doing so, adopted a flux-reclaiming episteme and discarded a permanence-reclaiming one.

But it is not sufficient to shift the index of the screen of realization and to immerse oneself in a ruling change to avoid *either* eidetic purity and atemporality, *or* indexical diflexion. In order to do so, one achieves a different discourse altogether, one which manages to maintain the possibility of flux in permanence-reclaiming. *One has to reach a method of description which neutralizes the reclamatory project from which it stems,* and yet still allows the valencing of its texts by the besouling presence of the philosophizing philosopher with his own index of realization.

Breaking Out of the Hermeneutical Circle by Means of Husserlian Eidetic Phenomenology. Such a discourse presupposes the neutralization of the lived valences of what is immediately and mediately resilient *both* for the writer, *and* for the reader. I submit that Husserl's serl's phenomenological method, with its requirement to suspend naive commitment and to bracket the contents of the presentation observed, forces its strict practitioners to perform just such a task. And I need only point to the path followed by Husserl himself who, by dint of scientific rigor under the strictest permanence-reclaiming ideals, discovered the "life-world" as the originary ground of scientific endeavour, therein joining across philosophic antipodes Miguel de Unamuno, perhaps the most consistent flux-reclaimer the West has produced.

Phenomenology, eidetic phenomenology, because it describes the operation of intentional focus as well as the object of each intention in its essential features, perforce places itself beyond any one valencing since eidetic features may take on either valence upon being lived. The lesson of the preceding description is that, as eidetic possibility of either stasis or flux neither the real nor the nonreal are eidetically either static or flowing. They "acquire" these qualities "really" (directly, in the case of the real; through proto-symbolic representation, in the case of the nonreal) in "living presence" when, being "lived," or "practiced," they receive in a sequence of lived experiences the reflexions of now this, now that ontological aspect. Inner time, as the actually lived "thickness" of the living present with its retentive comet's tail, is the locus of their manifestation and the record of its trace. It is where this manifestation *takes place*, is "embodied," so to speak, and actualized, actively by the living-awareness, and hence it is the "practical dimension of Being."

Eidetic description properly carried out escapes this practical dimension and although the phenomenological philosopher leaves as his "shadow" the indexed trace of his reclamatory enterprise, he does so in such a way that the eidetic realm can be clearly seen by anyone past all indexed reclamation, because *both* the following essential conditions are now met: one, the intentional operation and its focus are given; *and* two, the commitment to a particular ontological thesis is suspended. Should the phenomenological philosopher lapse into ontologically-coloured discourse, as I believe Husserl did unwittingly in his description of inner time-consciousness, the description of the operational structure alone enables another to focus upon the same objectivity and to complete the task of bracketing and of suspension.

The Bases of Eidetic Phenomenology in Mediate Resiliency. Why phenomenological discourse is able to achieve this is because it explicitly distinguishes between the contingent and the essential, between what is lived as it is lived, and its structure, *and it does so both* between what is lived as it is lived, and its structure, *and it does so both from the point of view of intentional operation and from the point of view of operational focus.* If the foregoing descriptions are correct, what eidetic vision eventually enables us to separate *are the valences* with which objectivities are lived within a particular reclamation project, from the essential structures thus experienced. What these structures "reduce" to, as we have seen, are the mediately resilient, the haunting aspect observed not in its valenced unitary appearing, only in its unitary appearing with no commitment to its valence which, along with all naive ontologizing, is suspended. The Husserlian distinction between the eidetic and the real (between the *reell* and the *real*) is an epistemic and doxic description of the distinction we have observed at the lowermost predoxic layer between the immediately resilient and the mediately resilient. The atemporality of the realm of essences thus uncovered, is originarily the alocality of the mediately resilient, its independence of the stream of lived experiences.

My abstractive regard, the "switch of the glance" which enables me to look upon a particular state of affairs from the point of view of the "categorial" and which Husserl describes in connection with the problem of abstraction, in the *Logische Untersuchungen,* (in particular, *L.U. VI,* chapter VI, VII, VIII.) is nothing other than the exclusive focusing upon the mediately resilient features "hovering behind" any immediately resilient inertial unitary appearings and "besouling" them. Thus, the abstraction may be "founded" on the concrete encounter, it is every bit as experiential as, though it may be based upon, the wider passive receptivity, as Husserl in fact maintains. In fact, as we have seen, the origin of its selectivity is in the immediate polarization of awareness in immediate dissatisfied resonance. Hence, every concrete awareness of whatever resonance, is the potential originary source of a "vision of essence" in full experiential clarity, though at the lowest predoxic layer, all that appears of the essence is its mediate resiliency as a source of protointentional satisfaction.

What appears thus mediately resilient is a unitary principle governing some elements of the primal perceptual upsurge passively fused for their ability to represent the missing valence of either flux or stasis. This unitary principle appears *through* the real but *not in* it and is, at the protodoxic level, the first glimmer of an essence, in its total phenomenological difference from the upsurging real of primal perception. The origin of this principle is in the mediately resilient realm which later proves to be the transcendental realm, the realm of essences (cf. on this Husserl's *Erfahrung und Urteil,* to which the present investigation constitutes a prolegomenon). Or, in other words, from the somewhat more complex description of the living present which we have attempted here, the realm opened by the intuition of essences at the epistemic level can be traced all the way back to the mediate resiliency of the haunting aspect of reality which organizes in passive synthesis elements retended and unitarily associated as they appear in the primal perceptual upsurge.

Resiliency, Mediate and Immediate, and the Traditional Distinction between the Subjective and the Objective. It should be noted however, that mediate and immediate resiliency correspond only partially to the traditional distinction between what is merely subjective and what is not. The subjective, usually so called, depends solely on the agent and his whim. The objective is viewed by distinction with this as independent of the agent. One may go so far as to distinguish degrees of dependence and independence between these two extremes, and scientific work, according to traditional empiricism, consists in reaching the point of view of the detached observer, or the point of view corroboratable by any agent whatsoever independently of his own whim and circumstances. A statistical compromise is struck in practice according to which what can be attested to by more than one observer is considered more acceptable as a potentially epistemic fact.

As against these traditional canons, one must observe that at the prepredictative level, mediate resiliency can only be attested to by the living-awareness experiencing it. No other awareness can have this very same experience, and hence, under the usual conceits this would appear to be a wholly subjective experience. In the same manner, and for the same reason, so can one characterize immediate resiliency. Nor can this be surprising considering the starting point of the Cartesian philosopher. But one must not allow the wholly subjective aspect of this experience (as per traditional canons) to blind one to the intrinsic non-subjective aspect of what is encountered—again, as per traditional canons. Although this experience is "wholly private," it is the encounter with something which *resists* my volition, with something which, though perceived by me, announces itself as other than, and independent of, me. "Resiliency," immediate and mediate, is the first appearance within subjectivity of what a later, and higher, constitutive level will call "objectivity," when intersubjectivity will have been constituted. Suffice it at this point that we have recognized at the heart of the Cartesian *cogito* the roots of "otherness."

One must accept, therefore, such seemingly paradoxical ascrip-

tions as "subjective experience of objectivity" and the like. The traditional "subject-object" distinction occurs wholly at the doxic and
predicative level of conscious life. It is a "later" distinction founded
upon the one we make here. Mediate and immediate resiliencies are
the prepredicative encounters with the foundation of what will be
later elaborated into the traditional distinction *from within a particular
reclamatory project.*

5. BY WAY OF A CONCLUSION

We have now recognized the two most fundamental forms of
otherness, and we have done so *within* the Cartesian *cogito* as used by
Husserl in his phenomenology. Thus an important step has been
taken in the attempt to demonstrate that the phenomenological
method is equal to the task of description required of the Cartesian
philosopher if he is to refute the accusation of *solipsism.* A careful
description of the seemingly solipsistic starting point of Cartesian
philosophy, the living present of the meditating philosopher, points
to the originary experience of otherness contained by such a living
presence at its simplest and lowest level of manifestation. In effect,
the ground for the accusation of solipsism is already removed. If the
Cartesian philosopher is not confined within his own *solus ipse* even
at the pre-predicative layer of experience, how could he be so confined at the higher level?

We must now show further in what way Cartesian philosophy in its
phenomenological garb not only escapes solipsism but also can place
itself at the one universal point of view Plato recognized as the apan-
age of the epistemic. Not only must I show that the Cartesian *cogito*
contains all it needs to refute the accusation of unavoidable solipsism
(this is a minimal claim and I consider the preceding description as
having conclusively met it); I must also show that it contains all that is
needed, when used properly, to make intersubjectively, universally
valid descriptions based on the contents of the *cogito* alone. *I must
show that the Cartesian philosopher can speak for all, legitimately and unambiguously without recourse to a divine presence of some sort.* From within
the Cartesian *cogito* those features which announce themselves as
moored to the actuality of my presence must be distinguished from
those which announce themselves as impervious to my presence or
to my absence. If there can be a vantage point to which any subjectivity whatever may pretend by virtue of being a subjectivity, this is the
vantage point which I must attain from within the *cogito.*

Now that we have seen the originary encounter with otherness,
this encounter must be shown to be accessible to any subjectivity

whatever *in principle*. In order to do so, *I must show in what way the point of view of the wholly other is accessible to me within my own cogito*. I cannot place myself merely at the point of view of the alter ego, because it remains at the same level of contingency as me: *I have to reach the point of view any subjectivity whatever must reach once it refuses the lures of its own contingency*. I term it "the wholly other" because it is other than any contingent subjectivity whatever. Seen through one of them, it is not *of* any one of them, *and exhibits clearly mediate resiliency*.

The task before me is thus clearly defined: first, through the genetic phenomenology of the "sphere of ownness," I must try to see whether or not an eidetic vision is possible enabling me to focus upon the besouling "meaning" *subjectivity* in its mediate resiliency. Then, I must try to corroborate this apprehension by attempting to describe phenomenologically the constitution of the intentional focus "alter ego," and, on the basis of that, attempt once again to apprehend eidetically the meaning 'subjectivity' in its mediate resiliency. This done, if it can be done, I shall have reached a proper foundation of the epistemic: transcendental subjectivity in its eidetic purity, in its mediate resiliency, that is to say, in its double independence from the accident of my apprehension of it, and I shall have done so through both my sphere of ownness and my alter ego, on the basis of the sole contents of my *cogito*.

FOUR

THE NEW HERMENEUTICS, OTHER TRENDS, AND THE HUMAN SCIENCES FROM THE STANDPOINT OF TRANSCENDENTAL PHENOMENOLOGY

I. INTRODUCTION

THERE IS INCREASING ATTENTION to the philosophical and methodological problems of the human sciences today. The different schools in hermeneutics, structuralism, and ideology critique have developed a Babel of theories of interpretation. The danger that the whole movement will end in an uncritical eclecticism is real. Critique is necessary—not a critique of texts but a critique of hermeneutical reason itself. Critique is the task of transcendental philosophy. The difficulty of such a critique is, however, that all the schools mentioned above seem to offer unanswerable challenges to transcendental phenomenology, which is the most developed form of transcendental philosophy. The urgent task now is responding to these challenges.

Given this situation it cannot be the purpose of this paper to give an interpretation of Husserl's thoughts about the human sciences and their significance for transcendental phenomenology. Two general remarks concerning the interpretation of Husserl's intentions are, however, necessary. The second already goes beyond Husserl's own considerations.

1. Gadamer showed as early as 1963[1] that the phrase in Appendix XXVIII of the *Crisis*, "Philosophy as a science, as a serious, rigorous, indeed apodictically rigorous science—this dream is over" cannot be understood as an expression of Husserl's own opinion. The phrase refers rather to a position Husserl believed to be a fatal corruption. In the meantime Gadamer's interpretation has been confirmed by

[1] H. G. Gadamer, *Philosophical Hermeneutics*, trans. and ed. David E. Linge (Berkeley: University of California Press, 1976), p. 158.

the publication of Husserl's letter to Roman Ingarden on July 7, 1935.[2] Husserl's real concern in the *Crisis* and related writings is that the theory of transcendental reduction and the transcendental theory of constitution cannot be completed without overcoming the paradoxes in the human sciences and history. These paradoxes are the roots of the irrationalism of the twentieth century, its crisis. *Ideas II* attempts to provide a theory of the basic structures, which methodical research in the human sciences accompanied by a naive trust in rationality, presupposes. *First Philosophy* and *Crisis* deal with the specific epoché, which is constitutive for the human sciences and its paradoxical consequences, which seem to destroy the ideal of objective research. A transcendental reflection on the presuppositions of the universal but mundane self-objectification in the human sciences must overcome these paradoxes and be able to serve as a path leading to the transcendental reduction, which reveals transcendental subjectivity in its concreteness.

2. The late Husserl introduced different paths leading to the transcendental reduction.[3] They do not share the disadvantage of the Cartesian path, which discovers the *cogito* in complete emptiness. The relations between the path via the lifeworld, which via psychology and via the human sciences have not been sufficiently explicated in Husserl's writings, and misunderstandings are possible. One of them is closely connected with the misunderstanding of Appendix XXVIII, mentioned above. The lifeworld, according to this misconception, is the new transcendental ground, and the Cartesian approach has to be abandoned entirely. The thesis of this paper is that the transition from the problems of the lifeworld to those of the transcendental reduction is possible only if mediated by the path through the human sciences and that this path implies the psychological path. There are, then, in principle, only two paths. One, the Cartesian, starts with reflections on the giveness of the world and the selfgiveness of subjectivity. The other is the result of reflections on the reflections through which subjectivity is given as subjectivity in the world. This is the path through the human sciences. How it implies the psychological path can be clarified only at the end of this paper, but a preliminary case can be made for the

[2] Edmund Husserl, *Briefe an Roman Ingarden*, ed. Roman Ingarden, (Den Haag: Martinus Nijhoff, 1968), pp. 92–93.

[3] Cf. E. Husserl, *Nachwort zu meinen Ideen*, Hua V, pp. 148f; *Cartesianische Meditationen*, Hua I, p. 107; *Krisis*, Hua VI, pp. 146ff, 157ff, 261f, 314, 297, and 363; *Erste Philosophie II*, Hua VIII, p. 139; cf. also pp. 317, 225f, 283, and 286f.

proposed reduction of the path through the lifeworld to the path of the human sciences.

The distinction between the lifeworld and the scientific world and the discovery of the subjective-relative character of different lifeworlds is in the *Crisis* and elsewhere the result of reflections on material prepared by the human sciences, history and the history of science, ethnological studies, and so forth. Such a human-scientific reflection does not, however, presuppose any transcendental reflection; it is possible even without any application of the phenomenological method in general. Simple methodical and philosophical reflections on the human sciences reveal that there are different cultural environments with different subjective-relative systems of norms, values, and truths, further, that the scientific world is connected with the specific development of our lifeworld, and, finally, that the development of the human sciences themselves, which leads to the discovery of such distinctions, is relative to certain types of cultural environments. If such reflections are pushed to the extreme, the end will be historical relativism, historism, and decisionism. The problem of every theory of the lifeworld and the attempt to consider such a theory as the new "transcendental ground" is that, even if phenomenological considerations are added, nothing is changed regarding the basis—the material provided by the human sciences. There is no other solution possible than some types of relativism and decisionism. A consistent theory of the lifeworld that avoids, in the last instance, what Husserl called the irrationalism of the twentieth century, can be developed only if the methodological problems of the human sciences are resolved in the transition to the transcendental reduction.

II. THE NEW HERMENEUTICS AND TRADITIONAL HERMENEUTICS

The problem of the relations between the human sciences and transcendental phenomenology can no longer be discussed in the present situation beginning from Husserl's writings alone. A new hermeneutics has arisen from Heidegger's hermeneutics of existence and being. A critique of the methodological Cartesianism of transcendental phenomenology and its forgetfulness regarding the question of being is part of the new hermeneutics. Its thesis is that the problem of interpretation (i.e., the basic problem of the human sciences) cannot be solved by a philosophy of reflection. A transcendental phenomenological account of the human sciences cannot be successful unless the hermeneutical problem is taken into account, and Husserl has not developed a theory of interpretation. The new hermeneutics is therefore of significance for the transcendental phenomenological approach. It is a question, furthermore, whether the new hermeneutics has found an answer to the paradoxes of the human sciences, which are a key problem for trancendental phenomenology, or whether they occur again on this level in another disguise. Certain other aspects of the new hermeneutics, especially those that are determined by the question of being including the theological implications, are not of interest here. The critique of certain theorems of the new hermeneutics is therefore not an immanent critique. The underlying interpretation here does not claim to be an adequate interpretation of the intentions of the authors. The critique is a reformulation of certain hermeneutical problems, which relates them to transcendental phenomenology. The common ground is the real activity of the human sciences.

It finally must be mentioned that the path to the reduction via the human science has the character of reflections on reflections. We do not need the guidance of the ideal of apodicticity in its scientific form on this path in order to make the transition from the natural to the transcendental attitude. What is necessary is that we perform the hermeneutical reflection in the natural attitude as explicitly as possible.

1. THE ANTINOMY OF METHOD AND ANTIMETHOD

The new hermeneutics has developed in two opposite directions, which may be called the *antimethodical* (Gadamer) and the *methodical* (Ricoeur).[4] The antimethodical position claims that authentic understanding in interpretation can be reached if only the insistence on method in traditional hermeneutics is abandoned. It is therefore a critique of method in hermeneutics. The methodical approach discovers the realm of being in the analysis of certain hermeneutical standards and accepts the demand for methodical standards. The analysis of this paradox is among the task of the following investigation.

From the viewpoint of traditional hermeneutics it can be said that

---

[4]Both authors are extremely rich in their development of viewpoints and aspects of the hermeneutical problem. An attempt to give a systematic explication of certain hermeneutical root problems implies, of course, certain abstractions and has to be to a certain degree unjust regarding the rich concrete content of the work of Gadamer and Ricoeur.

the antimethodical approach acknowledges the *second*[5] basic canon
of hermeneutics. This canon demands that the whole has to be understood from the parts and vice versa. The *first* canon is, however,
rejected. This canon demands that the text has to be understood out
of its own context and not out of the context of the interpreter. Only
the first canon allows the development of standards of confirmation
and falsification. The two standards, which are usually mentioned in
traditional hermeneutics, are the original intention of the author
and the perspective of the contemporary addressees of the text. The
first is rejected by the antimethodical approach because it is based on
unjustifiable psychological assumptions; the second, because it is
grounded in an idealization of the concept of contemporaneity
which cannot be realized.[6] The antimethodical approach has a radical and moderate reading. Authentic hermeneutic activity can, according to the radical reading, disregard standards of correctness. It
is a merging of horizons of meaning of the text and of the interpreter in the quest for truth. The radical reading is doubtless a
reincarnation of what Husserl called the "irrationalism of the 20th
century."[7] It has been used in criticisms that traditional hermeneuti-
cists have directed against the antimethodical approach. The reply
has been that the radical reading is a misunderstanding of the intentions of the author (!). The correct reading is the moderate reading.
According to this reading it is meaningless to apply the first canon as
well as method in general in the process of understanding eminent
texts. Hermeneutic theory must be primarily a theory of the process
of understanding eminent texts because this process is itself original,
authentic, and constitutive for the genesis of an original tradition.[8]
Understanding, when guided by method, degenerates.

[5]Extensive bibliographical material concerning the two canons is given by E. Betti,
Allgemeine Auslegungslehre als Methodik der Geisteswissenschaften (Tuebingen, 1967), p.
216f. Betti, following Schleiermacher, lists the canon of the separation of the context
of the text and the context of the interpreter as first canon and the canon of the whole
and the parts as second canon. His second canon is often referred to as "the canon"
and "the first canon," while the first is often neglected. Though I myself followed that
habit elsewhere ("The Problem of Hermeneutics in Recent Anglo-American Literature, Parts I and II," *Philosophy and Rhetoric*, Vol. 10, Nr. 3 and 4) I here return to the
original order.
    [6]Cf. H. G. Gadamer, *Truth and Method* (New York: Seabury Press, 1975), p. 356; see
also P. Ricoeur, *Interpretation Theory* (Fort Worth: The Texas Christian University
Press, 1976), pp. 92–93. Ricoeur has adopted Gadamer's viewpoints. About the problem of the relation of his and Gadamer's position, cf. my review of *Interpretation
Theory, Graduate Faculty Philosophy Journal* VII, 2 (1978), 257–269.
    [7]Cf. the letter to Roman Ingarden.
    [8]The radical reading is Betti's interpretation of *Truth and Method*. The moderate
reading is developed in Gadamer's answer to Betti. Cf. *Truth and Method*, pp. 464 ff.
Some further explications are given in *Philosophical Hermeneutics*. Cf. my review,
Philosophy and Rhetoric, XI, 3 (1978) 191–196.

Two levels of degeneration can be distinguished. The focus of interest on the first level, *the level of the philological-historical understanding*, is not truth but the meaning of the text. The interpreter tries to separate the truth claims of the text from his own truth claims. The second level is that of *diagnostic understanding*, which is modeled on the image of scientific understanding and is interested in the causes and motives of meaning. Its goal is the manipulation of the other. Methodical understanding is possible only within the framework of authentic understanding, which implies the question of truth. The philological interpreter presupposes his general understanding of the tradition in which the text is given to him. In this understanding of the tradition the question of truth cannot be eliminated. Diagnostic understanding presupposes the framework of a diagnostic theory and its unquestioned truth claim.

It can be said that the moderate reading of the antimethodical approach is in strict opposition to the methodical approach because the types of hermeneutics that are of greatest significance in the methodical approach, the hermeneutics of the latent, are diagnostic and hence most degenerate for the antimethodical approach. Furthermore it can be said that the antimethodical approach in its moderate reading is compatible with traditional hermeneutics, though it is apparently not aware of this. The moderate reading does not reject methodical discipline in understanding[9] but insists on the principle that the essence of interpretation is misunderstood if it is forgotten that the original concern is the question of truth and not method. According to traditional hermeneutics, the understanding of an eminent text, the work of a genius, is, on the level of generic hermeneutics and critique, not possible without asking the immediate question of truth and beauty. A merging of aesthetics and hermeneutics, of philosophy and hermeneutics, takes place in such a case. The philosophical difference between the traditional and the new hermeneutics is that the former is interested in the questions of why and how methodical discipline is possible and necessary. It is necessary because the uniqueness of the text for the situation of the interpreter can be properly understood only if all the means of methodical hermeneutics and critique on the grammatical, the historical, the individual, and the generic level have been applied correctly.[10]

[9]*Truth and Method,* p. 419.
[10]A Boeckh, *On Itnerpretation and Criticism,* trans. and ed. J. P. Pritchard (Norman: University of Oklahoma Press, 1968), pp. 47 and 164f. The book is an abridged version of Boeckh's *Encyclopaedie und Methodologie der Philologischen Wissenschaften,* ed. Bratuscheck (Klussmann, 1877).

The merits of the antimethodical approach are to have corrobo-
rated the structure of understanding in a living tradition and to have
shown the primacy of this structure. If method is possible, then it has
to be understood as founded in this structure. The difficulty is that,
because of its disinterest in method, the antimethodical approach
leaves us without any information about the place and the possibility
of methodical discipline. The arguments against the first canon have
furthermore completely destroyed the reasons that, in traditional
hermeneutics, could be given in defense of the possibility of methodical discipline. Though the radical reading was not the original intention of Gadamer, the author, it must be said that the destruction
of the first canon has the radical reading as its necessary consequence unless it is shown how methodical discipline is possible.

2. THE AMPHIBOLY OF THE LATENT AND THE PATENT

For the methodical approach in the new hermeneutics the confrontation of traditional hermeneutics as a *hermeneutic of patent
meaning* with a rival *hermeneutics of latent meaning* is characteristic.[11]
Both hermeneutics come together in general hermeneutics. The
mediating instance is the theory of polysemy, which can be understood as a modified version of that which in medieval times was
called higher hermeneutics (i.e., the assumption of a multiplicity of
layers of meaning in the scripture).[12] The hermeneutics of latent
meaning implies the existence of the unconscious. It is the unconscious that indicates the limits of the philosophy of reflection—of
the *cogito*—and the primacy of being in hermeneutical methodology.[13] It indicates in addition the limits of traditional hermeneutics,
understood as a hermeneutics of the patent.

It can be shown, however, that simple opposition of the hermeneutics of the patent to that of the latent implies equivocations
regarding the meaning of "latent" because it is not aware of how the
latent in some of its forms is dealt with in traditional hermeneutics.

---

[11]The opposition of a hermeneutics of the latent and the hermeneutics of the
patent, later developed into the opposition of a hermeneutics of belief and a diagnostic hermeneutics of suspicion, is present in P. Ricoeur's *Freedom and Nature*; cf. Don
Ihde, *Hermeneutic Phenomenology. The Philosophy of Paul Ricoeur*, (Evanston: Northwestern University Press, 1971), pp. 26 ff. Together with the principle of polysemy, it
is the *Leitmotiv* of Ricoeur's hermeneutics.

[12]P. Ricoeur, *The Conflict of Interpretations*, ed. Don Ihde (Evanston: Northwestern
University Press, 1974), pp. 3 and 29.

[13]The critique of the *cogito* and Husserl's transcendental phenomenology is primarily developed in P. Ricoeur, *Freud and Philosophy*, trans. Denis Savage (New Haven:
Yale University Press, 1970), pp. 375ff and 424ff; cf. *Conflicts*, 17ff and 101ff and
236ff.

The principle of polysemy, introduced in the methodical approach, transcends the realm of traditional hermeneutics only in the case of the most radical hermeneutics of suspicion—psychoanalysis.[14] Other instances of the hermeneutics of suspicion and the latent—structuralism and ideology critique—do not reach beyond that which is patent for traditional hermeneutics at all. "Latency" in these cases has to be distinguished from the latent, which is assumed in psychoanalysis and has quite different methodical significance and meaning in structuralistic analysis and ideology critique.

a. STRUCTUALISM AND TRADITIONAL HERMENEUTICS

The "unconscious" of structural linguistics[15] is, in principle, known in traditional hermeneutics. Birt's critical remarks about Boeckh's definition of philology as "knowledge of what has been known" refer to realms of philological knowledge that have not been known and are not known in oral and written speech. Grammatical interpretation presupposes grammer and lexicography, and both deal with relations that are not known as such in actual speech. This knowledge, presupposed in grammatical interpretations of texts, is linguistic knowledge.[16] Linguistic knowledge, already on the merely descriptive level, is guided by methodical principles, which are then made explicit in structural linguistics, which is in its origin nothing more than the result of methodological reflections of linguists on that which is done and has been done in their discipline. These principles are (a) the synchronic aspect is methodically prior; (b) the description of linguistic structures uses terms that belong to a metalanguage; (c) the structures are closed because the set of texts they hold for is finite; (d) irregularities are understood as violations; (e) if the diachronic aspect is introduced to deal with irregularities, change can be understood as bricolage; and (f) change in the history of language cannot be understood as intentional. What structuralist and, in general, modern linguistic have added to these principles are techniques of formalizations for the descriptions and a precise thematization of the difference between language and speech. The benefit for a further development of traditional methodical hermeneutics is the possibility of much more precise formulations of the *second canon*, especially of the concepts "whole" and "part" used here. They have different meaning and different methodical sig-

---

[14]Cf. *Conflicts*, pp. 148ff.

[15]Cf. *Conflicts*, pp. 22–97; *Interpretation Theory*, pp. 2f and 25f.

[16]Th. Birt, *Kritik und Hermeneutik: Handbuch der Klassischen Altertumswissenschaften*, ed. Iwan Mueller, Band I (Abteilung 3, 1913), pp. 4–5.

nificance if referred either to language as linguistic structure and language as oral and written speech in grammatical hermeneutics.

The application of structuralistic techniques in the interpretation of literary genre and even anthropology and culture is by no means incompatible with traditional hermeneutics. Generic hermeneutics presupposes metalinguistic terms in its description of generic forms. The synchronic aspect is again methodically prior. Especially in the case of the work of a genius in the fine arts it is often possible to understand its relation to tradition as bricolage. We are, however, in this case, not dealing with a savage mind, which lacks the possibility of a patent communication with its tradition through texts; we cannot exclude a priori interpretations, which understand such a text as answers to questions given in their tradition.

Structuralism is consequently not a rival of traditional hermeneutics but is rather a refinement of certain aspects of its methods. Thus in what sense is there something latent? An application of formalizations does not create any problem. The problem is the "latency," which is discovered by linguistic reflection in general. Since the different dimensions of such reflections—phonological, semiological, and syntactical—are all given through corresponding abstractive reductions, which disregard the concrete meaning of speech as a whole, it can be said that that which is latent here is latent in the way in which an abstract structure is latent in a concretum. If the concretum is patent, then the latency in question is given through the patent and is thematized by means of a corresponding reduction and reflection. The linguistic reductions, seen from the viewpoint of transcendental phenomenology, are in principle similar to those that lead to the discovery of formal apophantic structures in logic. Neither formal logic nor formal linguistics, though both are unknown in concrete arguments and concrete speeches, indicate in this sense an unconscious. To claim that there is any entity that is more than the correlate of an abstractive reduction must be rejected as uncritical hypostatisation by transcendental phenomenology. This rejection implies rejection of an unjustifiable methodological claim, the reduction of methodical interpretation to structuralist analysis. Transcendental phenomenology is incompatible with certain structuralist philosophies but not with sober structuralist linguistics, genre theory, and anthropology.

b. THE HERMENEUTICS OF SUSPICION AND THE PRINCIPLE OF POLYSEMY

The other type of hermeneutics of the latent, mentioned in the methical approach of the new hermeneutics, is the *hermeneutics of suspicion.* Two types can be distinguished—psychoanalysis and ideology critique.[17] The possible distinction between a left, Marxist and a right, Nietzschean version of ideology critique can be ignored here. The merit of the methodical approach is the discovery of a hermeneutical principle that allows the integration of the hermeneutics of suspicion into a general hermeneutics. This principle is *the principle of polysemy.* The new hermeneutics of suspicion has it in common with the older, higher hermeneutics, which was interested in the allegorical, anagogical, moral, and typological meanings of texts, which cannot be discovered in the analysis of their literal meaning. It is this affinity between higher hermeneutics and hermeneutics of suspicion that indicates the problem of the relationship between hermeneutics of suspicion and traditional hermeneutics.

Higher hermeneutics and hermeneutics of suspicion claim to be able to discover layers of meaning that cannot be discovered in the analysis of the literal meaning of a text. A principle of traditional hermeneutics introduced in the earliest stages of its development is, however, that any layer of meaning of a text can be discovered in an analysis of the literal sense. Furthermore, both presuppose doctrines about the nature of man and the history of mankind as a whole. These doctrines are the methodical tool of the discovery of the hidden meaning and at the same time an explanation of the genesis of different layers of meaning. The history of salvation and its implications about the nature of man have this function for the old higher hermeneutics. The new hermeneutics of suspicion uses doctrines about the nature of man that are supposed to be scientific, and theories about the history of mankind are derived from such doctrines.

Traditional hermeneutics is not able to confirm such theories. What the possibilities of man are is the object of research of indefinite extent. If they cannot be justified as scientific theories, doctrines that imply theorems about universal history are metaphysical doctrines for traditional hermeneutics. If they are scientific, they can neither be falsified nor confirmed through historical-philological research. What this research can do is investigate whether or not certain facts, explained by the doctrines, have happened in exactly the way in which the explanation presupposes it. An explanation can be rejected in demonstrating that the explained fact is not a fact at all. From this it follows that the application of the doctrines of the

---

[17]P. Ricoeur, *Conflicts*, p. 148. Ricoeur does not develop distinctions regarding different types of hermeneutics of suspicion.

hermeneutics of suspicion presupposes one-sidedly that the work of
the philological-historical method has been done and done correctly
(i.e., their relation to this research is not different from any other
application of scientific doctrines in historical explanations). On the
other hand, if the doctrines are really scientific, that which is latent
here for traditional hermeneutics is not latent for science; this means
that the doctrines would be patent for transcendental phenomenology because the constitution of scientific objectivity is patent for
transcendental phenomenology.

The problem of these doctrines, however, is that their claim to be
scientific can easily be challenged, and the methodical approach in
the new hermeneutics is aware of this. They imply assumptions
about history as a process of liberation and emancipation of mankind that are very near to those made in the history of salvation.
Furthermore, to claim to be able to give an account of history as a
whole is as dubious in the sciences as it is in the framework of the
philological-historical method. The methodical approach in the new
hermeneutics denies from the outset the scientific character of the
hermeneutics of the latent. At least it is not interested in it but rather
in its hermeneutical significance. The principle that is invoked here
is polysemy. To examine how the latent content of hermeneutics of
suspicion can be reached, it is useful to investigate the function of
polysemy in realms that can immediately be connected with traditional hermeneutics. The first would be the realm of linguistics; the
second, symbols as the realm of higher hermeneutics. It is the merit
of the methodical approach in the new hermeneutics to have shown
this possibility, but the necessary consequence has not been drawn.
The consequence is that latency cannot be understood as absolutely
opposed to patency, an assumption with which this approach starts.
Latency is always relative latency.

Two observations are essential for the linguistic aspect. Univocity
in meaning of words and symbols can be reached only by considering the context in concrete speech, and absolute univocity cannot be
reached in this process. The multivocity of words and symbols can be
discovered if different contexts using the same word or symbols are
compared. The study of polysemical structures presupposes the
collection and comparison of cases of actual speech. To take into
consideration that the structure of meaning is itself affected by its
application and, in the last instance constituted by it, is the methodical principle of the study of polysemy. This study of the process of
langage, which connects *langue* and *parole*,[18] is known to traditional

---

[18]Cf. *Conflicts* pp. 79f; also *Interpretation Theory*, pp. 2f.

hermeneutics as the interplay of lexicography on the level of grammatical and of individual interpretation. Individual interpretation is not interested in the individual as a psychic entity; it is interested in style, speech. What is latent here? Speech is not latent and neither is the semiological structure insofar as it is thematized. The process of *langage*, mediating between both, is known and is patent as far as the mediating factors are known. It is latent to the extent that semiological structures are not yet thematized and cases of speech are not yet realized. But this is the latency of every object of research, which is either not yet the object of actual research or does not yet exist.

The genesis of the polysemy of symbols in a tradition is accessible if a series of historically ordered texts is pregiven. The difference between higher hermeneutics and the study of polysemy in the framework of traditional hermeneutics is that, in the former the order of texts is at least partially determined by the historiosophical construction, which is characteristic for the presupposed doctrine of the history of mankind, while in the latter it is determined by philological-historical research, which belongs to the hermeneutics of the patent. In such research, latency has the specific meaning of being forgotten or, though present, no longer known in its genetic origin. This is, however, the latency that is continuously produced in a living tradition. It is, in general, the task of the philological method to overcome this latency. The guidelines of research are patent meaning in patent texts, which indicate references to patent meanings in other patent texts. There will always be, of course, a large realm of latency that cannot be reached by the method. But this is the latent, which is either patent in principle, although not yet known as such, or latent and will remain latent because it has never been documented in texts and in traces.

C. IDEOLOGY CRITIQUE AND PSYCHOANALYSIS

The principle of polysemy serves in the methodical approach of the new hermeneutics as the *explanans* of psychoanalysis and ideology critique. It is this realm in which the latent can be understood as a layer of polysemy, which is sedimented and hidden in principle but is nevertheless present as a determining factor. Psychoanalysis offers special problems. Ideology critique however, can be connected with methodical viewpoints in the human sciences. These viewpoints do not belong to hermeneutics in the narrower sense but rather to historical critique.[19] Historical critique works with hypotheses about relations that a certain text or activity has to other texts or activities. Such hypotheses can be confirmed if texts and traces can be found that tell us something about the relation. Hypotheses of this type can have the character of suspicions. The most simple case is the suspicion that a certain text does not tell the truth about certain events. More sophisticated is the suspicion that texts that tell us something about the self-understanding of activities and institutions have, regarding the values they refer to, disproportional relations to the spheres of power and property. Suspicions of this type belong to ideology critique, which, in this case, is a branch of historical critique. These suspicions may refer to misunderstanding the situation, self-misunderstanding, and dishonesty. They are mere hypotheses as long as they are not confirmed by other textual material. The whole process, methodically speaking, is one-sidedly founded on both sides in texts (i.e., in patent hermeneutics and in the interpretation of a meaning that is patent for some consciousness).

Ideology critique can serve as a source for the invention of hypotheses in historical critique. It is not necessary for this purpose explicitly to derive such viewpoints from some psychological or sociological scientific doctrine. Confirmation in historical critique is confirmation on the basis of patent meanings of texts. No additional confirmation of the hypotheses with the aid of a science is necessary. What is latent in such a process? Seen from *the side of the interpreter*, the latent always corresponds to hypotheses not yet confirmed. The reference is to a missing text. If it is found, everything is patent. The latency is again the latency of the objects of the human sciences, which are not yet objects of successful research. Latency on *the side of the text* entails psychological assumptions about the author or readers who have a "false consciousness." This latency is not yet a latency in the strict sense unless a further assumption is added: The author or the readers would not be able to free themselves from their false consciousness and conceive their real situation even if they were confronted with the patent meaning, which is sufficient for the interpreter to confirm his suspicion.

Latency, in all the aspects of its hermeneutics that have been considered, has either the character of an unconfirmed hypothesis of the interpreter or, on the side of the text, a layer of meaning that has not been thematized but could be thematized because it could be assumed that it is meaningful to search for a text in which it is

---

[19]Cf. Boeckh, p. 133, concerning historical critique. Boeckh does not, of course, deal with ideology critique, but its place in the system of methodical hermeneutics is exactly in historical hermeneutics and critique.

thematized, an assumption that is compatible with the fact that such texts often cannot be found or have never been produced.

Is there a realm for the human sciences that is latent in principle? If we understand by prehistory a culture of the savage mind, which has not yet produced a written tradition, then the realm of such a prehistory cannot be reached with texts; it is accessible only through archeological traces. The realm of the savage mind in the present can be reached, however, by ethnology. The hermeneutical peculiarity of ethnological research is that it itself produces the documents that have not been produced by the savage mind itself but which are necessary for research, which can be controlled intersubjectively. The process of understanding such documents and their production belongs to the realm of patent meaning. Applications of ethnological research to prehistory are hypothetical. Some confirmation is possible with the aid of archeological hermeneutics, the principles of which are patent. The latency of prehistory can again be characterized as the latency of an object about which we have a knowledge but which is not yet confirmed and allows us only indirect confirmation.

Strict latency, which is not reducible to relative patency, presupposes, on the side of the text, the psychological assumption mentioned above. The assumption marks the watershed between *simple ideology critique*, which can be understood as a part of historical critique, and *an ideology critique, which is grafted onto psychoanalysis*. The latency is strict because the layer of meaning in question can be reached *ex definition* only if certain psychological techniques are applied. To assume such a layer and polysemical relations between this layer and patent meaning is a hypothesis that cannot be confirmed by the human sciences. If there are scientific reasons for such an assumption no problems would be generated for traditional hermeneutics and transcendental phenomenology.

It is perhaps the lack of scientific character of the assumption that is responsible for the attempt to confirm this assumption with the aid of an hypothesis that belongs to the human sciences and introduces latency in principle. The consequences, however, are paradoxical. What is assumed in the hypothesis is that the savage mind is a layer in the genesis of the human mind and its contents should therefore be present in every layer. Hence every text has reference to them.

Regarding primarily the contents of the savage mind, such a hypothesis, however, can be verified only by the human sciences and hermeneutics of the patent. Even if it can be shown that the same contents that are now those of the unconscious are contents of the savage mind in a prehistory that is common to us all, it is not yet clear why they are unconscious now or in what sense. The very assumption, however, that they have been contents of a prehistoric savage mind has an interesting implication: they were patent. The brothers who killed the father knew what they did in the way in which the savage mind knows, and knowing can be known.

The riddle that is left for the hermeneutics of the patent is why and in what sense is that which was patent now latent and unconscious. The unconscious is discovered by psychoanalysis in the phenomenon of resistance and repression. Repression indicates a complete discontinuity in the genesis of meaning. Traditional hermeneutics presupposes continuity in the genesis of meaning, psychoanalysis and the human sciences can hence be brought together only if it can be shown how such a repression is possible or how the unconscious of psychoanalysis can be constituted within consciousness. This is a task for transcendental phenomenology.

III. THE SOLUTION OF THE ANTINOMY IN THE TRANSCENDENTAL REDUCTION

1. The Development of the Methodological Paradox

It has been shown that the hermeneutics of the patent (i.e., the methodical power of traditional hermeneutics) stretches far beyond the realm it is supposed to cover according to the methodical approach in the new hermeneutics. The hermeneutic of the patent is therefore the crucial problem for every methodical approach. The basic question with which the methodical approach has to be confronted, therefore, is whether it can solve the antimony of method and antimethod.

The paradox of the human sciences is present *prima facie* in the new hermeneutics as the opposition of the antimethodical and the methodical approach. A methodical approach has to give a justification of method. It has to insist on the critical distance grounded in the independence of the text and the legitimacy of genetic explanations. The treatment of the problem of prejudices in interpretation is the watershed between the two approaches. The prejudice on the side of the interpreter is removed for the antimethodical approach if the truth claim of the text is accepted as a question that challenges the interpreter. The methodical approach has to insist on the possibility of removing prejudices with the aid of an epoché, which neutralizes truth claims in general. The problem is, however, that the antimethodical approach asserts the priority of authentic interpretation over methodical interpretation and has backed this claim with arguments against the first canon. The first canon is the presupposition of the development of the epoché in the human sciences and of critical distance in general. Since the methodical approach has not refuted the arguments against the first canon, it has, on the contrary, recognized their validity, its trust in method remains unjustified. The radical reading remains an unchallenged possibility in the framework of the new hermeneutics.

This situation can be superseded only by means of a reflection on a higher level in which the whole context of the situation is thematized. The antimethodical approach has eliminated such a reflection. It denies the possibility of reflecting on oneself outside the context of one's own historicity, out of a living tradition.[20] The methodical approach has blocked such reflections because it considerably restricts the capabilities of reflections with regard to the contents, which belong to the hermeneutics of the latent. The above considerations have had the result that this restriction itself must be restricted. We must therefore attempt such a reflection, which will lead to the transcendental epoché.

Texts communicate meaning through a sign matter, which can be reproduced in original evidence. Hence a text can appear in different contexts. It is therefore as a text separated from the original intention of the author, from contemporary addressees, and from every possible interpreter. This description, introduced by the antimethodical approach and accepted by the methodical, is correct but incomplete.[21] It explains why texts and the historical past are understood in different ways in different phases of living traditions, but it is incomplete as a description of the structure of living tradition. The merging of horizons—the transition from distantiation to participation—does not always have results of the same type. Three ideal types can be distinguished: (a) the positive application of the text, (b) the rejection of its applicability, and (c) the inability of the text to provoke either an application or its rejection. In this case the text is without interest for the interpreter. The corresponding dimensions of a living tradition are the distinction between a true and a false tradition and a steadily growing realm of texts and meanings, which are forgotten in a living tradition.

The observation that, because of the sign matter, one and the same text can be received in different contexts of interpretation is

---

[20]Cf. H. G. Gadamer, *Truth and Method*, pp. 266ff.
[21]See note 6.

also incomplete. For the same reason it is possible that many texts can be present in the context of one interpretation. What can be discovered in this situation are relations between texts. One of them—which is inevitable if a tradition of texts were available that were themselves interpretations of other texts—is that texts refer to other texts in the same way in which the interpreter refers to them in a living tradition. They contain an answer to a question that has been opened up for them by other texts. For every text there is therefore a past horizon that determines the question of truth for this text and a future horizon in which the text determines questions for other texts, and, in the last instance, for the interpreter in the actual Now of a living tradition. The distinction of the horizons can be transformed into a methodical idealization, which is the second canon: a text should be understood out of its own context (i.e., its own past horizon). It is an idealization because it implies the ideal of the completely disclosed past horizon of the text, at least with regard to the texts to which the text refers. The first canon is nothing else but the result of a reflection on that which is given in living tradition. The epoché of the human sciences, which is the result of the decision to apply this canon to every text and every life expression, is therefore rooted in living tradition.

But the structure of a living tradition changes if the epoché is introduced. Methodical interpretation may change that which has been understood to be the truth claim of texts that have been applied, and a text, methodically understood out of its past horizon, produces new challenges and questions. Furthermore, since the method is interested in the answer the text gives in its own situation, it can be applied to texts that are of no immediate interest for the living tradition. The result can be an understanding that is of interest. The method works its way backward into the past horizon of a text, and that which it discovers are other texts to which the method can again be applied. The method works its way back through the continuum of forgotten text of the living tradition. That which has become latent is made patent again for a possible merging of horizons in a living tradition.

The correlate of the epoché is a universe of meaning that has to be understood out of its own context. It is an intersubjectivity of meaning in general. The epoché is developed within a living tradition, and this is the tradition of a lifeworld. The idea of an intersubjectivity in general is grafted onto this lifeworld. The attitude of members of this lifeworld toward alien subjectivity, alien lifeworlds included, is changed by the epoché. The idea of "understanding in its own context" is an attitude that is transferred as a possible modification to the actual encounter with others and with other cultures. The correlative idea is the idea of an understanding of all foreign cultures, of mankind. This correlate version of the epoché is the medium in which the formulations that are rejected by the new hermeneutics can be understood. They understand the interpreter-text relation and text-text relations as actual encounters. Though, as formulations of the first canon, they are misleading, the transference itself is a legitimate move of reflection of the situation generated by the epoché and the first step on the way that leads to historism.

The context of the interpreter is not included in the epoché of the human sciences when the epoché refers only to documents and traces. The process of interpretation may produce a document, but it is not itself a document. Such a reduction of the epoché to the professional attitude of the philologist and historian is, in the last instance, impossible. The epoché stands in a living tradition, in a lifeworld. A reflection on this origin of the epoché itself must include this lifeworld itself and all activity of interpretation in this lifeworld. Since the epoché restricts the claim to truth, to a certain context the level of historical relativism is reached: Every truth is relative because it is context bound, the truths of the own living tradition included.

Such a position is opposed to the self-consciousness of the actual Now of a living tradition. Truth is here known as an event that takes place in this Now without any restriction and relativity. It is there as original evidence. The antimethodical in the new hermeneutics is an attempt to restore this original claim of truth against method. It is, however, not able to overcome the paradox; it transforms it into the antinomy of method and antimethod. The critique of the claim for validity in method is rooted in two principles: (a) no interpreter is capable of moving himself out of his own context; and (b) no validity claim can transcend its own context. These principles are, however, results of reflections on the epoché. They presuppose that the epoché has taken place in the living tradition. Simple historism restricts itself to a relativism of truth claims in different cultures. The radicalized historism of historicity in the antimethodical approach is nothing more than the explicit inclusion of the process of interpretation itself in the epoché and hence the extension of the epoché which is most universal because it includes the epoché itself.

2. THE SOLUTION OF THE ANTINOMY

The presupposition of this whole movement of reflection, which governs the new hermeneutics as well as the old, is that all moments in the past that have been a Now of a living tradition, the actual Now of the living tradition in which we stand, and all future Nows are projected on one and the same level—the level of the genesis of reflection and interpretation, which takes place in mundane temporality. Such a projection is, on all levels, the result of a mundane reflection and self-reflection in the natural attitude. That means, however, that no actual Now that is not reflected upon this manner is on this level. The actual Now of a living tradition, which refers immediately to truth, can make its truth claims only insofar as it is the activity of interpreting and reflecting, which is not yet reflected upon and hence is not yet projected on the mundane level. What the antimethodical approach must presuppose if it is not to perish in the paradoxes of historicity is that every past Now can be apprehended in an attitude that is not mundane. The prerequisite for such an apprehension is knowledge about the transmundane character of the own actual Now. The epoché of the human sciences, thus far as it remains in the natural attitude, necessarily projects all truth claims of texts into contexts of mundane temporality at the very moment in which the epoché is understood to be more than a professional attitude, based on the first canon as a regulative principle. It is the inclusion of actual interpretative activity in this projection that leads to the paradox. Every interpretative activity, methodical as well as premethodical, implies truth claims. This immediate reference to truth, however, is transcendental. It cannot be found in mundane self-objectification. The epoché of the human sciences and the methodical activity of the human sciences can be understood in the transcendental attitude as an activity with its own universal truth claim.

The transcendental self-apprehension, which refers ideally to all past Nows, implies the unity of a transcendental genesis of truth claims in the form of a regulative idea. This idea refers to the horizons of meaning, which can be discovered and have been discovered before the transcendental turn under the epoché of the human sciences and the actual Nows belonging to them. If they are understood in their transmundane aspect, then the task, outlined by the idea, would be to conceive them in their relation to a universal transcendental genesis of truth in the transmundane actual Now. The structure of the regulative idea is discovered in the self-explication of the actual Now. What the actual Now is is known originally in the

Now of the living tradition, the Now of the actual process of interpreting and understanding. An approach to transcendental genesis and temporality is given only in this actual Now. To extend the unity and the form of this unity over all past Nows of alien living tradition is an idealization. It is justifiable because the way back to the Now of living tradition as transcendental leading to the analysis of a transcendental understanding of the temporality of this Now is the result of a chain of reflections, which is one-sidedly founded on the discovery of the universe of meaning given in the epoché of the human sciences. A more intrinsic analysis of this idealization will prepare the question of what is patent and what is latent for transcendental phenomenology.

IV. THE SOLUTION OF THE AMPHIBOLY: HUMAN SCIENCES IN THE FRAMEWORK OF TRANSCENDENTAL PHENOMENOLOGY.

The methodical approach of the new hermeneutics has criticized transcendental phenomenology as a philosophy of consciousness and the *cogito*. Regarding such criticism, it is useful to compare the Cartesian path to the transcendental reduction, to the path via the human sciences outlined above. The latter has the advantage of indicating the universal content of the residuum of the transcendental epoché. It has the further advantage of leading immediately to the stratum of genesis and temporality. The Cartesian path begins with the question of the thesis of the existence of the world and of the *cogito*. It reaches the stratum of genesis only via the analysis of the *cogito* and after performing the apodictic reduction to living duration. Only after reaching this level does it become clear that the *ego* and the *cogito* are constituted as units within the passive constitution of transcendental temporality. The *ego* and the *cogito* are transcendental because they belong to this unity and have the origin of their unity in it. The path to the reduction via the human sciences shows from the very beginning that transcendental phenomenology is not a philosophy of the *cogito* and consciousness but rather of their genesis and constitution.

1. HUMAN SCIENCES AS SCIENCES OF WHAT IS PATENT

What is patent for transcendental phenomenology? Patent in the sense of "adequate and original evidence of existence" is that which is given in living duration. Patent in the sense of "apodictic evidence of an eidetic structure" is the structure of living duration. This evidence includes the evidence of an indefinitely open and multidimensional continuum of retentions belonging to the living duration with contents not given in adequate original evidence. They can be reproduced in secondary memory. That which is given in secondary memory is not adequate, but it is sufficient for eidetic investigations of eidetic structures in the correlation *noesis-noema* and its genesis. Such investigations stretch beyond the realm of adequate and original giveness in a double way. The phantasy modifications, which are necessary for the constitution of eidetic self-objectification in the transcendental attitude, cover temporal phases that go beyond actual living duration, and the content itself, with which the modifications start, is in most cases pregiven by secondary memory.

For a correct understanding of the relationship between transcendental phenomenology and the human sciences the following point is crucial: contents of secondary memory are given originally in the natural attitude. They are contents available for the transcendental attitude only because they have been contents of secondary memory in the natural attitude. Two transcendental theorems have to be kept in mind:

1. the natural as well as the transcendental attitude is rooted in the transmundane actual Now; the difference is that this is known in the transcendental but not in the natural attitude.
2. Every oblique, reflective intentionality is one-sidedly founded in direct, object-related intentionality. The natural attitude is from the outset founded in direct intentionality; the transcendental attitude is the result of thoroughgoing, reflective, oblique intentionality.

The contents of secondary memory imply intersubjectivity, the lifeworld, and a living tradition in all cases of objects of higher levels of constitution. Some of the contents of higher order—among others, those that refer to the difference between lifeworld and science—are provided by the human sciences. The epoché of the human sciences implies the inhibition of the thesis of immediate truth claims and prepares the transformation of the contents to the transcendental level. That which has to be added in order to reach the transcendental epoché is the reflection on the presupposition of the possibility of the constitution of the truth claim in the actual Now.

With this in mind, we would be absurd to presuppose that contents such as the culture of the savage mind in the concrete form that it has (e.g., in the culture of the Zulu) should be patent for transcendental phenomenology as such. It is patent for it only because it has been made patent by the human sciences. Transcendental phenomenology is not and cannot be interested in the facts of this and that culture. It is interested in the *eidos* "lifeworld of the savage mind" and the ideal necessities and possibilities that connect this type of lifeworld with other types of lifeworlds. Transcendental phenomenology knows about facticity as the dark ground of irrationality in living duration. The facts themselves, however, are the domain of the researcher in the human sciences. He provides the material for eidetic variation in phenomenology. One of the temptations of the phenomenologist is to transform eidetic analysis into story telling (i.e., to confuse his business with the business of the researcher in the human sciences).

2. THE PROBLEM OF THE LATENT IN TRANSCENDENTAL PHENOMENOLOGY

If this is the case, then it is meaningless to criticize transcendental phenomenology for its inability to discover the concrete contents of the unconscious before they are discovered by psychology in specific encounters with the other in a specific cultural context. All content is given first in the natural attitude. Given this discovery, however, it is the problem of transcendental phenomenology to analyze the constitution of an unconscious as an ideal possibility. Such an analysis does not necessarily follow the self-understanding of this or that type of psychoanalysis. It can be a transcendental critique of this self-understanding. The next step would be the investigation of the eidetic necessities in the contents of the unconscious and their genetic relations to the development of other contents (i.e., to ask the question about the reasons of the assumption that the unconscious contains a level of meaning that is one-sidedly determinative for higher levels). The layer of meaning, of course, is for this purpose not presupposed as unconscious but as conscious again. A short outline of such an enterprise can be given.[22]

---

[22]Cf. H. Drüe, *Edmund Husserl System der phaenomenologischen Psychologie* (Berlin: De Gruyter, 1968), pp. 307–315, chapter on the "Genesis des Unbewussten," Drüe is a trained psychiatrist. His conclusion is:

> . . . a phenomenological psychology does not [need] to founder on the problem of the unconscious as has so much hitherto existing philosophy and psychology. . . . The factual investigation of depth-psychological events is, however, naturally the task of a depth psychology proceeding in an abstractively pure manner" (my translation).

I have seen no case in all the attempts to construct an opposition between psychoanalysis and transcendental phenomenology that can count as a convincing counterargument. On the contrary, Drüe's investigations are simply neglected.

The activity of the ego transpires in the hyletic field. Past activities constitute habits that determine present action. The genesis of habits is a process by which the ego receives a character. It begins on the lowest levels of constitution and takes place long before the ego is constituted as a person. The past activities themselves belong to the hyletic field. They are united with the ego in passive genesis and can be thematized by it. The thematizing of habits happens in acts of secondary memory, which trace them back to their origin. The power of private secondary memory is limited. The aid of the secondary memory of others and documentations of the past are often indispensable for the guidance of secondary memory. Investigations into the realm of the preconscious often presuppose intersubjective encounters. A first meaning of resistance and repression can be discovered on this level. Resistance against realizing in secondary memory that which is indicated by documents and memories of others is a repression of possible contents of secondary memory. Repressions of this kind constitute the objects of the hermeneutics of suspicion within the framework of historical critique.

A repression that constitutes an unconscious in the strict sense is something stronger. It must refer to a complete phase of the past, and it cannot be rooted in an intentional act of the ego. Repressions in the realm of the preconscious are intentional acts and can be identified as such. The false consciousness of ideology critique can be transformed into a bad conscience (i.e., the insight into the failure of adequate understanding of the situation). Repressions that constitute an unconscious are not intentional acts of the ego but something that happens to it. They are founded on traumatic experiences. The ideal possibility of such an event in the genesis of consciousness is conceivable in transcendental phenomenology. The hyletic field is constituted in the same temporality in which the ego is constituted together with its character, its habitual inclinations toward certain activities. The ego is not master over the hyletic field. It can be completely overpowered by it. Overpowering means that a new field of experience, demanding a new system of habits for positive responses and punishing the most essential habits of the old with traumatic responses, is forced on the ego by the hyletic field. In order to survive as a concrete unity, the ego has to build itself up as a new, concrete unity. The old unity no longer belongs to the new, concrete unity but is nevertheless there because it belongs to the same concrete unit of passive genesis. The old system is egoless, an id, but not because there was never an ego belonging to it. It is egoless because it is incompatible with the new system in which the ego understands itself as a concrete unity. This presupposes that it does not identify itself with the old system. The old system is present, but it is experienced as an alien and dangerous power that has to be repressed in the secondary and now deliberate intentional repression if its influence on activities are felt. To identify with habitual inclinations always means to recognize in general their temporal origin in ones's own past. Habitual inclinations, with which no identification is possible, are timeless. The unconscious is timeless in this sense.

The ideal possibility of repression and the constitution of the unconscious is conceivable and patent for transcendental phenomenology because the constitution of the ego as some concrete unity of habits is co-temporal with the constitution of the hyletic field and in its facticity one-sidedly founded in its facticity. The question is whether or not psychoanalysis has discovered an instance of such an event in the genesis of consciousness (i.e., a case of complete incompatibility of an already constituted system of habits and a sphere of new experience). The content of the unconscious can be characterized as a system of meaning in a symbolic imagery that is built up according to certain associative laws and in which no explicit distinction between object, desire, or symbol has taken place. Ego and alter ego are likewise represented in this system. They have no identity of their own. Transcendental phenomenology has thematized the eidetic structure of such a realm of constitution. It is the realm of synthesis in primordial constitution. Transcendental phenomenology has of course not conducted research about this or that concrete system of imagery.

The next prerequisite that has to be met for the constitution of an unconscious is a *sudden* encounter with a system of meaning that is discovered as already there in the structure of a widening experience. This would be an encounter with the correlate of an intersubjective constitution in which the ego discovers itself as already objectified and understood. The discovery itself is in the very beginning founded in the experiential responses in the hyletic field, which might be traumatic. The ego here discovers its superego as the new system of habits that are intersubjectively expected to be its habits and that it has to adopt. The two levels of constitution are patent for transcendental phenomenology, and the ideal *possibility* of a complete incompatibility is patent for transcendental phenomenology. What is patent for transcendental phenomenology is furthermore that there is no ideal *necessity* for the constitution of an unconscious, which is an unconscious of repression, in this situation. The constitution of such an unconscious happens in a specific cultural situation, and there is no law a priori that it always has to happen, particularly because the content of the system of meaning, which is intersubjectively constituted, is different from case to case; the question of whether or not, or if so, in what respect, it is incompatible with the imagery of a primordial constitution—and there might be different ones!—thus has to be answered differently in different cases.

The critical result of this analysis is that every application of psychoanalysis outside the cultural context in which it has been developed stands under the jurisdiction of the human sciences, the explanation of why an unconscious of a specific type has been constituted, in a certain context, included. Many empirical problems, especially those referring to the question as to whether or not the savage mind in human beings has developed the same system of desires, with the same system of desires in all cases, will remain latent, but only in the sense—developed above—in which something is latent for the human studies. One point is essential: the transition from the savage mind as such to higher levels of consciousness does not imply the constitution of an unconscious. The presupposition of the encounter between a system of imagery and a fully developed system of intersubjectively constituted meaning is not yet fulfilled in this phase. The genesis is in this case not yet a discontinuity. There is no discontinuity in the development of cultures. An abrupt discontinuity can happen only for an individual adapting to a culture.

The relationship between the path to the transcendental reduction via the human sciences and that via psychology can now be determined. As with every theory or doctrine, psychologies constitute different types of mundane self-understanding. As such they are included in the human sciences. The specific character of psychology is that its object itself can be understood as having its own genesis, and the analysis of this genesis is again an object of the human sciences. The genesis of psychology is implied in that of its object. Psychoanalysis is the level of psychological reflection at which it becomes inevitable to explicate psychological theory with doctrines that have a legitimate meaning only if they are understood as research hypotheses of the human sciences, which can be confirmed, however, only to a very low degree. The path to transcendental phenomenology via the human sciences implies, therefore, the path via psychology.

The critique of phenomenology implied in the methical approach in the new hermeneutics is based on doubtful explication of that which "patent" and "latent" can mean in traditional hermeneutics and in transcendental phenomenology. This approach, furthermore, neglects the fact that the problem of the unconscious is double sided in psychoanalysis. It is not only the clinical problem of the unconscious that shall become conscious again: where id was, there the ego shall be. If psychoanalysis is used beyond the clinical realm to produce hypotheses for the human sciences concerning prehistory and the savage mind, then it holds as well: where the id is the ego was. The brothers who killed the father knew what they did and they did not develop immediately after the killing of the psyche of a Viennese bourgois. The hypothesis generates a whole research program for the human sciences in which everything is patent that is an object of sucessful research, and the latent is exactly that which is not such an object. The methodological interplay of psychoanalysis and the human sciences, correctly understood, leads us to the correct formulation of the corresponding phenomenological problem. It is a problem of transcendental genesis: how is the unconscious constituted within the genesis of consciousness? The old principle, which implies a formulation of the epoché of the human sciences, holds for psychoanalysis as well: "Homo sum; humanum nihil a me alienum puto."

PART II

Heidegger

WALTER BIEMEL

FIVE

ON THE COMPOSITION AND UNITY
OF *HOLZWEGE*

(Translated by Michael E. Zimmerman)*

IN A HANDWRITTEN DRAFT of the foreword to the *Holzwege* essays, we find the passage:

> Taken externally, they are given as a collection of essays about objects which have no relation among themselves. Thought from the matter itself, everything stands in a hidden and rigorously developed unity.

This paper shall attempt to investigate this harmony to make visible the structural plan. For this it is necessary to call to mind the leading thoughts of the various contributions. This rapid survey is merely an expedient. To explicate fully what Heidegger says in them, a seminar of several semesters would be required.

The Origin of the Work of Art (1935–1936) poses the question as to the essence *(Wesen)* of art by bringing into view the "work-character of the work" (67 [80]). Art is understood in terms of truth: "The truth of being has set itself into the work" (25 [36]). And "to be true means to set up a world" (33 [44]). Here Heidegger unfolds a new concept of world in comparison with that of *Being and Time*. Truth

---

*The translator would like to thank Jeffner Allen, Keith Hoeller, and Theodore Kisiel for their invaluable assistance with the translation.

In referring to *Holzwege*, the German page number is given first, followed in brackets by the corresponding page number of the English translation. The translation of the various essays in *Holzwege* are found in the following volumes: "The Origin of the Work of Art" in *Poetry, Language,* and *Thought*, trans. Albert Hofstadter (New York: Harper and Row, 1971); "The Age of the World-Image" in *The Question Concerning Technology and Other Essays*, trans. William Lovitt (New York: Harper & Row, 1977); *Hegel's Concept of Experience* (New York: Harper & Row, 1970); "Nietzsche's Word 'God is Dead' "; in *The Question Concerning Technology*; "What Are Poets For?" in *Poetry, Language* and *Thought*; "The Anaximander Fragment" in *Early Greek Thinking*, trans. David Farrell Krell and Frank A. Capuzzi (New York: Harper & Row, 1976). The renderings given in these translations have been followed in many but not all instances.

itself gets taken as "clearing" (*Lichtung*) and as a twofold concealment (*Verbegung*). Untruth is the fundamental concealment. (Cf.
"mystery" in *On the Essence of Truth*.) Truth gets experienced as that
primordial strife "in which that open center is won within which
what is stands, and from which it sets itself back into itself" (43 [55]).

One mode of the happening (*Geschehen*) of truth is the work-ing
(*Werksein*) of the work: "The appearing articulated in the work is the
beautiful" (44 [56]). Preserving belongs both to the art work and to
its appearance. "Standing within the openness of being which happens in the work" and "the sober standing inside of the extraordinary awesomeness of the truth that is happening in the work" are
demanded (55 [67f]). Why does the truth that happens get characterized as "awesome"? Because we do not know about it (so I would
like to interpret this assertion) it is unfamiliar to us and, although we
stand in the midst of it, we do not ask about it at all. The leading
thought of this first text is the relationship of art and truth, where
truth is no longer understood in the traditional sense, and art is no
longer understood in terms of *mimesis* and the activity of enjoyment
(aesthetics).

The Age of the World-Image (1938). The event (*Ereignis*), which we
might call the founding of the modern age, is investigated here:
"The conquest of the world as image. Now the word image means:
the formation of the producing which represents. In this, man
struggles for the position in which he can be that being who gives the
measure to all beings and draws up their rules" (87 [134]). In the
supplements to this text we find the following instructive points:

> What is essential for a fundamental metaphysical position in-
> cludes:
> 1. the way and manner in which man is man and so himself; the
>   essential mode of selfhood, which does not coincide with I-hood,
>   but is determined from the relation to Being as such;
> 2. the essential interpretation of the Being of being;
> 3. the essential projection of truth;
> 4. the sense according to which man is here and there the measure
>   (96 [145]).

The emergence of man as subject is accompanied by a new projection of nature, whereby modern natural science necessarily becomes
mathematical science. This fashions the presupposition for modern
technology (*Technik*) since the latter is only a consequence of this
matephysical change. In and through technology man becomes
master over nature.

This transformation, the establishment of modern metaphysics,
fashions the presupposition for the modern form of science. Science

stands not in opposition to metaphysics but as a consequence of the transformed metaphysics. Here Heidegger concretely investigates how the transformation of metaphysics involves also a change in the knowledge of being—knowledge of man himself—and the dwelling of man in the midst of being. At the same time we have a change in the essence of truth. Truth becomes certainty; this change requires an approach to beings that guarantees certainty, and this in turn is a projection of beings, which makes possible their exact graspability —which is executed in the mathematical projection of nature. Metaphysics, science, technology belong together and are results of the essential change of metaphysically appropriated truth. (Cf. also Heidegger's lecture-course, *What Is a Thing?*)

Hegel's Concept of Experience (1942–1943). Heidegger provides a detailed interpretation of Hegel's "Introduction" to the *Phenomenology of Spirit*, and thus at the same time an interpretation of the unfolding of modern metaphysics from Descartes to Hegel, in which "true being has set itself up as the actual, whose actuality is spirit. But the essence of spirit rests in self-consciousness" (117 [27]). Why is the title "Hegel's Concept of Experience"? The fifteenth paragraph of the text explains: "Through this necessity the way to science is itself already *science* and moreover, with regard to its content, science of the *experience* of *consciousness*" (117 [26]).

The self-certainty of knowledge is the medium in which we move; self-consciousness forms experience and is that which first comes to self-consciousness in the formed experience. The first proposition about consciousness thus runs: "But consciousness is for itself its own concept." And with relation to experience: "Consciousness gives its own measure to itself" (155 [95]).

Knowing frees itself from the objects; this freeing (absolving) is the presupposition for self-certain knowing as Absolute. In this way science arrives at the *parousia* of the Absolute. Heidegger sketches the history of metaphysics, beginning with the determination of *on*, and refers in conclusion to the moment-of-willing, which also gets thought in Hegelian consciousness:

> The statement "The experience of consciousness is thoroughgoing skepticism," and the statement "Phenomenology is the Golgotha of absolute Spirit," join the completion of the work to its beginning. But what is essential in the *Phenomenology of Spirit* is not the work as the achievement of a thinker, but the work as the reality of consciousness itself. Because phenomenology is experience, the beingness of beings, therefore it is the gathering of self-appearance in concentration upon the appearance out of the light of the Absolute.

> But the gathering self-concentration is the unspoken nature of
> the will. The will wills itself in the *parousia* of the Absolute that is
> with us. "Phenomenology" itself is Being according to whose mode
> the Absolute is with us in and for itself. This Being wills, willing
> beings its nature (187 [147f]).

This quotation merits a seminar by itself. We content ourselves with
saying that Heidegger sees in Hegel's *Phenomenology*, and also in the
Logic, a decisive indication of the self-unfolding truth of metaphysics. Hegel is the highpoint of the position inaugurated by Descartes. Here consciousness has become absolute consciousness,
which is possible only if being as such is thought and understood as
Spirit. In this interpretation, Heidegger gives us at the same time a
look back at metaphysics from its beginnings on, and in particular at
modern metaphysics from Descartes through Leibniz to Kant,
Fichte, and Schelling, to end with Hegel as the high-point.

Nietzsche's Word "God is Dead" (1943). The interpretation points to
Nietzsche as the supposed final stage of metaphysics:

> In the overturning executed by Nietzsche, metaphysics is still only
> the inversion into its un-essence. The super-sensible becomes an
> unstable product of the sensible (193 [53f]).

Nietzsche himself interprets the course of Western history metaphysically as "the emergence and the unfolding of nihilism" (194
[54]). With the death of God, nothingness spreads. "Nihilism—'the
most uncanny of all guests'—stands at the door" (200 [62]). The
devaluing of the highest is for Nietzsche the lawfulness of history.

The expression "Nihilism" is ambiguous; incomplete Nihilism
fills the always empty place with substitutes: socialism, Wagnerism.
Nietzsche, on the other hand, wants a new principle of value
positing—the living (209 [70]). Preservation and enhancement are
the principles of life. The will posits value-points. "The will to power
is the ground for the necessity of value positing and the origin of the
possibility of value appraising." And further:

> . . . values are the conditions of the will to power which are posited
> by will to power itself. When the will to power comes to appearance
> as the fundamental trait of everything actual, i.e. becomes true and
> to that extent gets conceived as the actuality of the actual, only then
> does it become clear from whence values arise and through what all
> value—appraising remains supported and led (213 [75]).

Certainty as the principle of modern metaphysics is first explicitly
grounded in the will to power:

> Just as in Nietzsche's metaphysics the thought of value is more
> fundamental than the grounding thought of certainty in the

metaphysics of Descartes, insofar as certainty can only be valid as the correct (*Recht*) if it is valid as the highest value; so, in the age of the culmination of Western metaphysics with Nietzsche the insightful self-certainty of *Subjectität* proves to be the justification of the will to power according to the justice which prevails in the Being of being (227 [91]).

The super-sensible ground of the super-sensible world has . . . become un-real: That is the metaphysical sense of the metaphysically thought word, "God is dead" (234 [91]).

The Overman has not taken the place of God, but he works in the realm of *Subjeckität*:

All being is now either the actual as the object, or actualizing as objectification, in which the objectivity of the object is formed. Objectification poses pre-sentingly the object to the *ego cogito*. In this posing the *ego* shows itself as that which lies at the basis of its own act (the pre-senting posing), i.e. as *subjectum*. The subject is subject for itself. The essence of consciousness is self-consciousness (236 [100]).

This leads to the final conclusion:

The earth can only show itself as the object of attack, which is guided by the unconditioned objectification in the will of man. Nature, because it is willed from the essence of Being, appears everywhere as the object of technology (236 [100]).

Heidegger shows that what Nietzsche supposedly characterizes as the overcoming of nihilism, wherein Being becomes value, is instead the culmination of nihilism:

For now metaphysics not only does not think Being itself, but this not-thinking of Being cloaks itself in the illusion that it in fact thinks Being in the worthiest of ways, because it appraises Being as value. . . (239 [104]).

Indeed it is shown that the history of metaphysics taken together becomes Nihilism: "Being does not come into the light of its proper essence. . . . The truth of Being slips away. It remains forgotten" (244 [110]).

The Nietzsche-interpretation (cf. also the lecture courses later published as Volume I of *Nietzsche*) ends with the strange assertion, "Thinking begins only when we have experienced that Reason, which has been dominant for centuries, is the most stubborn adversary of Thinking" (247 [112]). This proposition makes Heidegger appear to be an irrationalist, as those opposed to him have always declared. But this is most certainly a remarkable irrationalism, concerned as it is with thinking. Do we really know what "thinking" means?

What are Poets For? (1946). Reference has already been made to the meaning of art in the Nietzsche interpretation; now it is thematized explicitly—not art in general but rather art in a specific historical moment. This moment, more precisely this epoch, is explicitly poetized by Hölderlin. It is the epoch of the absence of God, after the death of Christ and after the disappearance of Dionysius and Heracles:

> The absence of God means that no god any longer gathers men and things into himself, visibly and unequivocally, and by such gathering disposes the world's history and man's sojourn in it. . . The time of the world's night is the destitute time, because it becomes ever more destitute. It has already grown so destitute, it can no longer discern the absence of God as an absence (248 [91]).

In this time, poets are necessary who "attend, singing, to the trace of the fugitive gods" (251 [94]). After the introduction, which shows through an example of Hölderlin why the poet must purposely poetize the essence of poetry, the Rilke interpretation begins with the question whether Rilke is a poet in a needy time.

For Rilke, the time is needy because mortals do not know death, passion, and love (*Sonnets to Orpheus*, I, XIX). The *Sonnets to Orpheus* and the *Duino Elegies* are the genuine high points of Rilke's creative work. Heidegger chooses the poem that Rilke characterizes as "improvised verse" to explain his fundamental terms: nature as primordial ground (257 [101]), Being as a bold venture (258 ff [102 ff]), "pure difficulty," "ungranted middle," the "pure relation" (*Bezug*) (261 [105]), the "open" (262[106]). Yet this concept is clearly sublated (*aufgehoben*) by the open as Heidegger thinks it. For Heidegger, the open is the outstanding feature of man, but for Rilke, it is the outstanding feature of the creature. For Heidegger, Rilke remains in the realm of the truth of being (*Seienden*), which is also the realm of Nietzsche.

But, as the man who takes risks, the poet is not only oriented toward producing and arranging; this becomes clear from Rilke's explanation of the "gravity" (*Schwerkraft*) of pure strengths, which has nothing to do with natural scientific gravitation. The inner space of the heart stands in opposition to calculated world-space. For Rilke, the meaning of recalling (*Er-innerung*) is that it

> . . . converts that nature of ours which merely wills to impose, together with its objects, into the innermost invisible region of the heart's space. . . . The inner recalling is the conversion of the parting into an arriving at the widest orbit of the Open (285 [130f]).

But what can be more risky than life?

Language (die Sprache). "Language is the precint (*templum*), that is, the house of Being" (286 [132]). Because the venturesome risk language, turning back into the realm of the heart is possible. The angel has brought about the entire relation — the unity of both realms (of life and of death). The angels have taken together the visible and the invisible, and therefore Rilke poetizes angels. Indeed, according to Heidegger, Rilke's angels and Nietzsche's Zarathustra are metaphysically the same. (We shall come back to this.)

The venturesome — the legendary sayers, the singers: "Their singing is turned away from all purposeful self-assertion. It is not a willing in the sense of desire" (291 [138]). In the sonnets it is clearly said, Song is *Dasein*. But when are we? When we belong in the pure relation (*Bezug*):

> Because they convert the parting against the Open and inwardly recall its unwholesomeness into a sound whole, these poets sing the healing whole in the midst of the unholy. The recalling conversion has already overtaken the parting against the Open. It is "ahead of all parting" and outlives everything objective within the world's inner space of the heart (293 [140]).

At the end we find this passage: "They [the poets] bring to mortals the trace of the fugitive gods, the track into the dark of the world's night. As the singers of soundness, the more venturesome ones are 'poets in a destitute time' " (294 [141]). Because Hölderlin is the first one who has known this and said it in poetry, he remains unsurpassable.

The Anaximander Fragment (1946). First, Heidegger provides an account of the difficulty of translation. It is a matter of grasping the issue (*Sache*). Only thinkers can help here. But Hegel, who has experienced the history of thinking in a thoughtful way, says nothing about this saying. The fragment deals with *onta* in the sense of *ta panta,* but these are not the *physei onta. Diké, adikia, tisis* have a broad meaning and are not to be understood from jurisprudence. The question is, What remains in the fragment of Anaximander, and what is added to it from a later time? According to Heidegger, a literal translation of the fragment runs:

> But that from which things arise also gives rise to their passing away, according to what is necessary; for things render justice and pay penalty to one another for their injustice, according to the ordinance of time (303 [20]).

Of the original fragment there remains only, "according to necessity; for they pay one another recompense and penalty for their injustice" (314 [29]). But the part before, in which *genesis kai phthora* is spoken of, must not simply be left out. *Genesis* is thought from *physis,* to escape hiddenness. "The fragment speaks of that which, as it approaches, arrives in unconcealment, and which, having arrived here, departs by withdrawing into the distance" (316 [31]). Being is not thought of as the opposite of Becoming but as supporting and shaping Becoming. This is explained by Homer, by the meanings of *estin, en, estai, einai.* The seer sees that which is present and past and that which is coming to be. To this is added an elucidation of the ambiguity of *eonta,* which means both: what is presently coming-to-presence (*das gegenwärtig Anwesende*), and then also everything coming-to-presence—presently or not presently.

For the Greeks, being is "what presently-or-unpresently comes-to-presence, coming to presence in unconcealment" (322 [36f]). Since the presence of coming-to-presence is in itself already truth as "lighting-concealing gathering" ("*lichtendbergende Versammlung*"), the *einai* is "in a hidden way a property of truth" (322 [37]). *Eon* and *eonta* become the fundamental word of the thinking of Parmenides a few decades later: *hen.* And Heidegger says that in this view, "Only as a result of the destiny (*Geschick*) of Being, as the destiny of *hen,* does the modern age, after essential upheavals, enter the epoch of the monadology of substance, which completes itself in the phenomenology of spirit" (324f [39]).

Heidegger provides a penetrating interpretation of the fragment, which we will not follow in detail. Even with all the meaning that is given to this fragment, it still means already here at the beginning: "The essence of coming to presence and with it the distinction between coming to presence and that-which comes to presence remain forgotten" (336 [50]). And further:

> This history of Being begins with the oblivion of Being, since Being—together with its essence, its distinction from beings—keeps to itself. The distinction collapses. It remains forgotten. Although the two parties to the distinction, that which comes-to-presence and coming-to-presence, reveal themselves, they do not do as *as* distinguished. Rather, even the early trace of the distinction is obliterated when coming-to-presence appears as an instance of that which comes-to-presence, and finds its origin in a highest instance of that which-comes-to-presence (336 [50f]).

With the interpretation of *to chreón* as use, custom, usage (*Brauch*), Heidegger does not proceed etymologically; rather because he thinks through and conceives the state-of-affairs, he can translate (*über-setzen*).

> *To chreón* conceals in itself the still hidden (*ungehobene*) essence of the gathering which clears and shelters. Use is the gathering: *ho*

Logos. From the essence of *Logos*, thought in this way, the essence of Being is determined as the unifying one: *Hen.* Parmenides thinks the same *Hen.* He thinks the unity of this unifying one explicitly as *Moira* (Frg. VIII, 37). Thought from the essential experience of Being, *Moira* corresponds to the *Logos* of Heraclitus. The essence of *Moira* and *Logos* is thoughtfully intimated in the *chreón* of Anaximander (340 [55]).

The text ends with a reference to the essence of thinking—to the relation of man to Being. So much for the intellectual aids to the works found in *Holzwege.*

* * *

Now if we query the unity and the composition of this book of essays, the answer forces itself upon us: in the works "The Age of the World-Image," "Hegel's Concept of Experience," "Nietzsche's Word 'God is Dead'," and "What Are Poets For?" in a destitute time, Heidegger gives something like an account of the history of the metaphysics of the modern age. Indeed in "The Age of the World-Image," we perceive how the presupposition for natural science is fashioned—through Descartes' transformation of metaphysics, which involves the fact that truth becomes certainty and that beings become to-be-represented (*Vorgestelltsein des Seienden*). We also perceive how this presupposition leads to the decisive change in man's relation to beings, namely, beings become things to be dominated, mastered. We recall that the demand for certainty demands an exact projection of nature as well as how the demand is realized in the mathematical projection of nature. In this projection of nature there is already implanted technology, namely the determinate mode of dealing with beings in terms of their disposability. Only now does man become the subject, do beings become that which is represented by man, does truth become certainty, does man step onto center stage.

If in this essay ("The Age of the World-Image") we were situated at the beginning of the metaphysics of the modern age, in the Hegel essay we are at its high point. To refresh the memory, one passage may be cited:

> Earlier, truth had been regarded as the agreement of presenting with being. Truth is a character of presenting. But as certainty, truth is now the presenting itself, insofar as it posits (*zustellt*) itself and assures itself of itself as representation (*Repräsentation*). The state of being known, which has assured itself of its own knowledge, and indeed for and through itself, has thereby retreated from every particularized presenting of objects. It depends no longer on objects in order to possess the truth by that dependence (124 [38]).

Heidegger characterizes as *absolvence* (*Absolvenz*) the self-liberation of consciousness from the objective relationship. The autonomy of self-liberation, which is demanded here, a liberating in every respect, Heidegger calls absolving (*Absolvieren*). Absolvence and absolving make it possible for consciousness to make itself free "from the one-sided binding to the objects and from the mere presenting of them." This decree of freedom Heidegger calls *absolution*. The character of absoluteness, which is the issue for Hegel, is to be thought from the relation of absolvence, absolving, and absolution. "The true in the sense of unconditioned self-certainty is only the Absolute" (125 [39]).

In the *Phenomenology of Spirit*, Hegel wants to show "what science (i.e., philosophy) wants as absolute knowledge. Science wants in its way only what the Absolute wants" (125 [39]). Thus Hegel can maintain that it is the will of the Absolute, "in and for itself already to be with us" (ibid.). The work of the Concept, of which Hegel speaks, means "the Absolute's circling from out of itself in the absoluteness of its self-conceiving from unconditioned self-certainty" (127 [44]). Heidegger also provides a very sharp determination of the dialectical: Hegel

> . . . thinks the dialectical from the essence of experience. . . . The decisive essential-moment of the experience rests in the fact that there arises for consciousness the new true object. It is a matter of the origin of the new object as the origin of truth, not a matter of the fact that an object gets taken as an object for knowledge (159f [119f]).

We can understand the highpoint of the position of metaphysics only if we have first understood what has happened at the beginning of the modern age. Thus as different as the two texts, "The Age of the World-Image" and Hegel's "Concept of Experience" might be, they treat one and the same thing—the history of modern metaphysics. Surprisingly, we find in the Hegel text a not easily explained reference to technology, which is here simply quoted:

> Natural knowledge lives in all forms of the spirit, each of them lives in its own way, even and precisely that of absolute knowledge, which comes-to-pass (*ereignet*) as absolute metaphysics, but is only visible occasionally to a few thinkers. This metaphysics has so little crumbled before the positivism of the 19th and 20th centuries that, instead, the modern technical world in its unconditioned claim is nothing other than natural consciousness, which—according to its own opinion—executes the unconditioned, self-assuring producibility of all beings in the incessant objectification of each and every thing (137f [62f.]).

After the explanation of the highpoint, there follows the interpretation of the supposed end of metaphysics with Nietzsche. Nietzsche's ideas appear to be the reversal of Platonism. His philosophy is seen not only in the *"confrontive dialogue"* (*Auseinandersetzung*) with nihilism but is itself seen as a form of nihilism, precisely through the interpretation of being as value posited by will. With the disappearance of the authority of God, that authority has in no way dissipated.

> In the place of the vanished authority of God and of the teaching of the Church, steps the authority of conscience, and the authority of reason forces its way in. Over against this arises the social instinct. The flight of the world into the super-sensible get replaced by historical progress. The other-worldly goal of an eternal salvation is transformed into the earthly happiness of the majority (203 [64]).

What happens with Nietzsche is seen in the context of the history of metaphysics: "The *ousia* (beingness) of the *subjectum* becomes the *Subjektität* of self-consciousness, which now brings to light its essence as the will to will" (218 [79f.]). According to Heidegger, the connection between Nietzsche's two fundamental concepts, Will to Power and the Eternal Return of the Same, is the distinction in being corresponding to *essentia* and *existentia*.

If the agreement of the three works, which lead us to three decisive junctures in modern metaphysics, is undeniable, and if Heidegger's efforts to make this history comprehensible is also undeniable, then the question now arises: in this context, what place is the work that follows—the Rilke interpretation—to be assigned?

Chronologically, the Rilke explanation leads us into the present, because the question is posed, to what extent is Rilke a poet in a destitute time? In other words, what happens in Rilke's poetry with regard to illuminating this time? Here two things are shown. On the one hand, Rilke is interpreted by Heidegger as belonging to the metaphysical space of Nietzsche, which leads to the well-nigh provocative equation of Zarathustra with the figure of an angel. But on the other hand, Heidegger has shown how with Rilke something also happens, that we can characterize as a beginning of the overcoming of the metaphysics of the will. The inner-space of the heart of Rilke is understood in opposition to calculated world-space, even though Heidegger chides Rilke for not having considered more carefully the spatiality of the inner-space of the heart. Another point is also pertinent here. In this work we perceive something of what Heidegger calls the "dialogue" (*Zwiesprache*) between poetry and thinking.

Indeed the model of such a dialogue is given in the interpretation of Hölderlin. It is thus not by chance that the Rilke interpretation begins and ends with a reference to Hölderlin. But the Rilke interpretation is also a kind of dialogue in which the one partner remains by and large imprisoned in a domain that the other is striving to overcome. Moreover, we ought not to forget that for Heidegger art is a decisive way through which to institute a relation with Being. When Heidegger interjects into the Rilke interpretation a quotation from Hölderlin, which also crops up in other works, namely, the verse, "But where there is danger, there grows/also what saves" (273 [118]), then reference is made precisely to the possibility of art's grasping the danger, to save us from it and to find new ways.

The above named four works doubtlessly belong to the domain of modern metaphysics. Formulated more clearly: they provide thoughtful (*verstehende*) interpretations of the happening of modern metaphysics, from Descartes to Nietzsche and Rilke, and thus up to the present. That should be the moment which establishes unity. One would say that the structure follows an historical pattern, pursuing the course of metaphysics. This answer can be disputed only with difficulty, and yet it is inadequate. We ought not to stop with it, quite apart from the fact that the first and last works of *Holzwege* have not yet been taken into account in this attempt at a collective vision.

In this first movement, what have we overlooked or consciously passed over? It is now important to clarify this. It would be helpful to start from a point in the Rilke interpretation.

After the elucidation of the significance of the open for Rilke — about which Rilke says that the higher the consciousness the more exclusive is the conscious essence of the world (a thesis which is opposed to the Heideggerean meaning of the open, since for Heidegger only Dasein is "open") — Heidegger examines in an excursus the presenting of man since it is determinative for the modern age:

> It is by representing (*Vor-stellen*) that Nature is brought before man. Man places before himself the world as the whole of everything objective, and he places himself before the world. Man sets up the world toward himself, and delivers Nature over to himself. We must think of this pro-ducing (*Her-stellen*-literally "placing here") in its broad and multifarious nature (265 [110]).

The various modes of pro-ducing are the arranging (*Bestellen*) of Nature; producing in the sense of creating (*Erzeugens*) new things; the rearranging of things that disturb man; the arranging of things for sale; the display of (man's) achievement. Man is the one "who accomplishes all this producing with deliberation" (266]111]). This comportment of producing is a willing:

> By such willing, modern man turns out to be the being who, in all relations to all that is, and thus in his relation to himself as well, rises up as the producer who puts through, carries out, his own self, and establishes this uprising as the absolute rule (*ibid*).

Thus for Heidegger, in modern metaphysics there "appears the long-hidden essence of the long-since existing will as the Being of beings" (267 [111]). But this means nothing other than that, in this relation to the world, which must listen to the command of the subject, the essence of technology makes its appearance. Technology shows itself "as a destiny (*Geschick*) of the truth of the whole of being" (ibid.). Modern science is not the presupposition for technology but instead, like the modern state, its "consequence" (ibid.).

> Not only are living things technically objectivated in stock-breeding and exploitation; the assault of atomic physics upon the phenomena of living matter as such is in full swing. At bottom, the essence of life is supposed to yield itself to technical production (267 [112]).

And taking up the already familiar explanation from the "Age of the World-Image," Heidegger says:

> Even this, that man becomes the subject and the world the object, is a consequence of technology's nature establishing itself, and not the other way around (268 [112]).

Here we are far removed from the usual discussions about the benefit and danger of technology. Instead, technology now appears on a horizon that we might call that of "Being-as-history" (*seinsgeschichtlichen*). And as the discussion of the elucidation of the concept of the open proceeds, Heidegger can now say:

> By building the world up technologically as an object, man deliberately and completely blocks his path, already obstructed, into the open. Self-assertive man, whether or not he knows and wills it as an individual, is the functionary of technology (271 [116]).

And further:

> What is deadly is not the much-discussed atomic bomb as this particular death-dealing machine. What has long since been threatening man with death, and indeed with the death of his own nature, is the unconditional character of mere willing in the sense of purposeful self-assertion in everything (ibid.).

Here we perceive the fundamental danger of our world, which rests in the fact that the essence of man is reduced to willing, and in fact to a willing in the sense thought by Nietzsche: willing to power as the fundamental trait of all being:

> It is not only the totality of this willing that is dangerous, but willing itself, in the form of self-assertion within a world that is admitted only as will (272 [117]).

One might suppose that this danger can only be encountered from within the realm in which it grounds itself, namely, that of modern science. How then can Heidegger maintain that:

> ... above all, technology itself prevents any experience of its own nature. For while it is developing its own self to the full, it develops in the sciences a kind of knowing that is debarred from ever entering into the realm of the essential nature of technology, let alone retracing in thought that nature's origin (ibid.).

This assertion can be brought together with the other one, which easily becomes a reproach to Heidegger, to set him up as an opponent of science: science does not think. What does this mean? It can in no way mean that in science a spiritual achievement is not realized. Its impact has been no less than astounding. Indeed, we need refer only to the progress in the medical sciences, which have achieved results which fifty years ago would have been incomprehensible. That man can now send instruments to other planets, instruments that communicate to us information about the conditions there, is a unique scientific-technological achievement of which one can be proud.

But all of these achievements as well as the still more sensational and astounding ones to come do not bring man to ask about the essence of technology. They take the technological framework as given, as result, as progress; but they cannot ask what happens to man in the technological framework, or what happens to his world.

It is precisely the singular results, the efficiency, the usefulness, the unquestionable progress that prevent inquiry into what takes place in technology. For Heidegger this means that we remain hampered in getting at the essential realm of technology, or from going a step further and asking about the origin of the essence of technology. And this means nothing more than that the question about something like Being, about something like truth, cannot be posed because absolutely none of this lies within the horizon of science. The happening within which we stand without thinking it, can be concisely taken together in the following sentences: "The essence of technology comes to the light of day only slowly. This day is the world's night, rearranged into merely technological day" (ibid.).

These citations about the present, as the epoch determined by technology, could have only an exemplary character. They should in no way reduce the *Holzwege* essays to the question about technology, although this question comes up again and again in those essays, a fact which cannot be examined here in detail. Rather by this example, something else should be suggested—something that will allow us to grasp more accurately the aim of Heidegger's effort than was possible at the onset. Formulated in another way: In the *Holzwege* essays we not only find accounts of the history of metaphysics, metaphysics not only becomes more clearly accessible to us through the essays—which would already be a matter of importance—but in these works we find Heidegger's own position thematized. That will be clarified in that which follows. We might take the title: How Heidegger understands what he is doing. From the vantage he has reached, how can Heidegger experience more about metaphysics than it knows about itself?

In "The Anaximander Fragment," Heidegger poses the question about who we are and about what the epoch is in which we find ourselves.

> Are we the late-comers of a history which now moves precipitously to its conclusion, uniformities? [This is a resumption of the order-thought from the Rilke-interpretation, more precisely of the pseudo-ordering.] (300 [16])

There follows a whole series of questions, but what they now note is that our epoch is not to be seen merely as something like an end but as the possibility of a change, in the sense of a new beginning. "Do we stand before the evening of a night (which leads to) another morning?" (300 [17]).

> Is the land of evening now dawning? Will this evening-land, beyond Occident and Orient and on through the European, be the location of the coming, more primordially-destined history? (ibid.).

The series of questions, which stretch on for almost a page, ends with:

> Are we the late-comers who we are? But are we at the same time also the precursors of the dawn of a wholly different age of the world, which has left behind our contemporary historical representations of history? (300f [17]).

It is not by accident that these questions are expressed so clearly in the last essay. In the discussion immediately following, we shall try to show how from the first essay on what we have called Heidegger's own position it is expressed ever more clearly. This is shown by an

apparently restricted question, namely, how history is to be understood. But for Heidegger this question is the fundamental question.
"Historiography (*Historie*) is the continual destruction of the future. . . ." (301 [17]). How can Heidegger maintain the following?
"All historiography predicts what is to come from images of the past
determined by the present" (ibid.). History is constrained by that
which it knows of the past; more precisely, by the representations
which it forms of the past on the basis of the present. Grasped in
such a way, the past is regarded as a leading-image for what is to
come. More precisely, one can represent that which is to come as
nothing but a continuation of the past; indeed one predicts that
which is to come after this manner of repeating the past. What is the
result? Man becomes blind to a possible future that is not simply the
resumption of the past. Why is this fateful for Heidegger? The
above quoted citation is now given in full: "Historiography is the
continual destruction of the future and of the historical relation to
the advent of destiny (*Ankunft des Geschickes*)" (*ibid.*).

What does this mean? Stated concretely: If we were able to conceive history (*Geschichte*) in no other way than as an ever-repetitive
metaphysics, and if metaphysics (briefly expressed, in order to spell
out the context) were the oblivion of Being, then the possibility of
finding another access route to Being would be blocked from the
start.

In the Anaximander interpretation, Heidegger wants to understand the "dawn" (*das Frühe*) not from the present (thus necessarily
misunderstanding it) but as that which (as dawn) at the same time
surpasses and outstrips that which comes after. "But what if that
which is early outdistanced everything late, if the very earliest far
surpassed the very latest?" (301 [18]). In this connection, Heidegger
coins a new concept, namely, the "Eschatology of Being" (302 [18]).
What does he mean? He means that the hitherto concealed destiny
of Being would come to a parting of the ways. "The essence of Being
hitherto in evidence sinks into its still concealed truth. The history of
Being gathers itself together in this parting" (301 [18]). By way of
elucidation, Heidegger continues, claiming that the *Phenomenology of
Spirit* forms a phase in the eschatology of Being since in the *Phenomenology of Spirit* there appears "Being as the absolute *Subjektität* of
unconditioned will to will" (ibid.). But this means that Being, as it
was thought by metaphysics, appears in its most extreme form. I
understand the "decline into its still concealed truth" as something
being ushered in, something that is no longer metaphysically
thought truth but the truth of Being itself. Indeed, since history (*die*

Geschichte)—again, briefly formulated—is that which is "destined" (*das Geschickte*) by Being, Being itself is that which "sends" (*zuschickt*) itself in history.

Thus in another place in the Anaximander essay, in an effort to understand the Greeks in a Greek way and not in a modern way, Heidegger says:

> What is Greek is the dawn of that destiny in which Being illuminates itself in beings and so propounds a certain essence of man; that essence unfolds historically as something fateful, preserved in Being and dispensed by Being, without ever being separated from Being (310 [25]).

With the Greeks resulted what Heidegger calls the lighting of Being, the event which is authentically and historically formative. Through this lighting being becomes accessible to man, it becomes un-concealed. But that through which unconcealment first becomes possible—the light of Being itself—is not grasped, let alone thought. Thus what Heidegger calls the oblivion-of-Being, or metaphysics, can begin:

> As it reveals itself in beings, Being withdraws. In this way, by illuminating them, Being sets beings adrift in errancy. Beings come to pass in that errancy by which they circumvent Being and establish the realm of error (in the sense of a prince's realm or the realm of poetry). Error is the space in which history unfolds (310 [26]).

As evidence for this holding-itself-in of Being, Heidegger points to *a-letheia*. "As it [*aletheia*] yields the unconcealment of beings it institutes the concealment of Being. Concealment persists in the pull of that denial which keeps to itself" (311 [26]). For this Heidegger coins a new term: "epoché of Being." This is not to be understood as Husserl's bracketing and thus not as a concept that pertains to the methodological activity of philosophy but as an event which holds sway in Being itself:

> From the *epoché* of Being comes the epochal essence of its destining, in which world history properly consists. When Being keeps to itself in its destining, world suddenly and unexpectedly comes to pass. Every epoch of world history is an epoch of errancy (*der Irre*) [because the keeping-to-itself does not let Being become accessible] (311 [27]).

But now how does it stand with the relationship between man and Being or, put otherwise, how does *Da-sein* stand to Being? This is a difficult question, with which Heidegger himself wrestled for a long time. To sketch out the issue somewhat roughly: Is man nothing but the essence that has to endure the destiny of Being, or is Being itself allotted to man? In the first case, we run into the danger—again crudely put—that Heidegger thinks of Being as a new form of the divine. If this were taken as a fundamental variation of metaphysics, it would mean that he himself remains caught up in metaphysics.

At this point in the Anaximander essay, he says:

> For us, however, the most readily experienced correspondence to the epochal character of Being is the ecstatic character of *Da-sein*. [This can be understood such that Heidegger's explication of man in *Being and Time* is a first access to the thinking of Being.] The epochal character of Being lays claim to (*ereignet*) the ecstatic nature of *Da-sein*. The *ek-sistence* of man sustains what is ecstatic and so preserves what is epochal in Being, to whose essence the *Da-* and thereby *Da-sein*, belongs (311f [27]).

Here we have on the one hand the "appropriation" (*Ereignis*) of Being and on the other hand the contribution that *Dasein* also has to furnish. From this quotation, something like the reciprocal consignment of Being and *Da-sein* becomes visible for me.

In an earlier part of the Anaximander essay stands the sentence: "The poeticizing essence of thinking preserves the holding-sway of the truth of Being" (303 [19]). At first we are startled to see thinking connected with poetry.

By way of elucidation, let us draw on another passage: "The thinking of Being is the original way of doing poetry" (ibid.). This means that Being is to be understood in a double way: Being is that upon which there is thinking; and Being is at the same time that which addresses itself to thinking. As a result Heidegger can also say: "Thinking says the dictate of the truth of Being" (ibid.). In no way should the sentence be understood to mean that Being is a poetic fiction of thinking (i.e., a product of fantasy). But why does Heidegger in this connection use the expression "to poeticize", (i.e., to make poetry)? Because for him to make poetry means to open up the realm of language, to move into this realm, and this means at the same time to open up the realm of openness. Openness is not simply given but must expressly be opened up and, according to Heidegger, this happens in thinking, which at the same time can be characterized as doing poetry. What is said in poetry (*das Gedichtete*) is the truth of Being.

Do we have in the *Holzwege* essays, these "wood-paths," still other passages that point to the relation of Being and *Dasein*? This will now be investigated.

The account of the fragment of Anaximander ends with the reference; "But thinking is the poetizing of the truth of Being in the historic dialogue between thinkers" (343 [57]). Here the thought of poetizing is taken up again, but, in contrast to the earlier passage, it is said that this poetizing happens in the dialogue of those who think, which is not to say that that which has to do with Being can be completely poetized. And the situation in which we find ourselves is outlined:

> Man has already begun to overwhelm the entire earth and its atmosphere, to arrogate to himself in forms of energy the concealed powers of nature, and to submit future history to the planning and ordering of a world government. This same defiant man is utterly at a loss simply to say what *is*; to say *what* this *is* — that a thing is.
>
> The totality of beings is the single object of a singular will to conquer. The simplicity of Being is confounded in a singular oblivion (ibid.).

But what does this have to do with the question we posed about the relation of man to Being? With this question, the final essay of *Holzwege* comes to an end: "But what if Being in its essence *needs* (*braucht*) the essence of man consists in thinking the truth of Being?" (ibid.)

Once again we find the reciprocal consignment that we have encountered. Man must take over and preserve the openness, the clearing of Being; to that extent, Being needs man. Man himself, further, finds his own proper essence according to how he corresponds to the truth of Being, and that means how he is prepared to think this truth (i.e., truth in the sense of *aletheia*).

At the beginning of the Nietzsche essay Heidegger says, "Thinking through the metaphysics of Nietzsche becomes the meditation of the situation (*Lage*) and location (*Ort*) of contemporary man, whose destiny is still too little experienced with respect to truth" (194 [54]). Here, too, it is a question of the truth of Being, and Heidegger says explicitly, "For preparatory thinking it is a matter of lighting up the playing field (*Spielraum*) within which Being itself could once again assume an incipient relation to man with respect to this essence" (ibid.). Thinking should not be understood in the sense of an arbitrary act, but it can set something in motion with reference to man's position vis-à-vis Being, we can also say the experience of Being. And in this connection Heidegger clarifies what preparatory thinking has to do. He compares it with the activity of the sower, who strews the seeds without knowing whether he will ever see the fruit itself and who, in order to be able to sow at all, must make the field arable. In point of fact, he must first find the field,

> . . . which has to remain unknown because of the inescapable predominance of the metaphysical terrain. It is a matter first of divining this field, and then finding it and cultivating it. It is a matter of

> making a first path to this field. The still unknown field-paths are
> many. Yet for every thinking person there is assigned only one
> pathway, his own . . . to follow finally as his own, but which never
> belongs to him, and to say what is experiencable along this one
> pathway (194f [55]).

In this connection Heidegger refers explicitly to the difficulty that
this thinking requires that he be educated "in the midst of the sciences" (195 [56]) but without succumbing to their mode of procedure. "To think in the midst of the sciences means: to pass them by
without scorning them" (ibid.). In this text Heidegger provides some
hints about his procedure and his guiding-thought

> . . . that in the history of Western thinking, indeed from the begin-
> ning on, being is thought with respect to Being, but that the truth
> of Being remains unthought and as a possible experience is not
> only denied to thinking, but that Western thinking itself and in-
> deed in the form of metaphysics expressly conceals the occurrence
> of this denial, albeit unwittingly (195f [56]).

To say this, Heidegger must have already won a point outside of
metaphysics; this point is determined by the proximity to Being,
"which pertains to thinking in incalculable modes of destiny and
from a changing immediateness" (196 [57]). Or as he says in another
part of the same work, it is a matter of "thinking of the location of the
essence of man and experiencing it in the truth of Being" (205 [66]).
And with regard to the relation between man and Being, there is
posed the question whose concern is "whether man has so matured
to the essence into which he has been seized by Being, that he en-
dures this destiny on account of his essence and not with the
pseudo-assistance of mere precautions" (235 [98]).

Heidegger's critique of metaphysics can easily be understood as
though metaphysics had constantly abandoned something that
should be recovered. But toward the end of the Nietzsche essay, we
find in connection with Nihilism the following passage:

> Then it would lie in the essence of Being itself, that it remain
> unthought, because it withdraws itself. . . . For that reason,
> metaphysics itself would be no mere omission of a still to be consid-
> ered question about Being. It would not be entirely an error.
> Metaphysics, as the history of the truth of Being as such, would
> come to pass from the destiny of Being itself. Metaphysics would in
> its essence be the unthought—because withheld—mystery of
> Being itself (244 [110]).

If Heidegger formulates these assertions hypothetically, he might
want to say with them that preparatory thinking must also consider
this possibility. For if in fact history is supposed to be the event of

Being, then metaphysics cannot have withdrawn itself arbitrarily from this event. We must then rather think of this history together with the mysterious essence of Being itself. Then we must attempt to think from this history a trait of Being itself, namely, Being's self-withdrawing. Should we not add in anticipation that through this thinking there is introduced a change in the relationship of man to Being? I would like to interpret this state-of-affairs along these lines on the basis of various passages in the *Holzwege*. To recall only one citation: "For preparatory thinking it is a matter of clearing the space within which Being itself can once again assume an incipient relation to man with respect to his essence" (194 [55]).

Let us return to the initial question about the unity of *Holzwege*. In the beginning I referred to an unpublished introduction, from which I drew only one sentence. This introduction is now cited in its entirety:

> Facing man in the future is the confrontive-dialogue with the es-
> sence and history of Western metaphysics. Only in this meditation
> does the passage to the planetarily defined Dasein of man become
> realizable. Only then is the world-historical Dasein achievable as
> grounded.
> The wood-paths are attempts at such meditation. Taken exter-
> nally, they are given as a collection of essays about objects which
> have no relation among themselves.
> Thought from the matter itself, everything stands in a hidden
> and strictly developed harmony.
> None of the paths is to be travelled if the others are not tried. In
> their unity, they show a part of the path of thinking which the
> author of *Being and Time* has attempted in the meantime.
> They go into error; but they do not lead astray.

Now we ask, Wherein is found the unity of these texts? As an answer we suggest, In the thinking of the essence of history. In "The Origin of the Artwork," history is thought of as the strife of world and earth; truth itself is poetized as the primordial strife. The work-being of the work is itself grasped as occurrence (*Geschehen*). "The Age of the World-Image" provides the account of the begin-ning of the modern age—again, the occurrence, which itself comes to pass and co-conditions everything that follows: The Hegel in-terpretation provides its end point. "What Are Poets For?" shows the connection of poetry and thinking as well as the position of poets of the twentieth century, in which the metaphysics of Nietzsche is still decisive, though some attempts at a change are being made. In the Anaximander essay, Heidegger's thinking gathers itself in upon itself—in the confrontive dialogue with the first thinker of Western history. Here we experience also how Heidegger thinks history as well as what is proposed for this thinking. Indeed we experience that history cannot be equated with the history of metaphysics when we arrive at a new understanding of history through the confrontive dialogue with metaphysics and that which has come-to-pass in it.

Taken fundamentally, the unity of the *Holzwege* essays is the unity of Heidegger's thinking, and this thinking is the unique attempt to understand history as the destiny of Being. Longer, more careful, and assiduous work at interpretation is needed merely to bring us closer to this attempt. If Heidegger says that in his whole life he has investigated only one question, then this question is so decisive that it spans a manifold of phenomena—which should be manifest from the example of the *Holzwege* essays.

SIX

THE COILING PATHWAY OF
HEIDEGGER'S *ESSENCE OF TRUTH*

THE ESSAY *On the Essence of Truth* (*Vom Wesen der Wahrheit*) (*WW*)[1] is unique among Heidegger's works in several ways. Nowhere else has he made as thorough a study of truth, and we know how central to his thought that topic is. Again, while he is always a master of conciseness, I can think of no work in which he has said so much in so few pages; and the range of topics treated in the essay is immense. Not only do we learn a great deal about truth, but as the essay proceeds we are treated to profound observations on theology, freedom, history, and other things. Indeed a reader might be forgiven for wondering how all these things can possibly be connected. And herein lies the motive for the present paper. While each chapter of *WW* is able to bear the most minute interpretation, I believe that a view of that which unifies the essay overall will constitute a useful preface to interpretation. This is what this paper attempts. It is almost inevitable that a reader of *WW* will miss its overall plan in a first reading. It is only at the very end of the text that Heidegger himself gives any hint as to what the plan of the work has been (*WW*, 96–7; *Basic Writings* (*BW*) 140–141). What my paper aims to do is work through the essay, keeping this plan in mind, indicating the place of each part of the essay in the vista opened up by Heidegger's concluding remarks.

First, though, let me point out just one thing in the essay, which shows what an unusual literary character it has. Consider what

[1]*Vom Wesen der Wahrheit* (*WW*), in M. Heidegger, *Wegmarken* (Frankfurt: Klostermann, 1967), pp. 73–97, and in M. Heidegger, *Basic Writings* (*BW*), ed. D.F. Krell, trans. by J. Sallis (New York: Harper and Row, 1977), pp. 117–141. Text and translation are based on the second edition of the essay, 1949. *WW* was first presented as a lecture in 1930, and its text was revised and expanded during the years prior to publication. I am grateful to Professor Walter Biemel for letting me study the text of the lecture of 1930.

Heidegger says at a prominent place in Chapter 3, emphasized in the text: "The essence of truth is freedom" (*WW*, 81; *BW*, 125). Normally one would expect such a solemn assertion to be sustained and reinforced in the course of any subsequent reflections, but is that what happens? In the chapters that follow, one is hard pressed to see what status this thesis maintains. It is mentioned again at several points, but much of what follows seems to move away from it. Near the start of Chapter 4, we are told that there is another essence of truth that in some way lies deeper: "the more original essence of uniquely essential truth" (*WW*, 83; *BW*, 127). In Chapter 7 this is filled in for us. The claim is made that "the primordial essence of truth [is] the rule of the mystery in errancy" (*WW*, 93; *BW*, 137). This claim will concern us later on; here we merely note that by Chapter 7 it is difficult to see what has become of the thesis on freedom. It is never explicitly abandoned, and yet its validity comes to be restricted in some way.

Moreover, it is not easy to see how the solemn thesis of Chapter 3 is connected to the parts of the essay that *precede* it. We are told in Chapter 3 that "truth" is being provisionally identified with "correctness." We see too in Chapters 1 and 2 that attention is focussed particularly on statements, so that truth is understood for present purposes as correctness of statements. Heidegger deals with the traditional correspondence theory of truth in Chapters 1 and 2, according to which correctness of statements is explained as their accordance or correspondence to things. But what status is actually assigned in the overall strategy of the essay to this correspondence theory of truth? Does Heidegger mean to make it the presupposition for the solemn thesis of Chapter 3? If so, his thesis would lose its support if one were to raise doubts about the correspondence theory. Yet it does seem that such doubts are raised later on. So the question of how the thesis is connected to the correspondence theory of truth is a difficult one. These questions about Chapter 3 and the place of its thesis in the whole argument merely serve to illustrate the need for a study of the strategy of the essay as a whole. Comparable questions can be raised about every chapter, and some of them will come up as we proceed.

The case this paper means to make is that *WW* is not unified as a set of doctrines about truth. Its unity is that of a *pathway of thinking*. Attention to the pathway, then, is the proper preface to interpretation. Its form is that of a twisting or coiling pathway. This means that assertions made at one point along the route of the pathway do not necessarily hold at some earlier or later point, at least not with the same meaning. Thinking can be said to proceed on a pathway when it sets out to determine some subject matter, for instance, the essence of truth. But in the course of the pursuit, something can emerge that forces a rethinking of the opening question. Then the thinking itself is made to undergo a change of direction, to turn away from the pursuit of the initial subject and set out in pursuit of another; and such a change can be repeated again and again. The result of this sequence is that a pathway of thinking is constituted, rather than a series of assertions. It is one thing to proceed along a pathway of thinking, quite another to attain an overview of it. It is at the end of *WW*, after the pathway has been traversed, that one is able to form a picture of the changes that have befallen the thinking:

> Our thinking apparently remains on the path of metaphysics. Nevertheless, in its decisive steps, which lead from truth as correctness to ek-sistent freedom, and from the latter to truth as concealing and as errancy, it accomplishes a change in the questioning that belongs to the overcoming of metaphysics (*WW*, 97; *BW*, 140–141).

In the last sentence of the essay Heidegger touches on the point that the coherence of the essay is not that of a set of doctrines but that of a pathway of thinking:

> The course of the questioning is intrinsically the way of a thinking which, instead of furnishing representations and concepts, experiences and tries itself as a transformation of its relatedness to Being (*WW*, 98; *BW*, 141).

There are other of Heidegger's works where similar directives are given the reader right at the start. Here is the opening of "The Question Concerning Technology":

> In what follows we shall be *questioning* concerning technology. Questioning builds a way. We would be advised, therefore, above all to pay heed to the way, and not to fix our attention on isolated sentences and topics. The way is one of thinking.[2]

Admittedly such directives are difficult to fulfill. If it is a pathway of thinking that unifies an essay, this does not mean that its text is only the memorandum of a series of mental acts that the author has performed or only a series of guidelines for an exercise to be performed by the reader. As in the everyday use of the word "pathway," so here it must be understood to mean the direction of movement that has been *imposed* on travelers in a given territory by the most

---

[2]"Die Frage nach der Technik," *Vorträge und Aufsätze* (Pfullingen: Neske, 1954), p. 13; also "The Question Concerning Technology," trans. W. Lovitt, *Basic Writings*, p. 287.

prominent aspects of the territory itself. The route of the pathway of thought has been shaped by *what* it is that the thinker wants to know or to think. A pressure exercised upon the thinking by the subject matter of the thought has induced the twisting and bending that the thought has undergone. Thus attention to the pathway of thinking has to be accompanied by attention to the subject matter of thinking.

WW is constituted by three movements of thought, each of which accomplishes a redirection of thinking. In each, the thinking begins a movement in one direction and is forced to bend, inclining away from the goal first set, and to terminate in a surprising way at a point quite remote from the first goal. Thus each of the three movements describes an arc. The whole essay consists of a twisting of three great arcs—three bendings of thinking. Only because the thinking actually starts off in a certain direction can it encounter that which forces it to bend, so that each arc is delineated by a thinking that is already underway, like a bird on the wing.

At the very beginning, thought sets out in pursuit of the essence of truth (Introduction and Chapter 1), thereby entering the domain of essences themselves. But in the course of this pursuit, it is made to bend away from every essence altogether (Chapters 2 and 3), thereby describing an arc, which we shall call "From Essence to Freedom." Our description of this arc will show that the correspondence theory of truth has a provisional and heuristic value for Heidegger, not an absolute value; it serves only to give initial guidance to the question about truth's essence. By completing the first arc we quite outstride the limitations that pertain to any correspondence theory of truth.

In its next movement, seeking to determine freedom, thinking describes a second arc (Chapters 4 and 5), which we shall call "From Freedom to Being." We shall also call this the vindication of being because, as we shall see, the first movement of thought appears to endanger the principle of being. Particular stress must be laid upon this second arc and its distinctness from the first and the third. The first movement of thought has introduced the theme of freedom into the study of truth, but in its completion of the second arc thinking quite outstrides the limitations of all subjectivist, relativist, and pragmatist philosophies as well as their conceptions of truth. In the comment quoted above from the concluding page of *WW*, Heidegger does not make special mention of the vindication of being; he speaks of the first arc as the "step which leads from truth as correctness to ek-sistent freedom"; then he speaks of a step which leads "to concealing and errancy." The point will be made at length that the intermediate arc, the vindication of being, should be acknowledged before the step is taken to concealing and errancy in Chapters 6 and 7. Actually, it is implicitly contained in the notion of freedom being "ek-sistent," and it was explicitly mentioned (*Rettung des Wesens*) in the 1930 lecture.

In the third and final arc thinking, seeking to identify being and truth, is forced to bend away from that identity. This third arc we shall call "From Being to Untruth" (Chapters 6 and 7). The two forms of untruth—concealment and errancy—prove in the final analysis to constitute the ultimate and original essence of truth. Just how this astonishing result is achieved will be our concern in describing the third arc. With this step we have moved away from every sort of ontological and metaphysical thinking including the standpoints of classical Greek philosophy and Hegelianism, with their characteristic conceptions of truth.

I. FROM ESSENCE TO FREEDOM

Each stride in the pathway of this meditation accomplishes a change of direction only because the thinking is already proceeding in some direction. The arc of the first stride is accomplished when thought, beginning with a metaphysical push toward essence, is redirected away from essence. The essay begins with a distinction between the essence of truth and all particular truths. Attention is directed toward "the one thing that in general distinguishes every 'truth' as truth" (*WW* 73; *BW*, 177). Throughout the brief Introduction, Heidegger continues to polarize a philosophical ascent to generality against all thinking that wants to hold to the concrete, to the multiform realities of human experience, and to the urgent needs of humanity. Philosophy is thereby brought into a confrontation with common sense. Common sense is said to be deaf to philosophy and blind to the characteristic object of philosophy, which is always an essence. Nothing could be more traditional, more Platonic, than this ascent of thinking toward the essence of truth. Heidegger considers the objection that common sense makes to such philosophizing, that, leaving all concrete experience behind, it will be utterly abstract. Heidegger supposes the critic saying "We want to know what our situation is today. We call for the goal which should be posited for man in and for his history. We want the actual 'truth' " (*WW*, 74; *BW*, 118). But he will not yield to this objection, and gives a Socratic-

Platonic form of reply: If we want to know the actual truth, must we not after all know what we mean by "truth"? And if we really are ignorant of this, is it not better to admit it?

Guided thus by a traditional idea of essence, thought has pushed into a metaphysical dimension, and the focus upon the essence is faithfully preserved at the beginning of Chapter 1: " 'Truth' means what makes a true thing true" (*WW*, 74; *BW*, 118–119). Heidegger proceeds now with a major bifurcation: what is true may be on the one hand a thing such as gold, or on the other hand a statement. This bifurcation provides the occasion for a major excursion into essentialist metaphysics in Chapter 1, oriented not toward Plato but toward medieval theology. What Heidegger presents is a mighty vista, embracing God, the creation of the world, finite things, and the human soul. Its relevance to his argument (it was not in the 1930 lecture) is as follows: The truth of *things* (which is equivalent to genuineness: true gold is genuine gold) is their correspondence with their idea. The medievals construed the essence of something as an idea in the divine intellect to which the created thing conformed. True gold was what conformed to God's eternal idea of gold. What did not conform to it was false gold, a source of illusion to the human mind. Thus it was the belief that God had created the world that gave a clear sense to the notion of truth in things. The second case, of the truth of *statements*, was both similar to this doctrine and materially interwoven with it. The truth of a human being's statement or belief was also defined as a correspondence (an adequation of the intellect to the thing). But, more than that, the correspondence of statements to things depended on the prior correspondence of those things to the divine ideas. The things must first possess an ontological correspondence because if a thing were not held in the stable form of its essence, either the human intellect could not achieve a correspondence to the thing or, if it did, the intellect would itself be in an unstable state, unfit to express truth. The result of the analysis, then, is that for statements to be true a first correspondence of thing to essence must be maintained, then a second correspondence of human intellect to the thing must also be maintained. The thing must first really *be* that which it is taken as; second, it must be taken right. The metaphysical stride toward essence, whether in Plato or in medieval scholasticism, aims at a guarantee of being. It aims at securing ourselves and the things in the world about us against the pressure of fakery, illusion, and decay.

Surprisingly, however, Heidegger's reference to the truth of things does not prove decisive in the argument. At the end of Chapter 1 he proposes to set it aside. What is decisive at this point in the argument is the claim that in the traditional and conventional view, "true" is to be analyzed through correspondence. At the end of Chapter 1, he directs our attention to the second correspondence, the accordance of intellect to thing, which is the immediate definition of statement—truth. The task of Chapter 2 is to define how this accordance comes about. I believe that something very akin to the metaphysical theory, with its stride toward essence, continues to be operative throughout the first half of Chapter 2, but during the course of the chapter our thought is forced to bend away from the main principle of essentialism.

The mighty vista of medieval essentialism quite vanishes from Heidegger's argument from this point on. Leaving behind the doctrine of creation and the secularized versions of it, which Heidegger treats briefly, we zero in now on the most ordinary of scenes, a man in a room with a table before him where there are some coins sitting. The man says "The coin is round." What we are wondering is what makes this statement true.

Early in Chapter 2, Heidegger distinguishes the accordance that the statement has to a thing from the likeness of one thing (e.g., a coin) to another. He stresses that the statement must remain what it is if it is to be true; it must persevere in those very attributes that are its mark of unlikeness from the coin; it does not become at all metallic or tend to count as legal tender. There is a parallel to essentialism here. The very unlikeness of statement and coin that Heidegger emphasizes is akin to the unlikeness of the eternal essence with respect to particulars. Some indwelling virtue in the gold made it real gold, but that indwelling principle did not possess the same sort of reality itself. You cannot buy anything with a statement, but you cannot buy anything with an essence either.

The relationship that prevails between statement and coin, Heidegger lays down, is that of presenting or representing (*Vorstellen*). The statement presents the coin; therefore its accordance must be seen as one mode of that relationship. Heidegger introduces the idea of presentation in this context as a way of avoiding the view that the statement must resemble the thing it is about. Presenting is precisely not a sort of likeness, and serves to found a kind of accordance that is not a likeness. This unlikeness is important to the argument, and we shall discover an important echo of it a little further on.

What is it, then, to "present"? It means, we read, "to let the thing stand opposed as object. As thus placed, what stands opposed must traverse an open field of opposedness [*Entgegen*] and nevertheless must maintain its stand as a thing and show itself as something withstanding [*ein Ständiges*]" (*WW*, 79; *BW*, 123). We note here the attribution of some sort of agency to the thing; its appearing (*Erscheinen*) is being construed as a sort of traversing, but is the coin really and truly supposed to be in motion? Then there is the final clause of the sentence "while still holding fast in itself." The account of the passing-over unites two conflicting ideas. There is an Opposedness (*Entgegen*), which is said to be open (*offen*). Now an open would seem to be a volume that could be traversed in any number of directions, as one might pass through an open field; but an Opposedness seems to refer to something akin to two people facing one another. In such a case an area or zone between the two is set up, which closes off perspectives from the side. What does it mean to say that an Opposedness is open? The answer to this question lies in the thing's "standing fast in itself." It is not that an Opposedness somehow has the property of being open. Rather an Opposedness comes to be constituted in the midst of an open field. The standing fast of the thing in itself generates an Opposedness. By holding fast on itself the thing creates an Opposedness out of the open. Actually it is not just the thing that creates the Opposedness. Recall here that, in order to present a coin, the statement had to hold fast and persevere in its unlikeness from the coin. Both thing and statement, while venturing out into the open, also turn back to stand fast in self. Their standing fast in themselves is what first of all forms an Opposedness in the midst of the open. Thus it was the open that came first. This turning inward to stand in self links Heidegger's phenomenological account to the earlier Platonic version of correspondence. For it is by turning in on self that both statement and coin persevere in the constancy of their being; this is the guarantee of being. It is not that the thing is held in the stable form of its Whatness as in the older idea of essence; only that it is held in itself, perpetually accomplishes a turning in even while entering into the open.

When Chapter 2 began, it was the accordance of statement with thing that we needed to explain. What Heidegger now introduces is the explanation of this. Lying at the basis of the statement's rightness there is a correlation between the self-showing of a thing and a human bearing (*Verhältnis*), or comportment (*Verhalten*). *Verhalten* is an exceedingly abstract notion; fortunately some examples are immediately introduced: working at something, achieving something, acting, and calculating (*Werken, Verrichten, Handeln, Berechnen*). It is important to grasp what status the argument accords to such bearing of ours. I want to claim that human bearing takes precedence over the self-showing or appearing of the thing. The two are partners, as it were, in unconcealment, but they are not equals. This implies a dramatic shift away from the doctrine of essence.

For the statement to be true, it must have come under a directive (*Weisung*) to render the thing just as it is; following this directive the statement rights itself by the thing and thus is right or true. The thing's manifestation in the open has taken on the function of standard (*Richtmass*) to which the statement must approximate; the comportment, open as it is to the manifest thing, will acknowledge whatever standard the thing offers. It would thus be possible for Heidegger to say now that the standard of rightness for the statement stemmed from the one thing or from its manifestation. The truth of the statement, then, could be founded upon a kind of truth in the thing. We could call the truth in the thing the unconcealment of the thing, *aletheia*. Earlier in *The Essence of Ground* Heidegger spoke of "ontic truth" in just this sense and saw in it the basis of the possibility of the truth of statements. *But this is not what he says here.* He says that we must abandon the practice of locating truth primarily in the statement, but rather than making the unconcealment of the thing the proximal basis of statement-truth, he chooses man's open-standing comportment or bearing. Commentators on this passage have not pointed out that Heidegger has made this choice.[3] *There is no doctrine of ontic truth from this point on in our text.* Any notion of the truth of things is abandoned in the present arc of thought. The essentialism we studied first of all was aimed at protecting being, guaranteeing a stable world to which man's notions might approximate. But now we are heading for freedom and away from such security.

It is, of course, noteworthy that precisely in the present context Heidegger speaks for the first time in the essay about the thing as a "being" (*Seiendes*); in earlier pages it was always "thing" or "object." He adds that the sense of "being" is "what is present." But in no way does this suggest a doctrine of ontic truth here. Heidegger grants that the thing yields up a standard, but it is man's conduct that must take over the *posing* of this standard to the representation ("*es muss eine Vorgabe des Richtmasses für alles Vorstellen übernehmen*"). This phrase *could* be understood to mean that human conduct is the re-

---

[3]This refers particularly to T. Langan, *The Meaning of Heidegger* (New York, 1959); W. J. Richardson, *Heidegger: Through Phenomenology to Thought* (Hague, 1963); and E. Tugendhat, *Der Wahrheitsbegriff bei Husserl und Heidegger* (Berlin, 1967). On the particular point at issue here, see, for example, Richardson, pp. 212, 217, and 231.

ceiver of a pregiven standard: the *Vorgabe* (pregiving) *could* refer to
the thing's yielding up of a standard. However, the last sentence of
Chapter 2 definitely speaks of the comportment as pregiving a
standard (*ein Richtmass vorgebend*). And when in Chapter 3 we read
that the pregiving (comportment) has entered into the open (*das
Vorgeben schon freigegeben hat*), it can only be human bearing or comportment that is meant. It takes over the standard and poses it to the
presenting; it comes between the thing and the presentation, and its
standing-open is what makes it possible for the statement to be right.
The thing's ruling is only posed as authoritative, the thing is only
taken as a standard, and in general the manifest is taken as binding
for all presentation through that same source that assimilated the
initial directive (*Weisung*) to heed the manifest; this source is the
open-standing bearing. With greater justice, then, it must be called
the basis of the statement's truth (rightness). It is not just the self-
showing of the thing. The essence of truth is freedom.

So Heidegger's opening study of medieval theology was not made
with the intent of reviving it. The theological support for the concept of truth must be given up. Lacking a theological foundation,
accordance and correspondence are nevertheless possible on the
basis of human freedom. The directive to heed the manifest is more
general than any particular thing or any particular statement and
springs from an openness of the human being in his comportment
toward things. Only this open bearing can bind the presentation or
utterance. The thing itself, no matter how vividly it is manifest or
how unequivocally it directs us, is not capable of this.

Few commentators on Heidegger are more capable than Ernst
Tugendhat, especially on the question of truth. His general line is
that Heidegger's studies of unconcealedness do not succeed in ac-
counting for truth in the narrow sense of the term, (i.e., when it is
applied to statements).[4] But it would appear from the foregoing
analysis that Tugendhat's criticism is off the mark as far as *WW* is
concerned. Heidegger does not seek to eliminate statement-truth or
to reduce it to the thing's self-showing; statement-truth is constituted in its essence by that *freedom that holds to the directive to heed the
manifest*, not merely by the manifest itself. Likewise Tugendhat
maintains that no account of statement untruth can be made on
Heidegger's principles.[5] But by our analysis, once again, it would

[4]It is advocated not only in the treatise mentioned above but in a number of shorter
articles such as "Heideggers Idee von Wahrheit," in *Heidegger: Perspektiven zur
Deutung seines Werkes*, ed. O. Pöggeler (Cologne-Berlin, 1969).
    [5]Ibid., p. 290.

appear that a false statement is one that is not directed according to the standard of the manifest, but wanders away from its influence (i.e., errs, owing to a failure to hold to the directive to heed the manifest). Tugendhat's criticism would, however, apply to any interpretation that places ontic truth directly at the basis of statement truth.

II. FROM FREEDOM TO BEING

From the Platonizing introduction, then, Heidegger has reversed his direction. The external sign of it is that he turns to face a completely new objection. It says the exact opposite of that which we considered at the beginning, where the absolutism of philosophy was at fault. "To place the essence of truth in freedom—doesn't this mean to submit truth to human caprice? Can truth be any more radically undermined than by being surrendered to the arbitrariness of this 'wavering reed'?" (*WW*, 82; *BW*, 126). The thesis appears to make it entirely subjective, the objection says. While one might be ready to root untruth in freedom, as Descartes did, surely one must place the essence of truth in something beyond. The menace of subjectivism is the goad that animates the argument of the remainder of Heidegger's essay. He is at pains in Chapter 3 to show that when he says the essence of truth is freedom he means it in the strictest sense. It is not merely that freedom would be a psychic prerequisite for men to engage in the production of utterances. Making freedom the essence of truth is more comprehensive than that since it touches not only on the psyche of man but on the things the utterances are about. We may recollect that it was through the notion of *Verhalten* that Heidegger led up to the notion of freedom. But this means comportment and therefore action, behavior, working at something, or carrying out a task. It is no mere interior and intellectual freedom that Heidegger has in mind; he means it to cover the whole domain of practices whereby we break in upon the things in our milieu. If it should prove that this free comportment invariably involved some degree of intervention in the context of things, with some disturbance of the context, then it would be a serious matter. Human conduct intervening in the midst of things, shaping the world to its own purposes, would be an unquiet at the very heart of truth. It is possible for me to pocket a coin, to ignore it, to throw it away, to melt it down, or to use it in reckoning a sum of money. The truth of a statement, Heidegger is saying, is rooted in that openness, which for its part is inextricably linked to the practical projects of human life in which we deal with things like coins in ways such as I have mentioned—manipulative to a large extent, using and abusing them equally. Is it not, then, a materialism like that of Marx's second thesis on Feuerbach that we have now adopted? "In practice man must prove the truth, that is, the reality and power, the this-sidedness of his thinking." It might seem that we have clearly opted for a pragmatist theory of truth at the expense of correspondence, and adopted an extreme anthropologism in general philosophy. We seem now to be counting the essence and the being of things for nothing except as they might play a role within some project of man. It might be something akin to the humanism of Sartre that we have now adopted: "We are at a level where there is nothing for us but man."[6] From the old doctrine of essences we have moved to the extreme opposite pole. It is here that the second arc must be seen as starting. It is the vindication of being.

Heidegger has set out the fears of anthropologism and subjectivism that his thesis tends to evoke, but he says at the beginning of Chapter 4 that the fears rest on preconceptions that will vanish if we are prepared for a change in our way of thinking. It seems to me that Chapters 4 and 5 are a venture in a changed way of thinking and they have a unitary thrust, which I visualize as a second arc of thinking. It is a stride from freedom to being. I call it the vindication of being because the first arc did indeed lead us into perilous straights where being itself was endangered. The method of Heidegger's vindication is not to look further at the entity, the coin, which was described as a being during the course of the first arc, but to dig deeper into the very factor, human freedom, which appears to present the challenge to being. The argument is made in Chapter 4 that the essence of freedom is letting-be. The freedom for the manifestation of the manifest thing lets it be the thing that it is. The letting-be that infuses human freedom is not localized merely in acts that neglect or avoid something, nor merely in acts which are consciously therapeutic and conservational. Every way of involving ourselves with anything is informed by letting-be, whether or not we are conscious of it, since it is the very essence of our freedom and our action; it is our exposure to the world, our ek-sistence. This initial description of letting-be is oriented around our daily involvements with particular things.

---

[6]In the *Letter on Humanism* (*Wegmarken*, p. 165; *Basic Writings*, p. 213), Heidegger quotes from Sartre's *L'Existentialisme est un humanisme* the sentence, "Précisément nous sommes sur un plan où il y a seulement des hommes."

Now Heidegger makes the central point in his case, that there are more fundamental human conducts that vindicate being itself, being as a whole. He proceeds toward this by way of an account of the very early philosophical thinking in Greece. Let us look a bit into the philological background, which Chapter 4 presents.

> Still uncomprehended, indeed, not even in need of an essential grounding, the ek-sistence of historical man begins at that moment when the first thinker takes a questioning stand with regard to this unconcealment of beings by asking: what are beings? In this question unconcealment is experienced for the first time. Being as a whole reveals itself as *physis*, "nature," which here does not yet mean a particular sphere of beings but rather beings as such as a whole, specifically in the sense of emerging presence. (*WW*, p. 85; *BW*, pp. 128–129)

According to Heidegger, there was, in the early phase of Greek philosophy, an apprehension not merely of this or that thing but of the *totality* of what is. We have been speaking of a zone, an open, in which some thing or other becomes manifest. Now we see that a fundamental and universal unconcealing was also within the power of man, because it was achieved by the power of questioning of an early Greek philosopher. By analogy to what we have already said about one's dealings with ordinary things, we may understand the philosopher's question also as a venture or irruption into the open and as a self-exposure to the whole of being. We may therefore regard his question, too, as a letting-be—the letting-be of the whole of being. It is not Heidegger in his text who vindicates being. What Heidegger's text does is to show that there are conducts that vindicate being. He mentions the first thinkers who asked what being was and who experienced it as *physis*. Early on in Chapter 4, and climactically in Chapter 5, it is plain that it is the whole, *das Ganze*, to which the early thinkers exposed themselves.

The thinking that they inaugurated is first and foremost a free conduct of man. It involves nothing like tables of law being handed down from above, but depends upon the resolve of men (as Heidegger says in Chapter 8). It is an open resolve, and in this respect it shares in the open-standing of all human conduct. The poems or writings of thinkers are human works, free creations produced in language to which anyone can gain access if he knows the language. That eminently human conduct, philosophical thinking (at least as Parmenides and Heraclitus practiced it), is not just an intervention in which some entity or other is let be. It is a more radical intervention, not the letting-be of a thing but the vindication of being. A vindication is the dissolution of a suspicion at the very point where it arises. In antiquity there was a suspicion woven into language itself, to the effect that nothing really *is* in the eminent sense. What was that doubt that animated the thought of Parmenides and Heraclitus, that *doxa* they stood up against? In general, it was the suspicion that nothing really is but only seems, and no sooner is it one thing than it will present itself as another. They confronted the suspicion in the very spot where it was based, in reflective language, and produced vindications, one speaking of *to einai*; the other, of *physis*. Their work holds open a place in language where the manifest character of the whole can break in upon whoever reads it, where being itself, or the whole, can resonate. Yet they are the work of free men, not things of nature, and only for that reason do they deserve the name of vindications. Setting free from suspicion is an act of freedom; only the free can vindicate. And every such conduct is a vindication of freedom itself as well. However, the danger we have mentioned is *anthropologism*, so the vindication Heidegger undertakes in his time is not quite the same. When freedom itself is suspect, then *it is vindicative to show that free conduct such as thinking is vindicative.* The freedom which served initially in the argument as the basis of correctness, also proves to have the associated and enhanced capacity, by way of philosophy, of bringing being as a whole into unconcealment. It is this thesis that effectively banishes the menace of subjectivism. If human freedom were constrained by an unconcealment in which it had no constitutive part, this would not eliminate the menace at its root; because it is in the power of freedom to vindicate the totality of being (i.e., to bring it, too, into unconcealment, to let it be) then there is a stable core within human freedom that prevents us from regarding it as mere subjectivity, the "whim of a wavering reed." Since the connection of freedom and being is reciprocal, Heidegger is able to go on in Chapter 5 to say that the behaviour of historical man is attuned and by this attunement is raised up to the plane of what-is-in totality. Chapter 5 marks a switch in the relationship between being and man. He has been saying that man posed the question of being; now he says that being and its unconcealedness determine and attune man, all statements, and letting-be.

III. FROM BEING TO UNTRUTH

The vindication of being is not the final word of the essay. In Chapter 6 and 7 Heidegger pushes on to a discussion of two forms of untruth—concealing and errancy—and the text becomes very, very difficult. Words like "essence" and "non-essence," "truth," and "non-truth," are made to say things that run against all ordinary intuitions. But the main source of the difficulty of these chapters is that it is hard to see their overall thrust in the context of the essay. What should be discussed is why Heidegger wrote them, why he insists on tracing truth back to errancy and concealing. This is the final arc of thought in the essay, and it is on a descending path in the direction exactly opposite to the opening ascent toward essence but also opposite to the soaring vindication of the second arc. We follow the pathway now into the inner recesses of a cave of darkness, as Orpheus followed Euridice into the underworld. We proceed into the darkness of a primordial mystery of self-concealing, from which all and every unconcealing must necessarily have sprung and likewise from which all human errors and follies proceed. It is from self-concealing, from errancy, and from unconcealment that all human bearings and utterances have sprung, and all measure-taking. So it is from this primordial cave that every possible modula-tion of truth can trace its genealogy, each possible essence of truth (freedom, unconcealment, measure). In the primordial non-essence (i.e., pre-essence) to which we have now been led, the primordial self-concealing, a light breaks and is lost again; a way is struck and then abandoned; a veil is raised and falls again; an undulating movement of light crosses the enveloping darkness, to be lost again. It is only in this way that an unconcealment can ever come about. It is necessarily continuous with concealment, arising from concealment, returning again to it, and always preserving concealment within. Every event of unconcealing is in this way derivative from primordial self-concealment, mystery.

Why is it that the pathway of *WW* has led to this? It would seem to be because of the perspective of being in totality, which Chapter 5 introduced. All pathways struck by human beings, whether in thought or practice, are pathways through the totality, and they are events prompted and attuned by the totality of being. To speak of totality is to comprehend the human being (i.e., every agent and thinker) within the totality. Because Heidegger comprehends the human being in his cognitive capacity as in every other, as situated in the totality of being, he sees man's striving for truth as a particular determined event within the totality of being. Therefore the mix-ture of the true with concealment is the noneliminable situation of the human subject. In this argument it is not the finite power of human reason that is at work, as in the critical philosophy of Kant, but the movement or process of the totality of being. As the uncon-cealed arises ever again out of concealment, it can never eliminate the concealment that formed its origin.[7] Now untruth has another form: besides concealment there is errancy, which comprehends all errors and illusions and which is, properly speaking, a wandering astray. This form of untruth is essential to truth because it is impossible that the human being should attain cognition without an intervention in the midst of the things of the world, with the disturbance of the context of things as its necessary consequence. As Heidegger puts it in Chapter 7, ek-sistence is necessarily in-sistent, pushing its own claims and interests. For that reason, a wandering astray is the inevitable background of every truth and the terminus to which it will eventually lead.

We understand truth, then, as undulating revelations within a primordial sheltering darkness of concealment. It is no longer the bright arena of unconcealment, as thought by the Greeks, in which being itself showed itself. It is from this primordial mystery that all travelers are sent out and all pathways are struck; and Heidegger's view is that all the determinations of truth and all the determinations of untruth can be derived from the mystery. From it proceed all correctness, adequation, unconcealment, and letting-be. From it, too, proceed all illusions, concealments, errors, and insistence. Thus it is the proper terminus of a pathway into the essence of truth.

---

[7]Langan, pp. 134–140, argues that untruth comes into the course of the argument of *WW* because truth is necessarily finite, that is, that it pertains to every disclosure to leave much else undisclosed, whatever does not belong to it directly. Being focussed on only one thing, and that moreover from a particular perspective, every disclosure will be partial and one-sided. But Langan's account does not take sufficient note of the primacy of self-concealing.

THOMAS SHEEHAN

SEVEN

ON THE WAY TO *EREIGNIS*:
HEIDEGGER'S INTERPRETATION OF *PHYSIS*

THIS ESSAY SEEKS TO SHOW HOW Heidegger's interpretation of *physis* in Aristotle lays the foundation for his understanding of *Ereignis*. Specifically, I want to point out how Heidegger finds the meaning of *physis* to lie in movement, the meaning of movement to lie in *dynamis*, and the meaning of *dynamis* to be "retrieval" (*Wiederholung*) in the primary sense of that term. The structure of retrieval in the realm of *physis* underlies the structure of resolve (*Entschlossenheit*) in the realm of human existence. Resolve issues in authenticity (*Eigentlichkeit*) and is itself the entrance to *Ereignis*. The essay draws on Heidegger's lectures, published and unpublished, and particularly on his 1940 seminar, the protocol of which has been published as "Vom Wesen und Begriff der *Physis*: Aristoteles, *Physik* B, 1."[1]

The first step toward understanding Heidegger's interpretation of *physis* is to clarify how he reads Aristotle phenomenologically (Section I). Heidegger maintains that the Greeks, especially Aristotle, read entities as *phainomena*, appearances that show up in a correlative *noein* or *legein*, which manifests their meaningful presentness-as or is-ness (*ousia*, *Seiendheit*, beingness). The question of first philosophy concerns the analogical unity of is-ness as such. Heidegger's phenomenological orientation toward Aristotle led him to transform the Aristotelian question about is-ness or being-

---

[1]Originally published in *Il Pensiero*, Milano, 3 (1958), 131–156, 265–289, ed. G. Guzzoni; issued as a separate fascicule by the same press in 1960. Republished with slight orthographical changes in WEG (1967), 309–371. English translation by Thomas Sheehan, "On the Being and Conception of *Physis* in Aristotle's *Physics* B, 1," *Man and World*, 9 (1976), 219–270. In referring to Heidegger's works, this paper cites first the abbreviated title of the German work (following the list of abbreviations in William J. Richardson's *Heidegger: Through Phenomenology to Thought* [see n. 2, infra], p. xxxi) with the addition of "WEG" to abbreviate *Wegmarken*, 1967), then the German pagination and, after an "equals" sign, the pagination in existing English translations.

ness: he radically reinvestigates *logos* (in SZ: Dasein) and works out
the analogical unity of *its* beingness. This he finds to be a modality of
that which Aristotle called *energeia ateles* or *dynamis*, that is, a modality of movement, or, if the term be correctly understood, of "temporality." This was the task of *Being and Time*, Part One, Divisions
One and Two (the only sections of that book ever to be published),
and the results provided Heidegger with the horizon for understanding the meaning of being (*das Sein*) in terms of *dynamis* or
movement. The crowning section of *Being and Time*—the unpublished Part One, Division Three—was to have read the analogical
meaning of being as movement in the proper sense, which Heidegger at that time called *die Temporalität des Seins*, the time-character of
being. Section I of this essay only alludes to this program and then
goes on to elaborate what I call here an Aristotelian "phenomenological lexicon" for understanding *Physics* B, 1. This lexicon is, in fact,
the fruit of Heidegger's own rereading or retrieval of Aristotle from
the earliest courses in the twenties up through his interpretation of
Aristotle's *Physics* in 1940.

Section II of this essay turns to Heidegger's interpretation of *physis*
in Aristotle and focuses on Heidegger's characterization of *physis* as a
mode of *ousia*, or beingness. The clue here is Heidegger's reading of
kinesis (movement) as a mode of beingness. An investigation of
movement in terms of *energeia ateles* (incomplete appearance or beingness) shows that the fundamental meaning of *physis* is
Wiederholung, or retrieval, in the original and proper sense: regrasp-
ing possibility by letting it remain the relatively hidden source for
the appearance of a moving entity. It will be shown below that *physis*,
understood as this kind of retrieval, is called *Eignung*, the "appropriation" of possibility (as the relatively hidden source) into the limited appearance of natural entities. Heidegger's interpretation of
physis as retrieval and appropriation merely spells out his understanding of *physis* as *dynamis*.

On the basis of that reading of *physis*, Section III of this essay goes
on to show how *physis*, read as *dynamis*, lays the foundation for
Heidegger's understanding of *Ereignis* in his later works. A step in
that direction can already be found in *Being and Time*, where
Heidegger made use of the notion of *Wiederholung* for his understanding of the phenomenon of resolve. Section III shows that resolve, as the aware retrieval of existence's possibility as possibility, is
the core of the published portions of *Being and Time*, and it points the
way to Heidegger's later transformation of *Wiederholung* and *Eignung* into *Ereignis*.

As a whole the essay argues that the topic or *Sache* of Heidegger's thought—which he originally expressed as the problematic of "being and time" and which he later called *Ereignis*—is "movement," the movement of disclosure conjoined to and indeed initiating the disclosive movement that is man's nature. One way, and perhaps the most important way, that Heidegger worked out this topic was by way of a retrieval of the proper movement-character of *dynamis*. He found that *dynamis* as movement was itself a retrieval and hence that the answer to the question about the meaning of being was an ongoing retrieval of this primordial retrieval, that is, it consisted in letting possibility remain possibility, letting appearance appear by not directly appearing. This "answer" is a matter of simply "being-underway," *Unterwegssein*, where the only operative authority is the ineluctable movement of disclosure.

Before entering upon the subject matter of this essay, I wish to make some remarks on the sources for what follows.

It has long been known that Heidegger's reading of Aristotle was essential to his entire life's work. Richardson writes that "Aristotle has influenced him more profoundly than any other thinker," and Gadamer, Arendt, Szilasi, Tillich, Spiegelberg, Gründer, and Kaufmann report as much.[2] We know that his philosophical objectives were defined in terms of Greek philosophy in the context of Greek poetry and literature, and indeed that from the time he was eighteen years of age he spent an hour a day reading the Greek poets and historians.[3] Moreover, it is common knowledge that the Aristotelian problem of the analogy of being, first awakened in him by his 1907 reading of Brentano's dissertation on Aristotle, remained

[2]William J. Richardson, *Heidegger: Through Phenomenology to Thought* (The Hague: Nijhoff, 1963), p. 309. Hans-Georg Gadamer, "Martin Heidegger und die Marburger Theologie"; in *Heidegger: Perspektiven zur Deutung seines Werks*, ed., O. Pöggeler (Cologne: Kupenheur and Witsch, 1969), esp. p. 171. Hannah Arendt, "Martin Heidegger at Eighty," trans. Albert Hofstadter, *The New York Review*, 17 (Oct. 21, 1971) 50–54. Wilhelm Szilasi, "Interpretation und Geschichte der Philosophie"; in *Martin Heideggers Einfluss auf die Wissenschaften*, ed. C. Astrada et al. (Bern: Francke, 1949), pp. 73–87. Paul Tillich, *Theology of Culture*, ed. R. C. Kimball (New York: Oxford-Galaxy, 1964), p. 78. Herbert Spiegelberg, *The Phenomenological Movement: A Historical Introduction*, Vol. I (The Hague: Nijhoff, 1956), pp. 271–357, and esp. pp. 292–297. Karlfried Gründer, "Heidegger's Critique of Science in its Historical Background," *Philosophy Today*, 7 (1963), 22. Walter Kaufmann, *Critique of Religion and Philosophy*, (New York: Doubleday-Anchor, 1969), p. 29.

[3]Re Greek philosophy: US 134f=39. Also Manuel de Diéquez, "Chez Heidegger à Freiburg," *Les Nouvelles Littéraires artistiques et scientifiques*, Paris, 31, no. 1295 (June 26, 1952), p. 5. Re Heidegger's reading of Greek literature: Jean-Michel Palmier and Frederick de Towarnicki, "Entretien avec Heidegger," *L'Express*, Paris, 954 (October 20–26, 1969), 78–85, esp. p. 80.

"*the* ceaseless impetus for the treatise *Being and Time* which appeared two decades later."[4]

This impetus gained momentum in his lectures and seminars from 1919 on, when he seems to have taken to heart Hegel's words, "If philosophy were done in earnest, nothing would be more worthy than to give lectures on Aristotle."[5] It was in those early Freiburg and Marburg lectures that Heidegger tried out what he called "a transformed understanding of Aristotle," which was the basis for his eventual break with Husserl.[6] In 1928 Gibson recorded Heidegger's position (which was reported through Iskar Becker and went back at least to the 1923–1924 lecture course *Einführung in die phänomenologische Forschung*) that "Aristotle was really in *De Anima* phenomenological (without the explicit Reduction)."[7]

We know as well that Heidegger projected a book prior to *Being and Time*, one that was to summarize his interpretations of Aristotle, and that Paul Natorp got Heidegger hired at Marburg in 1923 on the basis of the introduction to that projected work.[8] And Aristotle's influence continued to work even on the later Heidegger. In the fifties he told his students, "It is advisable, therefore, that you post-

[4]*Frühe Schriften* (Frankfurt: Klostermann, 1972), p. x. Translation by Hans Seigfried, "A Recollection (1957)" in *Heidegger, the Man and the Thinker*, ed. Thomas Sheehan (Chicago: Precedent, 1981), 21f.

[5]Heidegger cites this sentence from Hegel's *Vorlesungen über die Geschichte der Philosophie* (WW, XIV, 314), in "Hegel und die Griechen," WEG 266.

[6]SD 86=78. Note: not "a seminar," as in the English translation, but "the seminar." Husserl realized that the cause of the break went back to Heidegger's (Aristotelian) beginnings in philosophy: "Ich hatte leider seine philos. Ausbildung nicht bestimmt, offenbar war er schon in Eigenart, als er meine Schriften studierte," Edmund Husserl, *Briefe an Roman Ingarden*, ed. R. Ingarden (The Hague: Nijhoff, 1968), p. 41. Husserl's strongest remarks on Heidegger are found in his letter to Alexander Pfänder, January 6, 1931 (Husserl Archives, R I Pfänder 6.I.31), soon to be published by Herbert Spiegelberg.

[7]W. R. B. Gibson, "From Husserl to Heidegger: Excerpts from a 1928 Freiburg Diary," ed., Herbert Spiegelberg, *Journal of the British Society for Phenomenology*, 2 (1971), 73. The winter semester course referred to here, which the prospectus of the *Gesamtausgabe* lists as "Der Beginn der neuzeitlichen Philosophie" and which the Marburg cataglogue (see Richardson, p. 665) subtitles "(Descartes Interpretation)," was recorded by Heidegger's students under the title "Einführung in die phänomenologische Forschung" and dealt at length in its opening lectures with Aristotle's *De Anima* B (November 2–22, 1923). Gibson (p. 72) went on to write, "Husserl is the Plato to Heidegger's Aristotle." Further information on Heidegger's relation to Husserl before SZ can be found in my article, "Heidegger's Early Years: Fragments for a Philosophical Biography," *Heidegger, the Man and the Thinker*, pp. 3–19.

[8]Gadamer, 170; Szilasi, 77; H. Knittermeyer, *Die Philosophie der Existenz* (Vienna: Humboldt, 1952), p. 212; Sheehan, *art. cit.*, p. 11f. Husserl wrote Ingarden on December 14, 1922: "In VII [the seventh volume of the *Jahrbuch*] erscheint eine grundlegende gr. Arbeit über Aristot. von Heidegger" (Ingarden, 25), but Prof. Mrs. Malvine Husserl wrote on February 25, 1924, "Der Beitrag von Prof. Heidegger hat sich durch seine Berufung nach Marburg verzögert...." Szilasi says that the introduction was written in the spring of 1923, but Gadamer, on the basis of a 1922 letter

pone reading Nietzsche for the time being, and first study Aristotle for ten to fifteen years" (WD 70=73). And to judge by an interview that the present writer had with Heidegger in 1971, Heidegger himself continued living out that program into his final years.

But if the influence of Aristotle on Heidegger is undeniable, the manner and degree of it remain among Heidegger's best-kept secrets. Sufficient index of the secret is the infrequency with which Heideggerian scholars elaborate the Aristotelian bases of Heidegger's work;[9] and this infrequency is not the fault of the commentators. Heidegger himself published only one essay devoted entirely to Aristotle ("Vom Wesen und Begriff der *Physis*"), and even there the theme is Aristotle and not his influence on Heidegger. Likewise, in *Being and Time*, where Aristotle's presence can be felt virtually everywhere, the nature of the influence is concealed behind the language of phenomenology.

The secret lies hidden in Heidegger's courses—chiefly those from 1919 through 1952—and, since it is not clear that his *Gesamtausgabe* will include the early Freiburg courses (1916–1923), the secret may be kept until Heidegger's *Nachlass* becomes available. But parts of it have leaked out. For example, the appearance of his 1925–1926 course *Logik: Die Frage nach der Wahrheit* revealed the deep influence of Aristotle's *Peri Hermēneias* (specifically the question of *logos apophantikos*) and *Metaphysics* Theta 10 (*alētheia*) on *Being and Time*. Likewise the publication of *Die Grundprobleme der Phänomenologie* has clarified Heidegger's reading of the meaning of *energeia* in Aristotle and the transformation of that meaning in the medieval problematic of *essentia* and *existentia*.[10]

---

from Heidegger, is correct in locating its writing in the year previous. In a conversation with me on January 27, 1975, Gadamer recalled that the work was to cover *Nic. Ethics* Z, *Metaphysics* A and Z, H, Theta, *De Anima* G, and *Physics* B. Before his death in 1924, Natorp gave his copy of the manuscript—typewritten with copious handwritten marginalia by Heidegger—to Gadamer, but this copy, along with Heidegger's letters to Gadamer, was destroyed in the bombings of Leipzig during World War II. Heidegger kept a copy without the marginalia, but it is not announced for publication in the *Gesamtausgabe*. Presumably it is in the Marbach Archives.

[9]Werner Marx's *Heidegger and the Tradition*, trans. Theodore Kisiel and Murray Green (Evanston, Illinois: Northwestern University Press, 1971), is a notable exception.

[10]*Logik. Die Frage nach der Wahrheit*, ed. Walter Biemel (Frankfurt: Klostermann, 1976); English translation *Logic: The Question of Truth* by Thomas Sheehan, forthcoming from Indiana University Press. *Die Grundprobleme der Phänomenologie*, ed. F.-W. von Herrmann (Frankfurt: Klostermann, 1975); English translation *The Basic Problems of Phenomenology* by Albert Hofstadter (Bloomington: Indiana University Press, 1982). Heidegger's 1931 course, *Aristoteles, Metaphysik Theta, 1–3: Von Wesen und Wirklichkeit der Kraft*, ed. Heinrich Hüni (Frankfurt : Klostermann, 1981), appeared after the present essay was completed.

Moreover, there exist secondary works that either grew out of the earliest courses or extend them or report their contents. Among these is Helene Weiss' *Kausalität und Zufall in der Philosophie des Aristoteles* (1940), which Heidegger recommended to his seminar students in 1951 as one of the few good works on the *Physics* and perhaps on Aristotle's thought as a whole. (This recommendation may have been influenced by the fact that Professor Weiss, a former student of Heidegger's, reports, often in close paraphrase, much of the content of Heidegger's lectures on Aristotle in the twenties.[11]) Among the unpublished seminars and lecture courses that inform what follows, the seminar of 1928, summer semester, entitled "Phänomenologische Übungen: Interpretation von Aristoteles, *Physik* II," is important, as is the major lecture course on Aristotle that Heidegger gave at Freiburg in 1921–1922, winter semester, and 1922, summer semester. However, since Heidegger's explications of *dynamis, energeia,* and *physis* are generally (and I emphasize that word) constant from the early twenties up through the winter semester of 1951–1952 (Übungen im Lesen: Aristoteles, *Metaphysik*, IV und IX, 10") and differ only in minor and generally contextual ways from "Vom Wesen und Begriff der *Physis*," attention will be directed principally to that last text.

I. READING ARISTOTLE "PHENOMENOLOGICALLY"

Crucial to the argument that will be developed here is a proper understanding of the "method" according to which Heidegger reads Aristotle at all.[12] To call this method "phenomenological," as

---

[11]Originally published in Basel, Prof. Weiss' book was reissued in 1967 by the Wissenschaftliche Buchgesellschaft (Darmstadt). Pages 20–29 closely follow sections of Heidegger's 1922 course on *Physics* A. Cf. also pp. 6, 52 n., and 100 n. Other works that follow Heidegger's interpretations to some degree are Rudolf Boehm, *Das Grundlegende und das Wesentliche: Zu Aristoteles' Abhandlungen über das Sein und das Seiende (Metaphysik Z)* (The Hague: Nijhoff, 1965); Walter Bröker, *Aristoteles* (Frankfurt: Klostermann, 1964), third expanded edition; Wilhelm Szilasi, *Macht und Ohnmacht des Geistes* (Bern: Francke, 1946), esp. pp. 285–291, which Szilasi (p. 76) calls "Eine durch die vielspäteren Bemühungen verdeckte Erinnerung" of Heidegger's early interpretation of *Peri Hermeneias*; Ernst Tugendhat, *TI KATA TINOS: Eine Untersuchung zu Struktur und Ursprung aristotelischer Grundbegriffe* (Freiburg: Alber, 1958); to some extent, Karl Ulmer, *Wahrheit, Kunst und Natur bei Aristoteles* (Tübingen: Niemeyer, 1953); Wolfgang Wieland, *Die aristotelische Physik* (Göttingen, 1962); see E. Tugendhat's review of it in *Gnomon* 35 (1963), 543–555, esp. p. 554; Fridolin Wiplinger, *Physis und Logos: Zum Köperphänomen in seiner Bedeutung für den Ursprung der Metaphysik bei Aristoteles* (Freiburg: Alber, 1971).

[12]"Method" is written in inverted commas to indicate Heidegger's self-distancing from the method of modern philosophy; see US 178=74, 197=91 and FD 79=102. Heidegger's "method" follows Aristotle's *methodos* (*Physics* G, 1, 200 b 13 and WEG

Heidegger indeed does, is not to drag Husserl's phenomenology back to an epoch where it does not and could not belong. Rather Heidegger claimed that his own phenomenological procedure is no more than the explicitation of Aristotle's own way of investigation and of the way of reading entities that was indigenous to Greek thought itself. This explicitation led to Heidegger's break with Husserl and the philosophical tradition and entailed as well a transformation of Aristotle's problematic.[13] Before spelling out the concrete shape of the phenomenological correlation that Heidegger found in Aristotle's works I will sketch a preliminary idea of phenomenology in Aristotle according to Heidegger and indicate how Heidegger used that idea to transform the Aristotelian problematic.

A. Phenomenology: Perspective and Program

According to Heidegger the Greeks were the first people to experience entities (*to on, ta onta*) as *phainomena*, as things that of themselves show themselves or appear. Professor John H. Finley, Jr., in an informative study *Four Stages of Greek Thought*, confirms from a classicist's point of view what Heidegger finds operative in Greek thought from Homer through Aristotle, namely, that the presence of entities in the world was experienced as the appearing or *phainesthai* of those entities, where *phainesthai* means that an entity brings itself to radiant self-manifestation (*sich zum Scheinen bringen*) and "is" precisely insofar as it shows itself in that self-manifestation.[14]

In appearing, an entity appears *as* something meaningful — as a shield that the warrior can use or as the ship that he can launch or as

---

341=246). For Heidegger's claim that his work remains "phenomenological" from beginning to end, see SZ 38=62f, SD 90=82, and his "Über das Zeitverständnis in der Phänomenologie und im Denken der Seinsfrage," *Phänomenologie — lebendig oder tot?*, ed. Helmut Gehrig (Karlsruhe: Badenia Verlag), p. 47; English translation by Thomas Sheehan and Frederick Ellison, "The Understanding of Time in Phenomenology and in the Thinking of the Being-Question," *The Southwestern Journal of Philosophy*, 10, 2 (Summer 1979), 201.

[13]Cf. SZ 28=51, 213=256 on *auto to pragma* (*Meta.* A, 3, 984 a 18f); also FD 62f=81f, US 134f=39f and WP 12=45. See Walter Biemel, "Heidegger and Metaphysics" in *Heidegger, the Man and the Thinker*, p. 164: "The word 'phenomenology' [in SZ] took on an interpretation that was tied into Aristotle more than Husserl." Cf. as well Joseph Owens, *The Doctrine of Being in the Aristotelian Metaphysics*, 2nd ed. (Toronto: Pontifical Institute of Medieval Studies, 1963), p. 132. On thinking "Greeker than the Greeks," see US 134f=39; also Heidegger's "Aus einer Erörterung der Wahrheitsfrage" (a selection from his course of winter 1937–1938, "Grundfragen der Philosophie: Vom Wesen der Wahrheit: *aletheia* und *poiesis*"), in *Zehn Jahre Neske Verlag*, ed. Günter Neske (Pfullingen: Neske, 1962), p. 20.

[14]Re *phainomena*, see US 132=38 and SZ 28f=51, EM 46=50, 54=59, 77=85, 79=88, 138=151, and WEG 345f=249f. See John H. Finley, Jr., *Four Stages of Greek Thought* (Stanford, Cal.: Stanford University Press, 1966), pp. 3, 5, 27, 29, and 53f.

the god that he can revere or challenge. This "as"-character bespeaks the arrival of meaning among entities, the irruption that
occurs only with the arrival of man. If man can deal with entities only
insofar as they appear as such and so, the philosopher is distinguished by the fact that he asks the question of their "appearing-as"
as such, the question of their being.

To say that much is to indicate two things:

First, whenever the Greeks speak of *to on*, they always imply *to on
hēi* . . . , an entity in terms of some modality of meaningful presence,
even if the "as" (*hēi*) is not expressly articulated. This as-dimension
of entities, which gets expressed in the "is" of apophantic discourse,
articulates the being-dimension of entities. Hence, *to on* always
means an-entity-in-a-modality-of-being, and so Heidegger correctly
translates *to on* as *das seiend-Sein*.[15] To express the togetherness of
entities and their given modes of being, Aristotle often uses *ousia*,
which, derived through the participle *ousa* from the infinitive *einai*,
can refer either to the particular present entity or to its presence or
being. When it refers to the *being* of an entity, Heidegger accurately
renders it as *Seiendheit*, that is, "beingness" or "is-ness." Therefore,
the question that defines first philosophy—"What is *to on*?"—must
be fleshed out to say "What is *to on hēi on*?" The *hei on* indicates that
the question points beyond the realm of the ontic (shields, ships,
gods) and seeks an ontological answer: "entities *as in-being*." The
question focuses on the is-ness of any given entity, and in fact Aristotle says that the question "What is *to on hei on*?" comes down to the
question "What is is-ness?" (*tis hē ousia*), and indeed not the is-ness of
any delimited region of entities but of all entities in terms of the
analogical unity of all possible modes of is-ness. Aristotle's aporetic
question about *ousia* is his formulation of the question about the
meaning of being (*Meta.* G 1 and Z 1, 1028 b 2).

Secondly, to speak of entities as *phainomena* is at least to imply the
locus of their meaningful appearance, the horizon within which that
meaningfulness is experienced. Entities as *phainomena* are in some
way correlative to modes of awareness (*Vernehmen*) in the broadest
sense. They comport a *legein* or a *logos* (a bringing-to-appearance)
that reveals them as what and how they are (without *logos*, no is-

---

[15]WP 31=97; cf. EM 24=25f. Also, "Vorwort" to Richardson, p. xi=x: "das
Seiende . . . hinsichtlich seines Seins." On *to on* as always in-being, see WEG 330=238
and Gottfried Martin, *Introduction to General Metaphysics*, trans. E. Schaper and I.
Leclerc (London: Allen and Unwin, 1961), p. 60.

ness).[16] The uniqueness of man as "the living being that has *logos*" (*to zōion to logon echon*)[17] is that his essence is the locus of meaning and he has access to entities only in terms of their appearance-as or being-as in *logos*. Aristotle thematizes the function of *logos* as *dēloun* (to make visible), as *apophainesthai* (to show forth) and most importantly as *alētheuein* (to uncover, bring out of hiddenness, bring into intelligibility).[18] For man *to on* is always *to on legomenon*; an entity is always interpreted or "read," more or less articulated according to one or many of the multiple modes of meaningful presence that we can discover in the implicit "as" of practical activity or the explicit "is" of apophantic discourse.

To summarize these two points we may say: If *to on* always implies a being-dimension or meaningful presence that is indicated by the "as" (*hēi*), the only locus of this being-dimension is man's essence as *logos* or *alētheuein*, disclosure. *To on* and *logos* are apriori correlative; man's very nature is to be ontological (*legein ta onta*) and phenomenological (*legein ta phainomena*). If man raises the question of first philosophy ("What is *to on hēi on*?"), the resultant ontology must be implicitly or explicitly phenomenological.

Before moving on, let us ask whether this alleged explicitation of the implicit phenomenological bases of Aristotle's philosophy is not merely a reading back of contemporary (specifically Husserlian) into Greek thought. We could, of course, raise the question as to whether or not any interpretation of Greek thought, whether carried out by Thomas Aquinas, Werner Jaeger, William David Ross, or whomever, can hope to be without presuppositions. But rather than opening up the important issue of the hermeneutical fore-structure, I will simply let Heidegger speak for himself, and I will leave open the question he poses. This paragraph is cited here at some length because it reveals the broad context within which Heidegger's reading of Greek philosophy moves.

> The totality of entities is the field from which the positive sciences of nature, history, space always get their regions of objects.

---

[16]Cf. SZ 212=255: "Allerdings nur solange Dasein *ist*, das heisst die ontische Möglichkeit von Seinsverständnis, 'gibt es' Sein." This paper prescinds from the question of *nous*.

[17]Cf. *Politics* A, 2, 1253 a 9–12, *Nic. Ethics* A 13, 1102 a 30 and Z 1, 1139 a 5.

[18]SZ 32f.=56f and the footnote thereto. Heidegger's reading is grounded in texts such as *De Interpretatione*, 4 and 5, esp. 17 a 15f (*apophantikos=delon*); cf. *Meta*. G 2, 1003 b 31f. (*dēloi*); *Nic. Ethics* Z 4, 1140 a 10f and 21f (*meta logou alēthous*), Z 5, 1140 b 6ff and 20ff (*alēthe meta logou*), Z 6, 1141 a 4 (*alētheuomen*), Z 7, 1141 a 17f (*alētheuein*).

Directed straight at entities, these sciences in their totality take charge of exploring everything that is. So it seems there is no field of possible investigation left over for philosophy, although from antiquity it has been considered the fundamental science. But doesn't Greek philosophy, since its decisive beginnings, make "entities" the object of its inquiry? It certainly does, but not in order to define this or that entity, but in order to understand entities *as entitities-in-being*, i.e., with regard to their *being*. The posing of the question and consequently the answers were for a long time caught in obscurities. But already in the beginnings something remarkable comes to light. Philosophy seeks to elucidate being via reflection on the *thinking* of entities (Parmenides). Plato's disclosure of the Ideas takes its bearings from the *soul's conversation* (*logos*) with itself. The Aristotelian categories originate in view of *reason's* assertoric knowledge. Descartes explicitly founded First Philosophy on the *res cogitans*. Kant's transcendental problematic moves in the field of *consciousness*. Now, is this turning of the gaze away from entities and onto consciousness something accidental, or is it finally demanded by the specific character of what has been constantly sought for, under the title "being," as philosophy's field of problems?[19]

The last question, which echoes Aristotle's *aei zētoumenon kai aei aporoumenon* (*Meta.* Z, 1, 1028 b 2f.), serves as Heidegger's starting point for radicalizing the Aristotelian question about the analogical unity of all is-ness. We may now proceed to show how Heidegger's explicitation of the implicit phenomenology in Aristotle also entails the transformation of the Aristotelian problematic.

Man has access to entities only in terms of their meaning in the broadest sense, that is, only in terms of some form of presentness-as in *logos*. This presentness-as, whereby entities are understood and eventually articulated (*legetai*), has many possible modalities. Thus: *to on legetai pollachōs*, "entities are revealed in their presentness-as in many modes."[20] In *Meta.* E 2 Aristotle gives an unsystematized list of

---

[19]This text is the opening lines of Heidegger's redaction of an introduction to Husserl's *Encyclopaedia Britannica* article on phenomenology: Edmund Husserl, *Phänomenologische Psychologie (Husserliana*, IX), ed. Walter Biemel (The Hague: Nijhoff, 1968), p. 256. An English translation of the entire redaction appears as "The Idea of Phenomenology, with a Letter to Edmund Husserl (1927)," trans. Thomas Sheehan, in *Listening* 12 (1977), 111–121; the present excerpt appears on p. 111.

[20]*Meta.* G 2, 1003 a 33; E 2, 1026 a 33ff; Z 1, 1028 a 10; Theta 1, 1045 b 33ff. Heidegger translates the Greek variously: "Das seiend-Sein kommt vielfältig zum Scheinen" (WP 31=97); "Das Seiende wird (nämlich hinsichtlich seines Seins) in vielfacher Weise offenkundig," "Vorwort" to Richardson (p. xi=x). Cf. "Seiendes kann sich nun in verschiedener Weise, je nach der Zugangsart zu ihm, von ihm, selbst her zeigen" (SZ 28=51); "birgt das 'ist', d.h. das Sein in sich selbst, die Vielfalt, deren Faltung es ermöglicht, dass wir überhaupt mannigfaltiges Seiendes in dem, *wie* es jeweils ist, uns zugänglich machen? . . . das 'ist' bekundet im Sagen eine reiche Mannigfaltigkeit der Bedeutungen" (EM 69=76). Cf. also Heidegger's redaction of the phenomenology article (previous note): "Dieses [Ding] stellt sich vielmehr in der Wahrnehmung durch mannigfaltige 'Erscheinungsweisen' dar" (p. 259=113).

four general ways that entities are revealed as in-being: (a) entities as being "accidental," (b) entities as being "true" or "false," (c) entities as being according to the schemata of the *kategoria*, and (d) entities as being in *dynamis* and *energeia*. But all of these four ways (and not just those within the schemata of the categories) are related analogically to a common term (*pros hen*) insofar as each is a modality of presentness-as in which entities are revealed as *being* this way or that. If there were a science that could reveal that analogical unity of being, it would be the science of all entities in terms of their is-ness as such—the science of *to on hēi on*.

Unlike Aristotle, Heidegger carried out a search for the common meaning that analogically unifies the many meanings of the being of entities by first thematically reinvestigating the very locus of any and all meaning: *logos* as the "faculty" of revealing. In so doing he transformed Aristotle's problematic. We may put the matter this way. If entities are present in *logos* in many ways, then those many ways are themselves modifications of *logos*, and hence *logos* itself appears in many ways. If *logos* in its revelatory function has a variety of ways of being (for example, the theoretical, the practical, and all their subdivisions), then the first and foundational step toward clarifying the meaning of being (the analogical unity of the ways in which entities appear) should be to question the unity of *logos* itself. *Logos* must, as it were, turn on itself and carry out an interpretation of the revelatory function that it itself is, and it must seek the essence of that function. And since the modes of *logos* are correlative to the modes of the appearance of entities, the discovery of the unity of *logos* would provide the philosopher with the a priori horizon for working out the analogical unity of all modes of the appearance of entities. This would be the meaning of being itself.

We can see here in a roughly Aristotelian formulation the program announced in *Being and Time*. And indirectly we can see how this program could not be carried out on Aristotelian grounds but only on the condition of a transformation of the Aristotelian problematic. To begin with, we must affirm, against misunderstandings of Heidegger's claim about the "forgottenness of being," that being *is* questioned by Aristotle with regard to its meaning. But the question is misplaced insofar as it does not investigate the being of *logos* deeply enough, and specifically insofar as it misses the *kinetic* meaning of the revelatory function and therefore the kinetic meaning of being itself. Aristotle did not get beyond the thematization of the being of entities as *ousia*, whether in the particular regions of entities or in the highest instance—the divine. Aristotle, as Heidegger reads him, understood *ousia* as the relatively stable presentness of entities

in a *logos* whose basic being is the relatively stable revelation of entities in their presentness. Given Aristotle's understanding of the
revelatory function of *logos* as a categorial-assertoric "making present" of entities, for him the analogical unity of the many modes of
the presentness of entities was pure presentness as such, pure
energeia. If Heidegger hoped to justify his claim that such a formulation does not disclose the authentic meaning of being, he would have
to reformulate critically the fundamental meaning of *logos* at a level
deeper than the categorial-assertoric unity of *synthesis* and *diairesis*, at
which Aristotle stopped. If it could be shown (as the course *Logik: Die
Frage nach der Wahrheit* attempts to do in terms of Aristotelian texts,
and as *Being and Time* attempts to do by a hermeneutic of "factical
life") that the apophantic *logos* of Aristotle is a derived form of a
more basic "dynamic" or kinetic (Heidegger says "temporal") form
of disclosure, then the way would be opened for stating the unified
meaning of being not as pure *energeia* but as *dynamis* and movement,
that is, as *energeia ateles*. In a non-Aristotelian formulation of the
same proposition, the meaning of being would be "time."

I state these matters programatically and in Aristotelian terms in
accordance with the limited aim that was stated at the beginning of
this section: to show the perspective within which Heidegger re-
reads Aristotle "phenomenologically" and to indicate the consequences of that reading for Heidegger's own program. Moreover,
stating Heidegger's program in roughly Aristotelian terms may also
have the advantage of demystifying some of the unique and difficult
language in which Heidegger formulates his own project of thought.
For example, as we shall see later, if an accurate translation of
dynamis were *Eignung* (roughly "appropriation"), as Heidegger
claims it is, then we might be able to find the justification for calling
the meaning of being *Ereignis* by investigating the meaning of
dynamis rather than by chasing the word *Ereignis* down the dubious
paths of German etymologies.[21] But that may be only a personal
preference. We turn now to the second topic of this first section,
namely, the concrete shape of the phenomenological correlation as
Heidegger finds it hiding in the key terms of Aristotle's philosophical vocabulary.

---

[21]Cf. Heidegger's etymology for *Ereignis*, ID 24f (omitted from the English translation at p. 36). For his claim that the word *Ereignis* is not arbitrary but demanded by the
issue, see "Vorwort" to Richardson, p. xxi=xxf). For his apologiae for his use of
language, see SZ 38f=63 and VA 27f (I, 19f)=20.

B. Phenomenology: An Aristotelian Lexicon

We have seen that all human knowing, as "phenomenological," entails knowing an entity in a mode of its presentness-as in *logos* (i.e., in a mode of its being). In Aristotle these modes of being can be expressed in terms of *eidos*, the "appearance" of an entity as what and how that entity is. It is not our concern here that Aristotle's thematization of the modes of being as modes of visibility (*eidos*: "the seen," derived from *horaō*, "I see") may carry over aspects of the Platonic emphasis on seeing. Rather, what is important is Aristotle's ontological transformation of Plato's *eidos*. Aristotle experiences entities so differently from the way Plato does that he radically changes the phenomenological correlativity of *eidos* and *logos*, which Plato already knew, and thereby achieves a more adequate ontological formulation (cf. N II, 228, 409=9f). Aristotle's *eidos*, as the being of an entity, cannot be some thing existing off by itself apart from *logos* (*ou choriston on...*) but rather exists only in *logos* (*...all' e kata ton logon — Physics* B, 1, 193 b 5). Both the Platonic *eidos* and the Aristotelian *eidos* are formulations of being, and both are correlative to some kind of awareness. But in Aristotle's unique formulation of that correlativity Heidegger finds a more adequate phenomenological formulation, which is at the same time a more adequate ontological formulation. Insofar as Plato's *eidos* (at least as Aristotle understands it) can stand off on its own, it lends itself to an ontical characterization (i.e., to being taken as an entity), whereas insofar as Aristotle's *eidos* appears only in the disclosive declaration about an entity (i.e., in the *legein* of an *on*), it has a properly onto-logical character — it names the being of an entity. We see here again how ontology is controlled by phenomenology. If Aristotle's ontology is more to the point (*zur Sache*) than Plato's, that is because his phenomenology is more properly formulated. And indeed, if Heidegger's ontology is to lay claim to more originality than that of Aristotle, this could be only because its thematization of *logos* would supposedly issue in a formulation of phenomenology that is more to the point.

But back to the lexicon. Granted that the phenomenological correlativity can be articulated as *eidos-logos*, the *eidos*, as the presentness of an entity in what and how that entity is, has the element of stability about it. Aristotle often speaks of *ta onta* (entities) as *synhestota* and *synhistamena* (respectively, *Physics* B, 1, 192 b 13 and 193 a 36). These participial forms are from the verb *histemi*, "I stand" or "I make to stand." With this clue Heidegger claims that the Greeks experienced entities as "the stable" (*das Ständige*) with the twofold meaning of (a) "that which has its stand in and of itself and therefore stands 'there,' " and (b) that which is stable in the sense of enduring and lasting (WEG 316=227). Another word that equally expresses the element of stability is *hypokeimenon*, which comes from the verb *hypokeimai*, "I lie before. . . . " An entity understood as *hypokeimenon*, "that which lies or is present" (cf. the Latin *subjectum*), can equally be called *hypostasis*, "that which stands of and by itself" (cf. the Latin *substantia*). Heidegger says that the "standing" and the "lying" indicate a common Greek understanding of what an entity is: it is "that which is stably present of itself" (WEG 331=239). There is yet another designation for the element of stability in being: *ousia*. In popular Greek usage, before it was taken up as a philosophical term, *ousia* designated one's present possessions, one's tools or property. These connotations were continued in the philosophical use of the term, especially by Aristotle, and the correct German translations of *ousia* as *die Habe* and *das Anwesen* ("present holdings") capture the sense of stable presentness that for the Greeks characterized the being of an entity.[22]

These words connoting stability can now be read in terms of *energeia* and *entelecheia*.[23] An entity that stands there, lies there, or is held in presence (*synhestota, hypostasis, hypokeimenon, ousia*) and shows itself as what it is (*eidos*) is seen as having "gathered itself up" into stability. The words *telos, peras,* and *ergon* point to this stable in-gathering. *Telos* does not mean primarily "aim" or "purpose" or "cessation" but rather "completion, fulfillment, accomplishment." (Cf. the Latin translation of *teleion* as *perfectum*.) Likewise, *peras* does not mean "limitation" in the sense of an externally imposed restraint and therefore a kind of deficiency; rather it means self-limitation in the sense of a "holding of itself together" in such a way that an entity can stand of and by itself and so *be*. To express the unity of all these modes of stability as modes of being we may say: An entity, standing or lying present (*hypokeimenon*, etc.) in its self-limitation (*peras*) and showing itself for what it is (*eidos*), "has itself" (cf. *echein*) "in its fulfillment" (*en telei*): *en-tel-echeia*. And because all of these meanings

[22]WEG 330=238, EM 47=50, 148=162. Cf. Martin, (note 15, supra), p. 112f, and Joseph Owens (note 13 supra), p. 152 n. 63. Also KM 216f=249.

[23]For what follows: On *peras* and *telos*: EM 46=49, 48=52, 87=96, 100=110; FD 63=81; VA 17 (I, 9)=8; WEG 321=231, 339=244f., 349=252, 354=256f.; N II 405=6; "Der Ursprung des Kunstwerkes" (Stuttgart: Reclam, 1960), 96ff=83f. For "das Gesprochene" as *telos* of "Sprechen": US 16=194. Confirmation of the fact that *peras* does not mean primarily "cessation" might be found in the verb *peraino*, "I bring to perfection." On *energeia* and *entelecheia*: EM 46=50, 146=150; HW 68=81; WP 15f=55; VA 50 (I, 42)=160; N I, 77=64, 404f.=5f; WEG 352-356=255-258, 361=261.

can also be expressed by the Greek *ergon*—not in the sense of the end-product of technical making but in the sense of what has been placed into the self-manifestation of its own *eidos*—then *en-erg-eia* says the same as *en-tel-echeia*. All of these terms express an entity-in-its-being, and as such are correlative with *logos*.

Two final lexical entries: *morphe* and *aei*. Heidegger reads *morphe* as saying the "same" as *eidos* (appearance), but with the added nuance of an entity's "placing itself into the appearance" (*die Gestellung in das Aussehen*).[24] What this nuance achieves is a delineation of the difference of Aristotelian *eidos* from the Platonic. "Overwhelmed, as it were, by the essence of *eidos*," Heidegger writes, "Plato grasped *eidos* itself in turn as something present for itself and thus as something common (*koinon*) to the individual 'entities' 'which stand in such an appearance'; thereby the individual, as subordinate to *idea* as the real entity, was displaced into the role of non-being" (WEG 345=249). In contrast, Aristotle grasps the individual as a real entity, that is, as something that has being insofar as it places itself into its own *eidos*, which appears in *logos*. Conversely: "The clue by which *eidos*—and thereby also *morphe*—are graspable is *logos*" (WEG 345f=250). "*Morphe* must be understood from *eidos*, and *eidos* must be understood from *logos*" (WEG 345=249). In summary:

> By translating *morphe* as placing into appearance, we mean to express chiefly two things which are equal in the Greek word but thoroughly lacking in our word "form." First, placing into the appearance is a mode of becoming present, *ousia*. *Morphe* is not an *ontic* property present in matter, but a mode of *being*. Secondly, "placing into the appearance" is movedness, *kinesis*, and this "movement" is radically lacking in the concept of form (WEG 346=250).

Finally a word about *aei* (See WEG 338–340=244f). Heidegger undertakes a reading of *Physics* 193 a 21–28 where *aidion* ("eternal," from *aei*) and *apeirakis* ("without limit"; compare *a* + *peras* and the Latin translation *infinities*) appear, and he argues that *aei* is to be understood not in terms of "limitless duration" (this would be the *apeirakis* that is the very opposite of *aei*) but rather in terms of presentness in *peras*. An entity that is *aidion* is not one that is "always going on without ceasing" but rather one that is authentically present for the time being. When Aeschylus has Prometheus speak of *ho aei krāton* (*Prometheus*, line 937), he does not mean "the eternal king" but "whoever is king at the time," the current king. If *aei* names an

---

[24]Gestellung: WEG 351=254. *Morphe*: EM 46=50, 131=144; HW 18=28, 27=38, 56=69; WEG 344–346=248–250, 357=258, 360=261.

ontological characteristic of entities-in-being (cf. the highest entity as *aei on*), it does not designate chronological permanence but rather primarily stability within *peras* — and for that reason perhaps permanence. Again, the focus of the Greek understanding of being is on presentness in unhiddenness (*aletheia*).

Here we may stop our preliminary sketch of how Heidegger reads Aristotle phenomenologically. What may seem like a complex journey through Aristotle's vocabulary can be briefly summarized as follows. The uniqueness of man among the animals is that with him there arrives meaning, indeed he has access to entities only in terms of their presence in *logos*. Man's very being is *logos*, and its revelatory function is that whereby and wherein the is-ness of entities becomes manifest. This is-ness is expressed equally as *eidos, ousia, entelecheia,* and *energeia*. Furthermore, the primary philosophical task is the determination of is-ness as such, the analogical unity that governs all possible modes of the presentness of entities. The question about the unified meaning of *ousia* rests on a prior (thematic or unthematic) understanding of the analogical unity of the being of *logos* itself. Heidegger's radical thematization of the being of *logos* is the basis of his claim that the authentic meaning of being remains overlooked in Aristotle, and it is as well the starting point for his own question about the meaning of being as *dynamis*.

II. HEIDEGGER'S READING OF *PHYSIS* IN ARISTOTLE

The preceding section is prologue to the present task of understanding how Heidegger interprets the meaning of Aristotle's *physis* as *dynamis*. The final goal of this essay is to understand how such a reading provided Heidegger with the raw material for understanding the meaning of being as *Ereignis*. We may put the argument briefly. The discovery that *physis* as *dynamis* is the meaning of the being of one particular region of entities (Aristotle's *physei on* or natural entities) raises the question of whether the heretofore undiscovered analogical unity of all the modes of being of all regions of entities may not itself be *dynamis*. To raise that question is to enter upon the project of *Being and Time*.

Our guide in the present section is the protocol of Heidegger's 1940 seminar (first published in 1958), "Vom Wesen und Begriff der *Physis*: Aristoteles, *Physik* B, 1." In form, this sixty-page protocol is a translation (and therefore already an intepetation) of and running commentary on *Physics* B, 1 with the exception of 193 b 9 (*dio kai*) through 193 b 12 (*ex anthropou anthropos*).

Heidegger divides the text into nineteen sections, on which he comments individually, but for our purposes the movement of his essay can be divided as follows.

A. An introduction that establishes the importance of the *Physics* as a whole and that shows, via *Physics* A, 2, 185 a 12 ff, that the clue to understanding *physis* is movement (WEG 309-315=221-226).

B. The delineation of that group of moved entities which makes up natural entities (*physei onta*) as over against that group which comprises man-made entities (*technei onta*) (*Physics* 192 b 8-32; WEG 315-329=226-237).

C. The decisive statement that *physis* is a kind of beingness (*ousia*) (*Physics* 192 b 32-193 a 2; WEG 329-332=237-239).

D. The ontological characterization of *physis* in terms of movement (specifically *genesis*) and the interpretation of the unified twofoldness of *physis* (*Physics* 193 a 3—193 b 20; WEG 332-371=239-269).

The first three divisions can be summarized briefly, more or less in thesis form. It is the last division that forms the major task of Heidegger's interpretation and so will require more attention.

A. The Optic: Movement

For Heidegger, Aristotle's *Physics* remains the hidden basis on which the entire metaphysical tradition of the West is constructed. Indeed, the *Physics* is itself a metaphysical work.[25] Not at all a book about what we call physics today, it is a regional ontology that inquires into the beingness (*ousia*) of a particular group of entities: natural as contrasted with man-made entities. But more than that, although Aristotle's *physis* is a regional narrowing of the originally broader understanding of *physis* as being as such, the work preserves an echo of those meditations on being that mark the origin of Greek thinking in Anaximander, Heraclitus and Parmenides. We may expect, therefore, that in interpreting *physis* in Aristotle's narrower sense, Heidegger will attempt as well to recall the original meaning of *physis*. We know, of course, that even such a thematization of the pre-Socratic meaning of *physis* is not the goal of Heidegger's thinking, but that it only sets the stage for a thinking about being that is even more original, a "second origin" that thematizes *Ereignis*.[26]

---

[25] For this paragraph: WEG 312=234; HW 298f=15, 305=21.

[26] On "first and second origins" see Joseph P. Fell, "Heidegger's Notion of Two Beginnings," *Review of Metaphysics*, 25 (1971), 213-237. The translation "Anfang" as "origin" is preferable, leaving "der Beginn" translated as "the beginning" (i.e., philosophy in Plato and Aristotle).

The decisive orientation in the determination of the meaning of *physis* in Aristotle is twofold: (a) *Physis* is a kind of beingness, and therefore the inquiry into *physis* is an ontological one; and (b) the clue to the ontological characterization of *physis* is *kinēsis* (cf. *Physics* A, 2, 185 a 12 ff: *ta physei [onta] kinoumena einai*). These two issues present a single task: the discernment of *kinēsis* as a kind of beingness (WEG 313f=225). We catch a glimpse here of the overarching problematic that controls all of Heidegger's thinking: being and "time," or in Aristotelian terms, *ousia* and *kinēsis*, where the "and" expresses the central problem. (To anticipate for a moment, we may say that the problem of the relation between each of the two will be worked out in terms of the time-character or, better, movement-character of *energeia*, which is stated as *energeia atēles* and which Heidegger reads as equivalent to *dynamis*.)

The crucial guidelines are established. The determination of the essence of *kinēsis* becomes the basis for determining Aristotle's *physis*, indeed for determining the pre-Socratic meaning of *physis* and ultimately *Ereignis* itself. Although *kinēsis* was surely investigated by Greek thinkers before Aristotle, that which makes his treatment of this phenomenon decisive for all later philosophy is the fact that he first elevated movement to a new level of questioning by grasping it as a mode of being — not just as the movement of entities but as their state of *being* moved. To designate such an understanding of *kinēsis*, Heidegger uses the word *Bewegtheit* in the sense of *Bewegtsein*. It shall be translated here as "movedness" or as "being-moved." These words designate the essence (being) of movement.[27]

B. Which Moved Entities are Natural Entities?

Whereas *physis* originally designated the being of all entities, whether those by nature or those by human *techne*, Aristotle limits the meaning of the word to the being of only a certain group of entities, natural ones as opposed to artifacts. Thus, prior to the main task of understanding Aristotle's *physis* as "kinetic beingness" (i.e., as a mode of *ousia* read in terms of *kinēsis*), we have the preliminary task of discerning which region of moved entities are natural entities.

Briefly stated, natural entities are those moved entities that have the origin and ordering (*archē*) of their movedness in themselves, in fact not accidentally but *of* themselves (*kath' hauto: Physics* B, 1, 192 b 20–23).

The words "of themselves" are crucial for distinguishing natural

---

[27]WEG loc. cit. Cf. *Physics* G 1, 200 b 12–15.

entities from artifacts. The origin and ordering of artifacts is their maker's pre-vision (*eidos prohaireton*) of the finished product. As a guiding principle, this prevision stands outside of the product, with the result that the product cannot "place itself back into its *archē* (WEG 328=236). The natural entity, on the other hand, "roots," in the sense of going back into and preserving its own *archē*.[28] The supreme importance of this dimension of returning to or staying with the origin of movedness (which ultimately is *Wiederholung* as the basic characteristic of being as such) emerges below.

C. *Physis* IS A KIND OF BEINGNESS

The decisive sentence of *Physics* B, 1, reads: "Everything which possesses that kind of origin and ordering 'has' *physis*; and all these things *are* (have being) of the sort called beingness (*ousia*)."[29]

The previous issues in chapter 1 of Book B have all been directed toward this ontological characterization of *physis*. The major task of Heidegger's interpretation can now be broached. If *physis* is a kind of beingness and if the clue to defining *physis* is movement/movedness, how is *kinēsis* to be characterized ontologically and how does this characterization lead to and effect the ontological determination of *physis*? The remainder of Heidegger's commentary is devoted to showing that Aristotle reads *physis* in terms of *kinēsis* and therefore that the essence of *physis* is the unified twofoldness of presence and absence: pres-ab-sence.

D. THE KINETIC-ONTOLOGICAL CHARACTERIZATION OF *Physis*

Heidegger's argument here is at once very complex and very simple. It is of the utmost importance that we constantly keep in view the goal of the demonstration. Let us call this goal the "kinetic-ontological characterization of *physis*" (i.e., the exhibition of the

[28]Cf. WEG 324=233: auf es zu; in ihre Wurzel zurück; 331=239: auf sich zu; 341=246: auf es selbst zu; 359=260: In-sich-zurück; 363=263: in sich zurückgehende Aufgang; 369=268: in sich Zurückgehen. For similar texts see KM 172=194: "zurückblickt; 173=196: Zurück-auf-sich; HD 120: "Diese zurückkehrende Gehen ist das Bleiben im Heimischen," and G 16=48: Bodenständigkeit; 26=57: Wurzeln.

[29]*Physics* B 2, 192, b 32f: *physin de echei hosa toiauten echei archen. Kai estin panta tauta ousia.* Heidegger renders the text: "*Physis* aber 'hat' alles, was ein so geartetes ausgängliches Verfügung enthalt. Und alles Dieses *ist* (hat Sein) von der Art der Seiendheit" (WEG 329=237). W. D. Ross translates: "Things 'have a nature' which have a principle of this kind. Each of them is a substance. . . ." The Latin "antiqua" translation renders *ousia* as "subjectum," whereas the "recens" translates it "substantia" (Aquinas *Omnia Opera*, vol. 22, *Commentarium in De Physico Auditu*, ed. Stanislaus Ferré and Paul Maré [Paris, 1889], p. 338). For Heidegger's polemic against the translation "substantia," see EM 40=50, WEG 330=238, N II, 429–436=26–32.

being-structure of *physis* by exhibiting the being-structure of *kinēsis*). The argument has the following formal structure: (a) beingness for Aristotle is always *entelecheia* or *energeia*; (b) but Aristotle reads the *energeia* that is *physis* in terms of *kinēsis* as *energeia atelēs*; (c) therefore Aristotle reads the beingness that is *physis* in terms of *energeia atelēs*. Clearly the central issue is the meaning of *energeia atelēs*, and it is here that we concentrate our attention.

1. *Physis* as *Dynamis*: "*Wiederholung*"

Since man has no access to entities except in terms of their being (i.e., their meaningful presence in *logos*), and since being for Aristotle is expressed as *energeia*, then man has no access to entities except insofar as they are in *energeia*. But because the *telos* of *entelecheia* and the *ergon* of *energeia* express the element of stability, it is clear that man has access to entities only insofar as they have stability about them. Although that does not preclude—especially in Aristotle— that movement (as nonstability) be a mode of being, it does inform us how moving entities must show up in *logos* if they are to show up at all. They must appear in the aspect of rest or constancy in being present. But if rest or stability means being *en telei* (in completion), and if the very nature of a moving entity is to be *ateles* (not in completion), then the movement of moving entities would indeed seem to be excluded from being (cf. *enioi . . . to mē on phaskontes einai tēn kinēsin*; *Physics* G, 2, 201 b 20f.). However, the genius of Aristotle consists in the fact that he grasps movement precisely as a kind of being, hence as a kind of *energeia* (cf. *energeia tis*, G, 2, 201 b 30f). If an entity can show up in *logos* only as *en telei*, and if a moving entity as moving is *ateles*, then the movement of a moving entity is *energeia atelēs*. A moving entity as moving is present in logos as somehow standing in its *telos* but as not yet having come fully into its *telos*.[30]

To understand a growing thing as what it fundamentally and properly is, namely, as growing, we must understand it as appearing (*en eidōi*), but appearing in such a way that the entity brings with it into the *eidos* a nonappearing. Moreover, the nonappearing is not simply absence from appearance. Rather "the wonder of it" (WEG 367=266) is that the nonappearance itself shows up and is present in *logos*. The presentness in *logos* of the nonappearance of the plant is the condition for the possibility of the presentness in *logos* of the plant *as plant*, as *on dynamei*. If *logos* does not reveal the privative

---

[30]WEG 355f=257: "Die Bewegung zeigt sich zwar als so etwas wie Im-Werk-Stehen, aber als ein noch nicht in sein Ende gekommen"—translating *Physics* G 2, 201 b 31f: *hē te kinēsis energeia men tis dokei, atelēs de.*

absence of the plant, it does not reveal the plant as what it fundamentally and properly is: an entity whose being is *energeia ateles*.

We can readily see the *appearance* of that green leafy thing over there; but how do we make present to ourselves its *non*-appearance in order that we may see it as a growing thing, a plant? The nonappearance is present, Heidegger says, as an *An-sich-halten*, as an *Abwesung* that is an *In-sich-zurück-gehen* (WEG 356=258, 369=268). The plant's "withdrawing into itself" has to do with the fact that it constantly stays in touch with the nonappearing source of its appearing. Such withholding from presence as the very condition for coming to presence is what is meant by *dynamis*, the mode of being of those entities that somehow "hide themselves" as the condition for presenting themselves. This interplay of appearing and hiding, of absence with presence, bespeaks a twofoldness in the being of moving entities: (a) the hiding is the source of the possibility of appearing; and (b) the appearing happens only by keeping the source of its appearance hidden, but hidden in such a way that the source remains source *for* appearing, and in this way indirectly appears.

A contrast of natural entities with artifacts will highlight this unique ontological character of *physis* (WEG 320ff=230ff). A house under construction has in itself no source of its appearance as house-under-construction (*on dynamei*). That source is the architect or builder and specifically his prevision (*eidos prohaireton*) of what the completed house will look like. Unlike the *technēi on hēi dynaton* (the house as under construction), a plant again and again draws up from its hidden source the possibility of its appearance as a growing thing. The plant keeps its *archē* within itself. Moreover, when the house under construction comes to completion and to full appearance as what it is (i.e., when one can articulate the *logos apophantikos* "Now it's a house"), then the *energeia* is *teleia*, then the house has left behind all the not-yet-ness of *dynamis* or *energeia ateles*, or better, then the house "has precisely brought it [*dynamis*] *forth along with it* into the realization of the fulfilled appearance" (WEG 357=258). But natural entities, insofar as they remain natural and therefore in movement, can never bring their not-yet-ness completely into *telos*. They must "let" their *dynamis* remain as *dynamis* if the natural entity is indeed to remain an *on dynamei*. By "letting" possibility remain possibility (i.e., hidden source for appearing), the entity appears as what it is, a moving entity, one that appears by not fully appearing.

We may hazard a word to describe this fact of "allowing" possibility to remain possibility. We may say that the natural entity, unlike the artifact, keeps on "repeating" its possibility (*re-petere:* to reach out for, again and again). But in reaching out again and again for possibility, the natural entity does not bring the hidden source out of hiddenness into full appearance. The reseeking of possibility is the retrieving (refinding) of possibility *as* possibility, as hidden-revealed source for the incomplete appearance of the moving entity. This "finding" or "retrieval" does not entail bringing possibility into actuality and complete appearance; rather it is a bringing forth again and again—a *Wiederholung*—of possibility as possibility. Such words as "repetition" and "retrieval" are Heidegger's halting attempts to enunciate the unique form of being that is *dynamis*, pres-ab-sence. The continual returning to or staying with or repeating-retrieving of absence as the source for presence is that mode of being which characterizes the *physis* of the *physei on*. Pres-ab-sence is the unified twofoldness of *physis*.[31]

2. *Physis* as *Dynamis*: "*Eignung*"

How Heidegger translates *dynamis* and the justification he gives for his translation are important to our argument that *physis*-as-*dynamis* provided the raw material for Heidegger's understanding of *Ereignis*. We have seen that the ontological clarification of *kinēsis* as *energeia atelēs* (incomplete being) is crucial to the understanding of *physis*. Natural entities have their being as being-underway-to-*telos*—in Greek, as *genesis*. A contrast of the generation of natural entities with that of artifacts will explain Heidegger's translation of *dynamis* as *Eignung* ("appropriation").[32]

All *kinesis* is *metabolē*, the change-over of something into something, such that the very act of change itself comes to appearance as what it is, namely, as *genesis*. Let us take the example of the construction of a table. Lying around the carpenter shop is plenty of "material" with the *eidos* "wood." But simply lying there, the wood is not yet considered *hylē* for, say, a table. In order for the wood to be read as *hylē*, the carpenter must have in mind (cf. *eidos prohaireton*) a new function for it, namely, as wood for a table. Precisely in its being ordered to a new *eidos*, the wood that just lies there becomes wood for . . . , or appropriated wood. Thus, in a similar example Aristotle distinguishes in *Physics* G, 1, 201 a 30ff between bronze simply as bronze (*hē tou chalkou entelecheia hēi chalkos*) and bronze seen as appropriate for making a statue (*ho chalkos dynamei andrias*). The latter

---

[31]WEG 365–369=264–268 and J. Sniezewski, "Wachstum," *Synergistiki* (Cracow), 9 (1974), 69ff.

[32]For what follows see WEG 352–364=254–264. For "Eignung," WEG 355f=257f.

state of the bronze is controlled by the prevision and prescription (cf. *kata ton logon*; ibid., 33f) of a new *eidos* for the bronze.

With that in mind we may now ask: How does one see the table's *genesis* as *genesis*? In the shop we certainly see various movements (the carpenter hammers, saws, carves), but our question concerns the movement of the wood itself into the *eidos* "table." We cannot actually see the table yet (although we might envision it), and if we are looking for generation, we do not see merely wood as wood. What we see is the appropriation of the wood unto a table: we see the wood as appropriated unto, as underway to, a table. The generation of the table as generation is the on-going appropriation-unto-a-new-*telos* wherein the wood changes from mere wood to wood that is appropriated for. . . . The kind of *kinēsis* that we call *genesis* is *hē tou dynatou hēi dynaton entelecheia* (*Physics*, G, 1, 201 b 4f). In generation, the wood is read from the *telos* "table" (*entelecheia*) but as not yet fully there (*hēi dynaton*). Its being is seen as the process of being-appropriated (*on hēi dynaton=on dynamei*). When one has said that much, the mention of *entelecheia* becomes superfluous because it is tautological. *Dynamis* by itself is enough to express *energeia atelēs*. "Appropriation"—Heidegger's word *Eignung*, which he uses to translate *dynamis*—suffices to define the being of an entity that is in the process of generation and hence in the state of pres-ab-sence.

If we move from the generation of an artifact to that of a natural entity, we find the same structure, but with an important addition. The *eidos* that controls the being-status of the table-under-construction (as *on dynamei*) is from outside that which is being produced: it is the carpenter's *eidos prohaireton*. Because it is external, this *eidos* of itself does not provide from out of itself the "appropriate material" for the table. Rather it sends the carpenter to the lumberyard in search of it.

However, in the generation of a natural entity (cf. "man generates man," *Physics* 193 b 8f), the controlling *eidos* is within the very generation itself, and hence the process of generation entails the *self-provision* of that which is "appropriate for. . . ." The "from which" (say: Smith, Sr.) and the "to which" (Smith, Jr.) have the same *eidos* ("Man"). The process of generation as a being-underway from Senior to Junior (*genesis* as *physēos hodos eis physin*—see 193 b 12f) never has to go outside of itself, but rather consists simply in deriving from one instantiation of the *eidos* (Smith, Sr.) the second instantiation of the same *eidos* (Smith, Jr.). Yet, as a being-underway of *physis* to more *physis*, natural generation is never a simply circling back upon itself (Smith, Sr. does not generate Smith, Sr.) but is always the production of a new and unique instantiation that never exhausts the power for yet more generation.[33] The inexhaustibility of *physis* as power of generation (*genesis*) can be expressed as "a going *back* into itself i.e., towards *itself* as a going forth" (WEG 363=263). *Physis* remains *physis*, an ever repeatable-retrievable pres-ab-sent source of possibility for the appearance of a *physei on*. Again we find *Wiederholung*. But as such it is "self"-appropriation of that inexhaustible hidden source into the limited appearance of its instance. Hence we have *Eignung*. We may draw the conclusion: *Physis = dynamis = Wiederholung = Eignung*.

3. Summary and Transition

We said in Section I that a "phenomenological" reading of Aristotle awakened the possibility of a radical restatement of the question, "What is the analogically unified meaning of the various modes in which entities appear in *logos*?" by calling forth the prior, foundational question, "What is the unified meaning of *logos* itself?" The explanation in Section II of Heidegger's interpretation of *physis* in Aristotle, although it did not deal directly with *logos*, has taken us a few steps in the direction of that foundational question.

We have seen that the being of a delimited region of entities—*ta physei onta*—is a unique mode of appearance in *logos*, the unified twofoldness of pres-ab-sence, where the absence too is a mode of presence and indeed the very condition for the presentness of entities. At least this much is clear: If *logos* is the revelatory function correlative to at least natural entities, then one of the modes of the being of *logos* must be a bringing-to-presence by the revelation of privative absence as the condition for presence. *Logos*, in at least in one of its modes of being, is itself a form of *energeia atelēs* or movement.

But Heidegger goes further. Although *Metaphysics* G, 3, holds the same position as *Physics* B, 1, namely, that *physis* is only one kind of *ousia* (see 1005 a 34f), nonetheless *Metaphysics* G, 1, 1003 a 27 reverses the perspective and says that *ousia* is a kind of *physis* (*physis tis*; WEG 369f=268; cf. EM 12f=13). Heidegger claims that this latter text in Aristotle is an echo of the original understanding of *physis* as the being of entities as such and in totality, and that *physis* as Aristotle

[33]Cf. James Joyce, *Ulysses* (New York: Modern Library, 1961), p. 731: "He is always the last term of a preceding series even if the first term of a succeeding one, each imagining himself to be first, last, only and alone, whereas he is neither first nor last nor only nor alone in a series originating in and repeated to infinity."

normally uses it is but a late derivative of that broader usage. Fragment 123 of Heraclitus, for instance, says *physis kryptesthai philei*, "Being loves to hide itself."[34] Heidegger interprets the sentence to say not that being is hard to get at and thus requires great effort if it is to be pulled forth from and purged of its concealment, but rather that self-hiding is of the essence of being and is the basis for its limited emergence into appearance. "And therefore the *kryptesthai* of *physis* is not to be overcome, not to be stripped from *physis*. Rather the task is the much more difficult one of allowing to *physis*, in all the purity of its becoming-present, the *kryptesthai* that belongs to it" (WEG 371=269).

Against such a background as this Heidegger projected the two-fold program of *Being and Time*:

1. Phenomenology was to take *logos* as its theme: *logos* was to turn on itself, as it were, and read its own revelatory function. The upshot was that *logos* was found to be intrinsically kinetic ("temporal," as Heidegger put it), "always existing in such a way that its 'not-yet' *belongs* to it" (SZ 243=287). Moreover it was found that *logos'* authentic self-appropriation of that not-yet "constitutes its uttermost possibility of being" and that this self-appropriation is achieved when possibility "is cultivated *as possibility*" and "*endured as possibility*" (SZ 261=306) in a retrieval of possibility. On that basis Heidegger was going to work out the meaning of being itself as possibility.

2. Part Two of *Being and Time* was to interpret the history of philosophy backward to Aristotle to show that the concealed meaning of being as *dynamis* underlay the whole tradition of Western philosophy; the kinetic character of being was to serve as the clue in this "destruction" of the tradition.

In short, *Being and Time* projected a twofold retrieval of the meaning of being—one focused on human existence, the other on the philosophical tradition—both of them grounded in Heidegger's understanding of the structure of *physis* as *dynamis* (i.e., as a primordial movement of retrieval in the original sense). This movement is called *Eignung*, appropriation, and it underlies Heidegger's key term, *Ereignis*.

---

[34]"Das Sein liebt es, sich zu verbergen" (WEG 370=269). Other translations by Heidegger of the same sentence: "Sein (aufgehendes Erscheinen) neigt in sich zum Sichverbergen" (EM 87=96). "Sein liebt (ein) Sichverbergen" (SG 113). "Das Aufgehen (aus dem Sichverbergen) dem Sichverbergen schenkt's die Gunst" (VA 271 [III, 67]=114).

III. *DYNAMIS*, RESOLVE AND *EREIGNIS*

Being and Time carries out a hermeneutic, a *legein* of *logos*. It lets *logos* appear to itself as what it is in order to clarify the meaning of appearance as such in its analogical unity. The book is a disclosure of the disclosive process itself for the sake of ascertaining the meaning of being.

To let something appear in *logos* is to appropriate it into its appearance as what it is. But in *Being and Time* that which *logos* appropriates into appearance is itself. In a certain sense the book can be read as a protreptic to a self-appropriation that only the individual can perform for himself. As a hermeneutic in which "the authentic meaning of being, and also those basic structures of being that existence itself possesses, are *announced* to existence's understanding of being" (SZ 37=62), *Being and Time* would be, in its own way, an "attestation to existence of existence's ownmost being-possible" (SZ 279=324), a second-order "call of conscience" unto self-appropriation or resolve.

Be that as it may, *Being and Time* in its published form culminates in the discussion of authentic time. The chapter on resolve bears a footnote that says, "These observations and those which follow after were communicated as theses on the occasion of a public lecture on the concept of time, which was given at Marburg in July 1924" (SZ 268 n.=495 n.). That lecture, entitled "Der Begriff der Zeit," has been called "the *Urform* of *Being and Time*," and it reaches its climax by transforming the question, "Was ist die Zeit?" into the protreptic question "Bin ich die Zeit? oder noch näher, bin ich meine Zeit?"[35] Clearly in that lecture the climax is the call to resolve, and the same is true, I believe, in *Being and Time*. In that book we see that in resolve, as the self-appropriation of the *dynamis* that one is, authentic time breaks forth as a repetition or retrieval of possibility as possibility. In that moment of insight (*Augenblick*)[36] one has not merely "understood" the analogically unified meaning of being in a distinterested and detached way, but rather one has been called into it as the very meaning of one's own being. In authentically appropriating one's own movement of disclosure (temporality), one is appropriated into being itself as the movement of disclosure (the time-character of

---

[35]Cited from a transcript of the lecture. See Thomas Sheehan, "The Original Form of *Sein und Zeit:* Heidegger's *Der Begriff der Zeit*, 1924," *Journal of the British Society for Phemomenology*, 10 (1979), 78–83, esp. p. 81 H.-G. Gadamer calls Heidegger's lecture the *Urform* of SZ in *art. cit.* (note 2 supra), p. 169.

[36]SZ 328=376, 338=387, 385=437, etc. This is the *kairos* of *kairologisch* temporality, mentioned infra.

being). The unity of *Zeitlichkeit* and *die Temporalität des Seins* is what Heidegger would later call the event of appropriation, *Ereignis*.[37]

In what follows I shall attempt to show (a) that resolve is the core of *Being and Time*, (b) how resolve is a kind of retrieval, and (c) how resolve is the entrance into *Ereignis*.

A. RESOLVE AS THE CORE OF *Being and Time*

The published portion of *Being and Time* is divided into two equal parts, the first exhibiting the unified structure of *logos* (existence) as disclosure, the second demonstrating that the meaning of that structure is temporality, the movement of becoming (*Zukünftigkeit*) that which one already is (*Gewesenheit*) and thereby being able to render entities present (*Gegenwart*). *Logos* is disclosure rendered possible by "temporality," and this is the horizon for all the ways that entities can be disclosed. We now take up "temporality" and disclosure to see their unity.

The word "temporality" could be misleading if one were to forget that by "time" Heidegger does not mean Aristotle's *arithmos kinēseōs*, the numbering of ontic movement, but rather *kinēsis* itself, movedness as the being of the unique moving entity that is man. Thus: "The movedness [*Bewegtheit*] of existence is not the motion [*Bewegung*] of something present at hand" (SZ 374f=427). As early as his 1921–1922 course, *Phänomenologische Interpretationen* (*Aristoteles "Physik"*), Heidegger set his task as the phenomenological clarification of *Leben* as the *Grundbewegtheit*, whose basic characteristic is *Sorge* (January 11, 1922). And in the 1922 continuation of that course (*Phänomenologische Interpretation ausgewählter Abhandlungen des Aristoteles zur Ontologie und Logik*) he said on July 25, 1922, that for the Greeks and particularly for Aristotle *logos* is a *kinēsis*, although not of a *physis*-type, and that its function of revelation (*alētheuein*) is a kind of *Zeitigung* or "temporalization." In his 1923 course, *Ontologie: Hermeneutik der Faktizität*, when he analyzed the *Zeitbestimmung* of existence, he studied curiosity as a form of movedness and, specifically, as one way of existence's "having-itself-there" (*Sich-Da-Haben*; June 20, 1923). In the same course this unique temporality was called *kairologisch* (July 25, 1923) to distinguish its existential-ontological character from the ontic "chronological" character of natural

---

[37]Cf. SD 23f=24 and Heidegger's answer to the first question in Prof. Joan Stambaugh's "Introduction" to Martin Heidegger, *The End of Philosophy*, trans. J. Stambaugh (New York: Harper and Row, 1973), pp. xif. This topic is addressed in Thomas Sheehan, "On Movement and the Destruction of Ontology," *The Monist*, 64, 4 (October, 1981) 534–542.

movement. In that course, when Heidegger investigated temporality, he found it embedded in what he called the *Bewegtheitszusammenhang des Lebens* (June 27, 1923). Clearly "temporality" in the early Heidegger is to be understood in terms of *kinēsis*, the unique disclosive movement that happens in man's essence. To say that disclosive existence is primordial temporality is to read *logos* as *energeia atelēs*.

But what of disclosure in relation to temporality? *Logos* achieves its proper being when it actively appropriates itself as the movement that it already is. For the most part *logos* functions as disclosure (*Erschlossenheit*) without being aware of it. The disclosure to *logos* of the fact that it is itself disclosive as finite possibility (the call to resolve, *Entschlossenheit*) is the preeminent mode of disclosure, and it is revelatory of resolve as the highest possibility of existence.[38] In fact, in resolve temporality is for the first time revealed; what is more, resolve *is* authentic temporality. Therefore, Richardson is correct in calling resolve the "core" and "culmination" of the published portions of *Being and Time*.[39]

In short, we may read the unity of *Being and Time* as *Erschlossenheit* and *Entschlossenheit*, disclosure and resolve. The basic structure of *logos* as disclosive temporal movement is the structure of resolve; and resolve is a unique mode of *energeia atelēs*.

B. RESOLVE AND RETRIEVAL

It is clear from *Being and Time* that existence is through and through nothing other than being-possible (SZ 143=183) and that this being-possible, as opening up a world, is the structure that accounts for the disclosure of all encounterable entities in their being. As being-possible, existence (even when it does not know it) is "ahead of itself," where the "itself" designates its unauthentic self.[40] This being-possible is first of all not something that existence has chosen for itself; rather it is already de facto operative. To express the de-facto-ness of being possible, Heidegger speaks of "already projected possibility" (*geworfene Möglichkeit*) or simply "projectedness" (SZ 144=183, 135=174). Insofar as projected possibility effects

---

[38]SZ 287=334: "Das Dasein ist rufverstehend *hörig seiner eigensten Existenzmöglichkeit.*"

[39]William J. Richardson, "Heidegger's Way Through Phenomenology to the Thinking of Being," in *Heidegger, the Man and the Thinker* (see n. 4 supra), pp. 86 and 89. In the original German version (*Philosophisches Jahrbuch*, 62 [1965], 391) Richardson writes "Kern" (core); in the English, p. 86, this is translated as "culmination."

[40]SZ 193=238: "Im Sich-vorweg-sein meint daher das 'Sich' jeweils das Selbst im Sinne des Man-selbst."

disclosure, we may equally speak of it as "projecting" or "project" (*entwerfend, Entwurf,* SZ 145=185). But the active voice does not indicate some different kind of possibility.[41] Projectedness (thrownness) and projection, facticity and existentiality, are Heidegger's retrieval of the Greek and medieval problematic of possible and active intellect (*ho nous tōi panta ginesthai, ho nous tōi panta poiein —De Anima* G, 5, 430 a 14f) within the framework of the disclosive movement of existence, and both modalities of possibility are grounded in the area of intelligibility called *Rede* or *logos.*[42]

If *logos* as *Rede* is underdeveloped in *Being and Time*, in Part One, Division One, this is because its proper function emerges in Division Two as the call to resolve. As projected-projecting disclosive possibility, existence first of all has been "brought into" possibility, but "not of its own accord," "not as itself," "not through itself," not "understandingly," and hence "forgetfully."[43] The preeminent role of *logos* is to make transparent to existence, as projected but unappropriated possibility, its very nature as possibility. *Logos* as conscience is "an attestation to existence of existence's ownmost being-possible" (SZ 279=324). As such it is a "calling back" (*Rückruf*). But that to which it calls existence is existence's own being-already-ahead-of-itself. The calling back is in fact a calling forward (*vorrufendes Rückruf*).[44] More specifically, in calling existence back to its ahead-ness, conscience summons existence to take over its own projectedness understandingly, to seize upon it authentically, to own it as its own. If existence does so, it does not become something different, but rather repeats or retrieves itself and becomes understandingly what it already is.[45] It comes back to its already-projectedness by taking up this "ground" anew so as to *be* it authentically.

> And how *is* existence [authentically] this already projected ground? Only in that it [understandingly] projects itself [i.e., discloses itself] in terms of possibilities into which it has already been projected (SZ 284=330).

---

[41]SZ 145=185: "Und als geworfenes ist das Dasein in die Seinsart des Entwerfens geworfen," and "als Dasein hat es sich je schon entworfen und ist, solange es ist, entwerfend."

[42]SZ paragraph 34 and 133=172: "gleichursprünglich bestimmt durch die *Rede*."

[43]SZ 284f=329f: "nicht von ihm selbst in sein Da gebracht"; "*nicht* als es selbst"; "*Nicht* durch es selbst." SZ 326=373: verstehend. SZ 339=388: "dass sich das Dasein in seinem eigensten *geworfenen* Seinskönnen *vergessen* hat."

[44]On "Rückruf": SZ 277=322, 280=325. On "vorrufendes Rückruf": SZ 280=326, 287=333, 294=340, etc.

[45]SZ 326=373: das verstehende Zurückkommen auf das eigenste Gewesen; 385=437: der Rückgang in Möglichkeiten des dagewesenen Daseins; 386=438: "Die Wiederholung *erwidert*. . . die Möglichkeit der dagewesenen Existenz."

The moment of self-appropriating insight (*Augenblick*) that is resolve is described as "the taking over of projectedness" and as "the
self-aware return to the alreadiness of one's ownmost being," i.e., a
self-disclosive retrieval and appropriation of the projected possibility that existence already is. This "retrieving-repeating of itself" is
the event whereby existence "discloses . . . possibility as possibility."[46]

Such a retrieval that discloses possibility (*Eignung*) as possibility
is original authentic temporality—the first goal toward which *Being and Time* moves.[47] The already-dimension (*Gewesenheit*) of everyday unappropriated existence is its de facto state of being the already projected possibility that discloses entities. This already-
projectedness, even in its unappropriated state, has an intrinsic
futural dimension to it. As projected possibility, existence is never all
at once and static, but is always becoming, always on-the-way, not to
some goal but simply to more of itself: "existence, *as being*, is always
becoming itself" (SZ 325=373). *Geworfenheit* is of itself *zukünftig*, the
unity of these two dimensions constituting the presentness of existence as disclosive temporality. But if existence's very structure
(*geworfen—entwerfend*; *gewesen—zukünftig*) is temporal, its temporality
is generally and for the most part closed off from existence. *Logos* as
conscience makes that structure transparent by disclosing disclosive
possibility to itself so that, in resolve, existence may retrieve and
appropriate its own possibility. Resolve frees up (cf. *Sichüberliefern*)
that structure for existence so that existence can take it over.[48] When
it does so, existence does not draw already projected possibility (*das
dagewesene Dasein*) into full present appearance (cf. *nicht, um es aber-
mals zu verwicklichen*; SZ 385=437) but brings it into presence by
leaving it possible, i.e., in relative absence.

In brief: Resolve as authentic time is the self-appropriation of
one's own being as *dynamis*, it is a self-aware allowing of oneself to
appear by "not appearing." Existence regrasps itself as already projected possibility by letting that possibility remain the ever repeat-

[46]For this paragraph: SZ 325=373: die Uebernahme der Geworfenheit; 326=373:
Zurückkommen auf das eigenste Gewesen; 306=354: Möglichkeit als Möglichkeit.
[47]On "Wiederholung" see: SZ 308=355, 339=388, 343=394, 344=395, 385=437,
etc.
[48]On "Sichüberliefern": SZ 383f=435f. The existing English translation of
"Sichüberliefern der Möglichkeiten" as "handing down to oneself possibilities" misses the nuance of "to *free* possibilities *for oneself*." "Liefern," derived from the Latin
"liberare," has overtones of "to free up," that Heidegger means the reader to hear.
See WP 8=35: "Ueberliefern, délivrer, ist ein Befreien, nämlich in die Freiheit des
Gespräches mit dem Gewesenen."

able pres-ab-sent source for the appearance of existence as being-possible. In yet other terms, it is the concrete acceptance of and entrance into the *alētheia*-process itself, a process that is always grounded in a *lēthē*, a privative absence that allows for presence.

The very language we are using here encourages us to compare resolve with what we saw earlier as the meaning of *physis*: *Wiederholung* and *Eignung*. But comparison reveals that *Wiederholung* and *Eignung* have a meaning in *Being and Time* that goes beyond that of *physis* as Heidegger interprets it in *Physics* B, 1. When *logos* reads a moving natural entity, it brings it to appearance (appropriates it) as what and how it is: an appearing-present entity that retrieves its own relative absence or nonappearance. But when *logos* reads and resolutely appropriates itself, it appropriates its own appearance-presence as the retrieval of its own relative absence. In resolved existence, *dynamis/Eignung/Wiederholdung* is on a higher ("self-aware") level than in nonexistential natural entities. *Eignung* resolutely reveals itself to itself as *Eignung; Wiederholung* resolutely retrieves itself as *Wiederholdung*; existence as pres-ab-sence allows itself to be pres-ab-sence. The "paradigm" for resolve is *dynamis*, but resolve is a transformation of *dynamis* into "self-aware" possibility. This unique form of *Eignung*, which resolutely reveals itself as *Eignung*, is intimately bound up with that which Heidegger later called *Ereignis*.

C. RESOLVE AND *Ereignis*

But beyond mere comparison of words, we must spell out the issue for itself. The being of an entity is its disclosed presentness in *logos*. The meaning of being-as-such can be had only if *logos* reads and appropriates the unified meaning of itself as disclosive presenting. Such a disclosure of disclosive presenting is a hermeneutics of the revelatory process, and since the disclosive process is fundamentally bound up with existence as possibility, this hermeneutics of the revelatory process shows that the unified meaning of being is possibility as possibility, disclosure/presence rooted in nondisclosure/absence. But the authentic disclosure of the unified meaning of being is not some disinterested act of knowledge. It does not happen by simply reading and understanding, say, *Being and Time*. The final point of this work is to allow the reader to hear a protreptic, a call to his own personal, *existentiell* self-appropriation of the unified meaning of disclosure. Concretely, such self-appropriation means living in the *alētheia*-process, letting oneself be drawn into absence as the condition for all presentness of entities, including one's own. To appropriate *alētheia* means to let oneself be appropriated into *dynamis* as such by returning to one's already projected possibility and letting it remain possible. To let one's own being be is at the same time to let being-as-such be, i.e., to let it be the pres-ab-sent and ever retrievable source for all presentness of entities. To live resolutely in the *alētheia*-process is to experience being (the disclosed presence of entities) as given in oneself but only by experiencing withdrawal from presence as such. One knows this withdrawal from presence only insofar as that withdrawal is registered in one's own movement of being drawn out ahead of oneself (early Heidegger: *Geworfenheit*; later Heidegger: *Angezogenheit*, etc.[49]). One knows the giving (or "there is") of presence only insofar as that giving allows and is registered in one's presenting of entities in their givenness. There is no place here for the hypostasization of "someone" who withdraws or gives, no objectification of "something" that disposes over the movedness of one's temporality as *dynamis*. There is only the resolute experience of the self as not being ultimately at its own disposal. To say this is not to import some romantic mystery into philosophy, but simply to take seriously and rigorously the meaning of being as *dynamis*.

To put this another way: If one brings entities "to language" (i.e., to meaningful presence in *logos*), one does so precisely by not having language (*logos* as *dynamis*) at one's disposal. Not that some "voice" then tells us what entities are. There is no such voice, only the silence that characterizes the absence that makes possible the meaningful presence of entities in *logos*. And the most authentic response to such silence is "to keep silent about silence" (*Geschwiegen . . . über das Schweigen*) by letting the absence be absence.[50] Such a stance toward silence might be called a "hearing," but the message one hears is that there is no message other than the already givenness (*Geschick*) of meaning in the space of man's own self-absence. Such a stance might also be called "reverence" or "piety," but there is no authority to revere other than "the retrievable possibilities of existence" (SZ 391=443), indeed the retrievable possibilities of possibility itself.

Phrases like "silence about silence" and "reverent attentiveness"

---

[49]Cf. Heidegger's other terms for this "already-dimension": SZ 134=172: Stimmung, Gestimmtsein; WP 24=77: Entsprechen, be-stimmt sein, être disposé, in die Bezüge versetzt, Gestimmtheit; HD 124: die lautlose Stimme; WD 5=9: Angezogenen, 23=77: Gestimmtheit, Stimmung; US 112=122: Stimme.

[50]US 152=52. Compare SZ 173=218: "wer in echten Weise einer Sache 'auf der Spur ist,' spricht nicht darüber." On the "unsayable" see US 251=120: "was ungesprochen bleiben muss im Sinne dessen, was dem Sprechen vorenthalten ist"; 253=122: Ungesagten, Unzeigbares im Verborgenen, Geheimnis; 100=113: Unbestimmten, im Unbestimmtbare zurückbirgt.

are but halting ways to describe *die Sache selbst*, i.e., ways of describing how, in appropriating one's own being as *dynamis*, one gets appropriated into the center of meaning, *dynamis* itself. "The question of existence," Heidegger once wrote, "is never settled except through existing itself" (SZ 12=33). Further: "Every answer keeps its force as answer only so long as it is rooted in questioning" (HW 58=71). The two sentences say the same thing: only in concrete *existentiell* appropriation of oneself as the act of questioning does questioning find its answer, namely, that the meaning of being is questionableness itself. Only in resolve does one enter *Ereignis*; only by taking up personally one's own movement does one authentically discover the movement that is being itself. The meaning of being, as Richardson has said, is not a doctrine to be learned but a risk to be taken.[51] And if one does not take that risk, Heidegger told his students, "all talk and listening is in vain. And in that case I would urge you to burn your lecture notes, however precise they may be—and the sooner the better" (WD 160=158).

IV. CONCLUSION

The purpose of this essay has been to show how Heidegger's understanding of *dynamis* and *Wiederholung* in his reading of Aristotle's *physis* lay the foundations for his understanding of "the issue itself," *Ereignis*. We have concluded that Heidegger's work is not a "doctrine" except in the unique definition Heidegger gave that word: a teaching about an essentially "unsayable" to which man is opened up "in order that he might spend himself on it without counting the cost" (WEG 109=250). For all the information they provide, Heidegger's works remain a protreptic. Man is already "at" the issue itself, already "at" the ec-centric center of meaning, but in such a way that he needs to appropriate his own essence if he is to be authentically where he already is. To heed that protreptic is to enter upon a path with no goal, for *Alles ist Weg* (US 198=92).

For those who finally want more, this is not very much. But philosophy never accomplishes much. As long as it is philosophy and not some other art or science, it remains a search that does nothing so much as cultivate the search, precisely because being itself remains a path that leads only to more path—an experience perhaps captured by Heraclitus' *Agchibasie* or Aristotle's *physeōs hodos eis physin*

---

[51]Richardson, p. 551.

or James Joyce's "almosting it" or Heidegger's *Unterwegssein*.[52] Walking along such a path, one may find that he has to say, "I hardly know
any more who and what I am," only to reflect, "None of us knows
that, as soon as we stop fooling ourselves" (G 35=62). Is this the
defeat of rigorous science? Or does the path require more rigor than
science can muster? Perhaps rigor means, in the words of the poet,
that

> We shall not cease from exploration
> And the end of all our exploring
> Will be to arrive where we started
> And know the place for the first time.[53]

[52]Heraclitus, Fragment 122 (G 70=88f). Aristotle, *Physics* B 1, 193 b 12ff (WEG
361f=261f). "Unterwegssein": SZ 79=110 (cf. 437=488) and WEG 361=262. James
Joyce, *Ulysses* (see n. 33 supra), p. 47.
   [53]"Little Gidding," V, (*Four Quartets*); in T. S. Eliot, *The Complete Poems and Plays of T.
S. Eliot* (London: Faber and Faber, 1969), p. 197.

EIGHT

HEIDEGGER (1907-1927): THE TRANSFORMATION OF THE CATEGORIAL

> Yet they show the beginnings of a way which was then still closed to me: the question of *being* under the guise of the problem of the categories, the question of *language* in the form of the doctrine of signification. How these two questions essentially belong together remained obscure. The inevitable dependence of the way in which these questions were treated upon the standards of the doctrine of *judgment* prevalent for every onto-logic prevented me from suspecting that there even was an obscurity.
>
> Heidegger (1972), upon republishing his
> *Frühe Schriften* (1914-1916)

HEIDEGGER'S MORE AUTOBIOGRAPHICAL STATEMENTS of the last decade or so make it crystal clear that his point of embarkation into philosophy in general and ontology in particular is centered on the "problem of the categories." Brentano's dissertation on the manifold sense of being in Aristotle (1862), which set the gymnasium student Heidegger on his philosophical way in 1907, is devoted primarily to the articulation of being into its categories. Husserl's *Logical Investigations* (1900-1901), which Heidegger began to read as a university student in 1909, culminates in the doctrine of the categorial intuition. Emil Lask's *Die Logik der Philosophie und die Kategorienlehre* (1911) calls for a logic of philosophy directed toward the elaboration of the "categories of categories." In the same vein, Heidegger, in his dissertation (1916) on the doctrine of the categories of being and of signification in Thomas of Erfurt alias Duns Scotus, identifies *ens commune* as the "category of categories" and sees in the medieval doctrine of the transcendental properties of being—the one, true, good, and beautiful—a reflection of the philosophical categories par excellence.

This line of development is destined to expand into a concern for the existential categories in *Being and Time* (Heidegger-I) and to Heidegger-II's penchant to seek out the fundamental concepts of the West emerging from their pre-Socratic roots, in particular the *topoi* of *logos, aletheia,* and *physis,* which, as basic names for being, display a peculiar convergence akin to the "convertibility" of the medieval transcendentals.

165

If we can hybridize Richardson's Roman numerals with a crucial Arabic notation, this point of embarkation coming to fruition in the early writings (1912–1916) might be designated as Heidegger-Zero (i.e., before Heidegger became *Heidegger*, not yet charged with all of the contrary emotional reactions that this internationally recognized name still arouses).

In "my way to phenomenology," Heidegger has himself underscored the importance for his early development of Husserl's notions of intentionality and categorial intuition. But another profoundly significant link, nowadays by and large ignored by Heidegger scholars on this continent, between the student Heidegger concerned primarily with logical problems and the more hermeneutically oriented Heidegger-I is Wilhelm Dilthey. Dilthey's lifelong quest for a "logic" (i.e., epistemological foundation) of the historical and human sciences eventually led him to seek an articulation of the "categories of life," the basic structures of historical life. Such categories find their roots in the textures immanent in life itself. Ideally, they are first of all the very articulations of life before they emerge from this soil into our judicative structures. The operative task is to let experience come to a natural conceptual blossoming without imposing upon it concepts that have their origin in alien soil.[1]

It is this different kind of category—formulated in a language indigenous to life and thus stemming from the earth out of which language springs—that motivates Heidegger to a radical reorientation of the classical question of being. The assumption of an autochthonous language locates this classical question at the very threshold of language and being, the moment of incipience for the being possessed by speech, the very "event" of articulation and contextualization in human existence, the emergence of the matrix, texture, and tissue of human experience. Ultimately, this "grassroots" development of the classical "problem of the categories" raises the question as to whether or not the soil of experience is itself tractable to conceptualization.

The following development of the transition from Heidegger-Zero, by way of Dilthey's categories of life and Husserl's doctrines of intentionality and categorial intuition to Heidegger-I—*Being and Time* will function throughout as the retrospective basis of this commentary—is intended to follow some of Heidegger's first steps toward his own shift in orientation from language to that which

[1] J. L. Mehta, *The Philosophy of Martin Heidegger* (New York: Harper, 1971) p. 14.

comes to language, to the process of disclosure which precedes and supports speech, to dimensions of experience which at first are only *sprachmässig* but which are accordingly amenable to language—in short, to the "underside" of "language, which, in its own way, *itself* "speaks" of *itself*.

HEIDEGGER-ZERO

"Being is said in many ways." Appearing on the frontispiece page of Brentano's dissertation, this quotation is taken from Aristotle's discussion in the *Metaphysics* (Book VII) of the categories of reality. For the young Heidegger, it suggested the more basic question: what is the unity and simplicity of being which then articulates itself in manifold fashion? What is the leading and fundamental sense that manifests itself in and through the amazing polyvalence of the single little word "is"?

Such an ontological principle of identity is at once a principle of differentiation and is accordingly always accompanied by the problem of the articulation of the manifold modes of being. Heidegger's dissertation on psychologism (1914) is concerned particularly with the distinction between psychic and logical reality. The second dissertation (1916) broadens the discussion to include physical, metaphysical, mathematical, and linguistic reality but is ultimately concerned with their coherence in a unified and articulated whole in the form of a "doctrine of categories," a theory of the fundamental divisions of reality. This is closely connected with the more grammatically oriented "doctrine of significations," which is concerned with the fundamental divisions of our discourse about the world, sometimes called the "semantic categories." The connection between the two doctrines resides in the fact that the categories are traditionally the most fundamental concepts and most universal predicates that can be applied to (said of) a particular realm of beings.

Paradigmatic for Aristotle's division of the categories into substance and the nine accidents is real physical being. For Kant, who more unequivocally than Aristotle oriented them toward the synthetic function of judgments, the categories became the apriori forms of the understanding, which serve to constitute the flux of experience into a judicative context. Thus after Kant the categories can become the most universal determinations of any object whatsoever, while retaining their traditional role as predication-forms of a subject matter.

The limits of Aristotle's paradigm are brought out particularly in the modern discussion of "logical reality" or of "meaning" by the opponents of logical psychologism at the turn of the century.

Logic deals with the laws of thought. But "thought" is an equivocal term. It can refer to the actual psychic activity of, say, judgment made by an individual at a certain point in time, or it can have reference to the object intended by such an activity (i.e., to the meaning or logical content of the judgment, which belongs to an ideal order not subject to temporal fluctuation and variegation). The object of thought (e.g., a sentence in its sense) accordingly remains identically the same in and through any number of acts that think it. From this it follows that logic and psychology have distinctively different topics and problematics. The identical ideal content of meaning is the proper topic of logic, the real psychic activity in time is the topic of psychology, and the confusion of the latter with the former topic is logical psychologism. Nowadays such confusions of levels of being are sometimes called "category mistakes." Such difficulties are circumvented only if logic single-mindedly concentrates on the stable identical factor of meaning pervading the dynamic flux of mental activity like a continuous thread. Meaning has a way of "taking hold" and "standing fast" in judgment again and again in and through a manifold of individual acts. *Pure* logic moves strictly in its own allotted sphere of the meanings thus contained in judgments.

And so "meaning" comes to the center of Heidegger's thought for the first time, never to yield that place, though the tenor and the direction of its problematic goes through a number of permutations. In first asking the question "What is the meaning of meaning?"[2] Heidegger selects examples—a businessman planning and evaluating a promising new venture, the effect of a particularly "meaningful" artwork upon the beholder, a "sensible" gift thoughtfully chosen for its appropriateness—that stress the reflective character of meaning and are accordingly led to tie the phenomenon of meaning closely to thought, in which judgments are made and evaluated. In other words, emphasis falls on the moment in which judgments are themselves judged in their meaningfulness and thus appear as if they were standing before us like independent objects. The following question may now be asked: What kind of "reality" do such ideal objects have? What is their ontological status? To be sure, an ideal object is not real and temporal like the psychic activities that

---

[2]*Die Lehre vom Urteil im Psychologismus* (1914), Sec. V, Chap. 2, para. 2. Cf. Martin Heidegger, *Frühe Schriften* (Frankfurt: Klostermann, 1972) pp. 112ff.

evoke it, inasmuch as it remains the same throughout a manifold of such numerically distinct activities. As Lotze put it, "es *ist* nicht, sondern es *gilt*." In this sense, the identical moment does not "exist," but simply "holds" (*gilt* = "is valid"). It is precisely this pervasive holding *power* that then constitutes the mode of reality of the logical, of the meaning of judgments. The reality of meaning is to be found in the tenacity and stability of its valence, in its capacity to "take hold" and "stand fast" in a judgment and thus "remain in force."

Is it possible to specify the nature of this holding relationship any further or do we have here an ultimate and irreducible dimension that cannot be illuminated by a more comprehensive genus? What exactly is the ontological status of logical reality, of a meaning that holds to the point of obliging us to repeatedly consent to it, if it is neither psychically real nor suprasensible in a metaphysical sense, in view of the immediacy with which we become aware of such meaning as it exerts itself with compelling force upon our consciousness? Heidegger confronts these questions in terms of the structure in which logical meaning appears, namely, the judgment in which meaning "takes place" and thus "takes hold" of its object. Meaning appears here as a structured or "articulated" phenomenon. This point is already implied in the specification of the reality of meaning as a holding *relation*. What (or whom) does the meaning of a judgment hold? Close analysis of the structure of a judgment yields a two-sided answer to this question. There is (1) the holding relation of the predicate to the subject internal to the judgment and (2) the hold on the mind that a true judgment exercises.

1. In a predicative proposition, a certain content of signification (*P*) is said to hold for a specific object (*S*). The state of affairs thus comprehended is expressed through the copulative "is" in the unified whole of the judgment (*S is P*). If the judgment is truly an articulated unity, then its component parts are not fully disparate and unrelated but must already, in their content, "demand" each other to the point of assuming the intimacy of a form-matter relation. This internal hold finds its focus in the "is," which is thus a relation that precedes its relata, the most essential element in the judgment and not just a superfluous third element standing in as a mere sign of identity. It is in the "is" that the form of reality of the judgment is situated. For example, the sentence "The bookbinding is yellow" in effect says that "Being yellow holds for the bookbinding." One might also say that "Being yellow is true of the bookbinding" (though not the converse) and thus give a specific interpretation to the classical definition of truth as adequation of

"thing" (the matter or object of the judgment, stated in the subject position) and our knowledge (the form or determination manifesting itself in the predicate of the judgment). The unity of the two, the "is," constitutes the meaning under consideration. The "is" is accordingly the actual bearer and locus of truth.

2. The holding relation of the copulative being of a judgment placed in the perspective of truth naturally leads to a consideration of the hold on the mind, which the true statement exercises to the point of obliging us to assent to it and of compelling our acceptance again and again, depending on how much "weight" it carries and how long it "remains in force." The question of the meaning of meaning thus leads to the question of truth, and the relation of truth shifts our consideration from the hold internal to the judgment to the "intentional" hold between the judgment thus described objectively and the judicative activity, since through judgment we have knowledge and accordingly, in perfect correspondence with the judicative meaning, there is an essentially cognitive awareness, which is not the same as the real psychic activity. This essentially cognitive activity is to be viewed as a "meaning-realizing activity," or better, as a "performance meaning" (*Leistungssinn*), which is in strict conformity with the judicative meaning (*Urteilssinn*) immanent in the relation between the members of a judgment. Viewed as a cognitive performance in direct correlation with the judicative structure, knowledge is the activity of taking possession of an object by bestowing a meaningful determination upon it. In knowing an object, we arrest it from the stream of experience and fix it in a definite form (a category). Positing an object is at once a matter of setting it into a form and thereby giving it meaning. "Reality can become meaningful only when it is somehow *grasped* by means of the logical; something is broken out of the real and thus distinguished, delimited and ordered."[3]

If at first the logical realm was found to be somewhat deficient in being in relation to the real order of things, it now appears that the real is dependent on the logical for its meaning. For if the real is not somehow held in meaning, we would in fact not know that it exists. Accordingly, to receive its due, reality in all of its modes must be given in and through a context of meaning, which in effect holds it in being. We must live in meaning in order to know that which exists.

[3]*Die Kategorien-und Bedeutungslehre des Duns Scotus* (1916), First Part, Chap. 2; *Frühe Schriften*, p. 222.

The logical, at first characterized as "unreal," now appears as the very condition of possibility of the real and thus more rightfully deserves the name of being.

But no less important than its hold on the real is the compelling hold on the mind that judicative meaning exercises. Being in its most efficacious manifestation is thus to be situated in the median realm between reality and the mind, and it is this realm of intentionality that holds the real secret of the "meaning of being" contained in our judgments.

The concluding chapter of the Scotus book,[4] written after the work was accepted as a dissertation by the University of Freiburg, sets the stage for things to come. The chapter entitled, "The Problem of the Categories," makes plaint with the lifeless sterility of past systems of categories and calls for their rejuvenation by setting them back into the meaningful coherences and continuities of the immediate life of the subject in complex correlativity with its objects. The logical problems of category and judgment are to be reinserted into the "translogical" context of the "living spirit" in which meaning is first realized, where the theoretical attitude is only one possibility and by no means the most significant. The rich and variegated life of the spirit includes within itself the fullness of achievements of its history, which must be made operative in order to work out the "*cosmos* of categories," which is to displace the empoverished schematic *tables* of categories hitherto proposed. One might then interpret an historical epoch in terms of its categorial structures (i.e., in terms of the manifold senses of direction, which determine the "form of life" of, say, medieval man, whose acts realize the meanings that vectorially structure his context and the living spirit of his language). The concept of the living spirit thus takes us to a fundamental level in which the uniqueness and individuality of *acts* and the self-sustaining validity of *meaning* are brought into living unity, where the character of this unity in and through its differentiations poses the most difficult of ontological problems. But only with the "breakthrough into true reality and real truth" will it be possible to arrive at a satisfying answer to questions such as how "unreal" (ideal) meaning grants true reality to us, and to determine the sense and the limits of the form-matter relationship as an account of how categories structure our judgments.

With this entry into his new problematic of historical life experience, Heidegger's logical themes of his student days—centered on

4Ibid., pp. 341–353.

the judgment in its internal composition and its interweaving with
other judgments into the fabric of the sciences—are now to be as-
sessed in terms of a larger context in which they lose their priority,
assume a derivative status and at times recede completely into the
background. As Heidegger notes some years later, "the very idea of
'logic' disintegrates in the vortex of a more original questioning."[5]
Nevertheless the larger view never loses sight of the smaller units of
logical concern. A recurring theme throughout these later years is
the question of the nature of the judgment, particularly with regard
to the meaning of its being, of the "is," which is said in many ways.

Manifestly, the discussion of these issues will undergo modification in the changing perspective. After all, a sense of meaning that
holds fast in its validity is a static sense promoting a rigidity of being,
which Heidegger in his burgeoning opposition to the priority of
being as object will now methodically strive to mitigate and delimit.
Instead he seeks to uncover a more historical dimension of the
meaning that precedes and underlies the "holding action" of judicative meaning. Hence, "validity" (*Geltung*) as the deepest sense of
meaning and truth, at first lauded as "this felicituous expression"
from "our German vocabulary,"[6] becomes "this word idol" (*SZ* 156),[7]
which only stands in the way of the effort to ontologically clarify the
problem of the meaning of meaning. The phenomenon of meaning
no longer finds its center of gravity in the content of judgments,
especially theoretical statements about things, and truth is seen to
"take place" not only in the judgment but also more fundamentally
in the question, particularly if it is oriented toward the basic issues of
existence. The meaningful sentence is thus oriented to the contextual and vectorial meanings of existence, and the meaning of the
sentence is determined first by what it *shows* of that meaningful
fundament (*SZ* 154). It is only through this apophantic function of
judgment that the internal structure of predicative determination of
subject matters acquires its meaning. At the center of this structure is
the phenomenon of the copula, which gives expression to address-
ing something as something, and it is this schema of "as" that must
now be existentially demarcated and ontologically interpreted
against the background of the temporal character of linguistic pat-

---

[5]"What is Metaphysics?" (1929); in *Existence and Being*, ed. Werner Brock (Chicago:
Regnery, 1949) Gateway Paperback, p. 342.

[6]*Frühe Schriften,* pp. 211 and 111.

[7]Martin Heidegger, *Sein und Zeit* (Tübingen: Niemeyer, (8) 1957), p. 156. References to this book hereafter are incorporated into the body of the text.

terns and contexts (*SZ* 159, 349, 360); and the question of truth in the sense of correspondence between ideal and real becomes extremely problematic through the sharp separation of these two realms that the polemic against psychologism promotes (*SZ* 216–217). Moreover, the very tenor of the critique of psychologism resides in the assumption of the timelessness of the being under consideration. The polemic is accordingly softened by considering judicative meaning not simply as a logical content but more as an intentional content implicated in a living discourse in which the ideal and real once again merge (*SZ* 161). The temporal interchange between subject and object through the mediation of language thus serves to thrust the ideal object back into life. The task that Heidegger takes upon himself is to elaborate the proper concepts to articulate this "between."

This line of development passes through Husserl's doctrines of intentionality and the categorial intuition and Dilthey's attempt to articulate the categories of life.

A PHILOSOPHY OF LIFE

Wilhelm Dilthey, biographer of Schleiermacher, historian of ideas and art forms, proponent of a descriptive psychology comparable to Husserl's, saw his many endeavors converging in his lifelong quest for a "logic" of the historical and human sciences as a whole. At first seen as a critique of historical reason paralleling Kant's effort to found the natural sciences, Dilthey's project gradually found itself on the trail of a reason in history that ran counter to Kant's notion of reason. Not the anemic transcendental ego, "in whose veins flows no real blood" (I, XVIII),[8] but a kind of "logic" immanent in life itself is to be the source for the categorial articulation of the human sciences, which would thus have access to "predications out of life" itself (VII, 238). To paraphrase Pascal, one might say that "life has its reasons which the reason does not have." Thus before they are the apriori theoretical forms of objectivity that enter into judgments, as in Kant, the categories are "forms of life," or better, the spontaneous articulations of the structural coherences and temporal continuities of life itself. Life itself, considered as an active and nevertheless perduring

---

[8]References here are to the following volumes of Wilhelm Dilthey's *Gesammelte Schriften:* Vol. I, *Einleitung in die Geisteswissenschaften;* Vol. V, *Die Geistige Welt: Einleitung in die Philosophie des Lebens;* Vol. VII, *Der Aufbau der geschichtlichen Welt in den Geisteswissenschaften* (Stuttgart: Teubner, [7]1959, [6]1957, [6]1958).

Zusammenhang (context, coherence, continuity) is the subject of the
sentences of the human sciences, whether the sentence refers to the
course of an individual life or to that of societies, nations, cultures,
historical worlds, and times, and finally to the whole of human reality, which brings us to the sentences of philosophy, whether these be
anthropological, epistemological, or ontological in import.

An ontology of life would be distinguished not only by its breadth
but also by a penetration into the depths of its subject matter to the
point of drawing the possible predications about it into such an
intimate unity that subject and predicate would well become one.
For it would serve to counter the flow of the categories into the
sciences and refer them back to their convergent locus in the effective continuity and working context (*Wirkungszusammenhang*) from
which they spring. This would in fact be the culmination and highest
achievement of Dilthey's own methodological dictum "to understand life from out of itself."

Dilthey liked to reiterate, almost as a formula, that life is that
behind which thought cannot go. Its negative formulation is directed against any and all metaphysics that would seek a reality
behind or beyond the appearances; in particular it sought to counter
the other-worldly thrust still present vestigially in the Kantian attempt to delineate an atemporal realm behind the "appearances" of
time. The converse of the maxim serves to develop a much more
positive sense of the phenomenon of life itself. Relegating thought
to "this side" of life does not necessarily dash it against an opaque
wall. That life finds itself amenable to thought suggests the alternative that life is a much richer resource than philosophies, prone to
drive a wedge between the two, have been willing to concede. The
conviction that thought is inherently compatible with life is brought
out most tellingly by the methodological principle of immanence,
"to understand life from life itself," which Dilthey identifies as "the
dominant impulse in my philosophical thinking" (V,4). Life is to be
understood through categories derived from life itself by "entering
ever more deeply into the historical world" (V,4) (i.e., into the meaningful structures of artworks, human institutions, and customs as
well as the written documents that we more properly call texts).
Where do such meaningful structures come from? Nowhere else
than from life *itself*, replies Dilthey. *Das Leben legt sich aus.* The principle of immanence thus functions as a kind of "principle of identity"
fraught with consequences for the methodology not only of the
historical sciences but also of the philosophical exploration of the

nature of life itself, for which the most basic issue is the very character of this "identity," which now appears as the most radical category of life, defining the very way in which it manifests itself, the "logic" of its appearance.

It is but a short step from here to *Being and Time*, where phenomenology is formally defined as a matter of permitting "that which shows itself to be seen from out of itself just as it shows itself in itself" (*SZ* 34). Even more emphatically than in Dilthey's principle of immanence, this formulation views thought as a function of life, the phenomenon par excellence, "the guiding-thread of all philosophical inquiry at the point where it *arises* and to which it returns" (*SZ* 38). Accordingly, the phrase "philosophy of life" is as pleonastic as the "botany of plants" (*SZ* 46). Rightly understood, philosophy is always and only about life not only as end but also as source. Life is that out of which all philosophic inquiry develops as well as that to which it directs all of its questions. If one takes seriously the reversal of priorities that ensues from considering thought as a function of life, then life becomes the issue that gives rise to thought in the first instance, which calls for thought and thus provides the food for thought that sustains it and carries it through to its destination. To understand life from out of itself is therefore to cultivate a certain intimacy between life and thought, already inherent in life itself, to the point where—in Droysen's pregnant phase—"life thinks and thoughts live."[9]

But this path in the later Heidegger's meditation on the relationship between being and thinking, implicit in Dilthey's dictum to understand life from out of itself, has obviously short-circuited a crucial middle term in the process of life's understanding itself. Heidegger's shortcut here stands in sharpest contrast to Dilthey's detour of self-understanding through all of the expressions of human life, which establish the proximate conditions for the development of that understanding which is first of all a way of life issuing from the familiarity of existence before it is a mode of knowing.

Even the formulation of the bypassed intermediate question bears a qualitative difference because Dilthey does not ask "How does life disclose (show) itself?" but rather "How does life objectivate itself?" Yet the coherence and continuity between life-experience, expres-

[9]Cited by Hans-Georg Gadamer, *Wahrheit und Methode: Gründzuge einer philosophischen Hermeneutik* (Tübingen: Mohr, ²1965) p. 199.

sion, and understanding, which form the basis to Dilthey's answer, are obviously conceptual predecessors to the co-originality of the disclosures of disposition, discourse, and understanding, which lie at the basis of Heidegger's analysis of Dasein. (In the same vein, the later Heidegger speaks of "dwelling, building, thinking.") Dilthey, moreover, sees life as fixing itself in meaningful wholes through the interpenetration of three types of objectivations: (a) the conceptual textures of language proper, (b) the action textures of public institutions, and (c) the emotive textures of personal styles whose controlled expression leads to works of art. In a similar vein, in *Being and Time* the meanings articulated in action and emotion precede and underlie more cognitive and theoretical meanings. Thus the meaningful relations woven in the pragmatic space of action found the possibility of words and language (*SZ* 87) and the attunement of mood first made possible the cognition of something within the world (*SZ* 137). "Meanings grow into words. It is not the case that word-things are invested with meanings" (*SZ* 161).

Thus the basic category of meaning, first encountered in a logical framework and identified there as the content of judgments, is now found to be indigenous to life itself. Life is at once the meaningful context in which any particular experience becomes meaningful and the movement of development that makes sense. Before it is a holding action in judgments, meaning is the cohesion of context and continuity of direction of the *Wirkungszammenhang* of life. Meaning first gets its force and carries weight from the efficacy of a life-context before it becomes effective in human judgments; and if meaning is a fact of life before it is the content of logic, then meaning is first of all not imposed from above upon experience as a form upon matter but is rather drawn into judicative structures by being explicated from the textures immanent to life. If this emergence of meaning occurs spontaneously in the context of life, then the scientist and above all the philosopher must learn how to follow and continue this process of explication by inserting himself into the operative context and entering into the process by which life articulates itself, which calls for (*heisst*) thought. *Heissen* takes us to the theory of meaning of the later Heidegger, which converges with his reflection upon life as the principle of identity. Mediating between this later notion of meaning and the more orthodox sense of meaning as validity is the notion of meaning in *Being and Time* as both efficacious context and temporal continuity, beautifully captured in the single German word favored by Dilthey, *Wirkungszusammenhang*.

INTENTIONALITY, TRUTH, AND
CATEGORIAL INTUITION

From the *Logical Investigations* Heidegger learned that categories of objects likewise cannot be situated in the judging subject but are to be traced back to a prepredicative dimension of being. The doctrines of intentionality and of the categorial intuition in the Sixth Investigation become for Heidegger the "formal indicators" to the structures of this new apriori realm of being. The theoretically oriented intentionality is set back into the more "interest-laden" dimension of Being-in-the-world and care and, like them, is to find the condition of its possibility in the transcendence of temporality. Categorial intuition is, as it were, turned upon itself into a prior understanding of being and its modes so that, for example, the "empty" intention of signification now becomes the project that throws forward an outline of structured meaning that "can be filled" (*SZ* 151) by the beings that are discovered in and through this provisional space of disclosure.

"Intentionality" is another name for the phenomenon par excellence of phenomenology and poses for it the most difficult of ontological problems. For what precisely is the reality of intentionality if it is not a coordination of the psychic and the physical, the inner and the outer, the ideal and the real? Here one must first learn to consider only the structure as such. Yet to say that the doctrine of intentionality merely affirms that consciousness is always a consciousness *of* something is almost trite, and certainly far too static in describing the structure of what is fundamentally an activity. Basically, intentionality describes the structure of directing-itself-toward, a movement of "meaning" tensed between emptily signifying and fully bestowing meaning; and, contrary to terminological appearances, the "empty" intention is the more basic of the two, inasmuch as it determines that which the possible fulfillment can be, and not vice versa. In and through the signifying intention, the directing-itself-toward is given a sense of direction (*Richtungssinn*), which the early Husserl calls the *Auffassungssinn* and which Heidegger will later call the *Vorsicht*. This provision of meaning is precisely that which categorial intuition adds to intentionality.

The signifying act finds its fulfillment in an act of intuition in which (a) the object itself is present *just as* it is in itself, and (b) this presence is *just as* it was initially intended in the signifying act. The second "as" is the experience of truth as agreement, which takes place in the intentional act of identification of the signified and the intuited on the basis of and out of the originally given thing itself. Truth as correspondence is the noematic correlate of the act of identification, the act of self-evidence. But in the act of fulfillment, we are thematically directed toward the thing *itself* and not the self-sameness of identification. What we apprehend is the *identical* object and not its identity with the signified. The *self* is grasped thematically, but not the selfsameness, which in direct, naive, straightforward living is not thematically intended but simply experienced in the apprehension of the thing itself. We thus live in the state of identity and continuity between the signified and the intuited, a state that we continually experience but do not grasp.[10] This is what it means "to be in the truth" (*SZ* 221) without knowing it thematically, whereby we understand the structures of our world as "self-evident," (i.e., as a matter of course in a straightforward living of them without considering them thematically).

That which we thematically grasp is the object itself "just as it is in itself" (the first "as"), which gives fullness to the signifying intention and thus makes it true. The object itself "is experienced as the true-making thing."[11] Because it provides the basis for truth as identity and agreement, *die Sache selbst* is the more basic truth. For it is the thing itself toward which the signifying intention is directed, and it is the thing itself that is itself given in intuition. In short, it is the thing that underlies the entire process of identification. Heidegger will go further and try to show how an advance notice of the thing itself in some way even prompts the initial signifying intention and thus provides it with its sense of direction.

Only on the basis of the above two notions of truth is it possible to then speak of the truth of judgment, truth in the sense of correctness. A judgment is correct if it is directed toward the true thing: "It says that it is so, and it really is so."[12] The "is" of the "really is" refers to truth thematically grasped as a stasis of identity and is not to be confused with the first "is," the copula of the categorial judgment, which refers to a structural moment of the true state of affairs articulated by the judgment.

[10]Cf. "Evidenz und Wahrheit," para. 39, Chap. 5 of the Sixth Logical Investigation. The internal reference here to paragraph 8 on static unions (i.e., habitual and matter-of-fact identities) underscores the fundamentally nonthematic character of the initial experience of truth.

[11]Ibid. ". . . als wahrmachender erlebt ist." This is the third conception of truth discussed in this paragraph.

[12]Ibid. The fourth conception of truth here, taken from the standpoint of the noema of the signifying intention.

If we consider the categorial judgment *This S is P* as an assertion of a perception, it contains the categorial elements *this* and *is*, which themselves are not perceived. What is the source of this surplus of senses that sense intuition does not cover? As Kant said, copulative being is not a real predicate; it can find no objective correlate in acts of perception in the strict sense. Nor is it apprehended by reflection upon the acts of judgment through which it appears but rather in the experience of the objects of these acts, the states of affairs of the judgment. The categorial form is neither a real predicate of the object nor a result of reflection upon the conscious activity of judgment but an ideal structure of the object under judgment, the same object given straightforwardly in sense intuition because perception gives the whole object explicitly, but its real parts are thus only implicitly given. To highlight these adumbrations calls for the categorial act of predicative explication, which explicitly articulates the parts and sees them *as* parts of the whole. Not covered by sense intuition, the categorial elements thus evoked nevertheless receive their fulfillment in the perceived thing under judgment through the categorial intuition founded upon sense intuition and operating in unison with it.[13] Even though founded, the ideal structures thus intended can be given originally in the perceived thing. This suggests that the categorial is implicated in every "simple" and "direct" experience down to ordinary perception, so that such experiences are after all not so simple at all but developed out of highly structured contexts. Disengaging such categorial states from their founding objects would serve to explicate their comprehensive structures and permit them to be grasped as categories proper or concepts. Such is the task of the "universal intuition" of ideation, which brings out the categories of the various regions of objects.[14] Judgments are accordingly explicated out of prior contexts of meaning, and their differentiation into regions compensates for the seeming indifference of the pervasive "is," which in each case must be understood in terms of the particular region that it articulates and thus *shows*.

Heidegger will view these categories not only as contexts or regions of being but also, more temporally, as projects that already anticipate and guide our understanding of the objects that appear in their respective regions. It is the projective "fore"-structure of the categorial that establishes the indissoluble unity between the doc-

[13]Cf. "Charakteristik der kategorialen Akte als fundierte Akte," para. 48, Chap. 6 of the Sixth Logical Investigation.
[14]Ibid., para. 52. This is Husserl's first account of eidetic intuition, the method of describing the material apriori of various regions of experience.

trines of intentionality and categorial intuition. Intentionality is a "categorizing" movement, which articulates a context of meaning within which things can appear. Categories are first of all incipient presuppositions of an operative context that carry us forward in the movement of interpreting that context. Categories are at work before they are seen, and we attempt to see them to put them to work all the more effectively, for example, in the form of a "productive logic," which guides scientific inquiry (*SZ* 10).

But if intuition in general can thus be taken back to a more fundamental operative context, then sense intuition is itself a founded mode of knowledge. The directing-itself-toward of all perception arises out of a more basic indwelling in which we are already familiar with the world (*SZ* 61). Husserl himself has shown that evidence is a universal phenomenon that reaches beyond the theoretical into more practical and emotive comportments; and these may even possess a measure of primacy over the theoretical. If noncognitive comportment underlies our more cognitive behavior, if our more cognitive stances are drawn from our noncognitive comportment, then this expository movement is a mode of knowing more basic than intuition. Perception itself is to be viewed as a process of specifying something that has already been laid out in other ways. Interpretation and not intuition is the most basic mode of cognitive behavior.

The movement of intentionality is thus situated in a concretion of precedented structures that are operative as projective anticipations before they are explicitly uncovered by us. In short, before we intuit them, we understand them, where understanding first describes a way of existing rather than a mode of knowing. The basic form of intentionality is therefore not the subject-object relationship but what Kant called the "pure self-affection of time," which articulates its categories as "schematisms" operative in a realm of meaning between conception and sensation, the ideal and the real. The "categorizing" movement of intentionality, more originally thought, becomes the transcending movement of time.

CATEGORIAL INTUITION AND
THE QUESTION OF BEING

Some recently published texts serve to specify more closely the role played by Husserl's doctrine of categorial intuition in Heidegger's "transformation of the categorial," especially in the climactic period of 1925–1927, while *Being and Time* was being written. Heidegger's lecture courses of this period, now being published in the *Gesamtausgabe*, indicate that it is also a time in which years of attempts to interpret the *Logical Investigations* are likewise coming to a climax for Heidegger. The lecture course in the summer semester of 1925 couples the most intensive exegesis of the Sixth Logical Investigation Heidegger has ever published[15] with a first draft of the early portions of *Being and Time*. A retrospective view of some of the elements of this exegesis is provided by the recently published protocol of Heidegger's "Seminar of Zähringen (1973)."[16]

In the seminar at Zähringen, Heidegger observes that the Husserl of the *Logical Investigations* broaches the question of being in the strict sense only in his doctrine of categorial intuition, which accordingly becomes for Heidegger "the kindling point of Husserlian thought."[17] To arrive at this doctrine, Husserl took his point of departure from the then philosophically commonplace notion of sense intuition, in which direct access to "hyletic data" is obtained. If one also speaks of categorial intuition, then, contrary to Kant, "categories" too are to be regarded as in some sense directly *given*. In the intentional fulfillment of the categorial judgment *This S is P*, the *S* and the *P* are loci of sense intuition while the *this* and *is*, the categories of substance and being, are not given through the senses but are nevertheless given in their own way. In analogy with sense intuition, Husserl maintains that they are "seen" in a way that exceeds sense intuition. What is this "seeing" that is not of the senses? How are "categories" such as substance and being given? Or, in more phenomenological language, how do they appear? The doctrine of categorial intuition points out that "substance" and "being" are no less phenomena than are tables, chairs, trees, and things,

---

[15]The publication of this lecture course, entitled *Geschichte des Zeitbegriffes*, appears to be imminent as of this writing, but the basic lines of the exegesis of Husserl that it contains has been public since 1975, in a paper by Walter Biemel, one of the editors of Heidegger's *Gesamtausgabe*, first presented the Heidegger Conference at Wilfrid Laurier University in Waterloo, Ontario, under the title "Heidegger and Phenomenology." Already published as volumes 21 and 24 of the *Gesamtaugabe* are the lecture courses of Winter Semester 1925–1926 and Summer Semester 1927. The first, *Logik: Die Frage nach der Wahrheit*, treats intentionality and intuition in conjunction with Husserl's critique of psychologism. The second lecture course, *Die Grundprobleme der Phänomenologie*, announced as the hitherto unpublished Third Division of the First Part of *Being and Time*, uses intentionality as the operative concept in a phenomenological critique of the basic thesis of traditional ontology.

[16]Martin Heidegger, *Questions* IV (Paris: Gallimard, 1974) pp. 309–339. An interpretation of this seminar is to be found in Jacques Taminiaux's "Le regard et l'excédent: Remarques sur Heidegger et les 'Recherches logiques 'de Husserl," *Revue Philosophique de Louvain LXXV* (February 1977) 74–100. An English translation of Taminiaux's paper has just appeared in *Research in Phenomenology* VII (1977).

[17]Ibid., p. 311.

accompanying these more mundane phenomena without appearing in the same way. In Husserl's words, the categorial accompanies ordinary perception as a "surplus of meaning."[18] This for Heidegger is "Husserl's essential discovery and at once the essential difficulty,"[19] since being as such is not a phenomenon in the same way as particular beings.

What then is the nature of this "categorial" phenomenality? In the first instance, it is to be situated precisely in its "excessiveness" in regard to particular beings. Being appears (a) in conjunction with particular beings, (b) in a way that exceeds them, much like a context in which they can appear, (c) accordingly, as the very condition of their appearance, and (d) so that it must in some way "precede" their appearance. The later Husserl will describe this more subtle presence of "categorial" structures as a compresence of horizons that are "apperceived" or "appresented" with perceived things. As late as the summer semester of 1925, Heidegger is still using the distinctly Husserlian term "appresentation" to describe the relationship between a thing and the meaningful context or "world," which enables the thing to appear as it is, where priority is clearly placed in the world that "appresents" the thing or tool (i.e., permits it to come to presence).

Soon after Heidegger replaces the term "appresentation" with "disclosure;" and to describe the empowering presence of being—thus a "category" which is more verbal than nominal in its mode of givenness—and to distinguish it from the mode of givenness of a particular being (i.e., that which *is*), Heidegger resorts to a literal interpretation of the German idiom *es gibt*:

> Perhaps no other being *is* except that which is, but perhaps something is given which itself *is* not, but which nevertheless *is given* in a sense still to be determined. Moreover, in the end it *must* be given in order that we can have access to beings as beings and relate to them, in order that we may experience and understand something like beings at all.[20]

This reversal of perspective from beings to being and from a thing to its world points to the importance for Heidegger of another anal-

---

[18]"Überschuss in der Bedeutung," Paragraph 40 of the Sixth Logical Investigation. The translation is Findlay's; Taminiaux translates Überschuss as *excédent* (excess). Similarly, in paragraph 14 of the Fifth Logical Investigation, Husserl says: "Apperception is for us the surplus which is present in experience itself, in its descriptive content as opposed to the raw existence of sensation."

[19]*Questions* IV, p. 314.

[20]Martin Heidegger, *Die Grundprobleme der Phänomenologie* (Frankfurt: Klostermann, 1975) pp. 13–14.

ogy in the *Logical Investigations,* which in effect reverses the analogical move from sense intuition to categorial intuition. The analogy first appears in a discussion of meaning-bestowing acts in the First Investigation, in a paragraph (§ 23) entitled "Apperception in Expressions and Apperception in Intuitive Presentations." Here the objectifying interpretation that occurs in acts of intuition such as perception, in which a complex of sensations is invested with meaning, is compared with the more familiar "understanding interpretation" (*verstehende Auffassung*) of acts of expression, in which the meaning of a word is realized. This new analogy suggests that something like an expression of meaning occurs even in intuitive acts of perception. It emphasizes the understanding of meaning rather than the intuition of a givenness or presence. But ultimately the two, expression and intuition, are placed in continuity and become phases or moments of a single and complete act of intentionality. This leads to a hybridization of the two analogies, which permits one to speak of the presence of meaning and of "categorial" understanding and exposition, in particular the understanding of being, which is precisely the outcome of Heidegger's "retrieve" of the *Logical Investigations.* Thus, the "appresentation" of significance becomes a rudimentary form of expression, if indeed "expression" means any exposition and articulation of meaning, which is not always a matter of words. Here, the tradition of hermeneutics, made actual for Heidegger by Dilthey, no doubt played its mediating role.

The Heideggerian retrieve opposes Husserl in situating the understanding and exposition of meaning not in acts of consciousness but first of all in a preconscious realm of a being-in-the-world, which is already pervaded by "expressivity." All of our experiences are already articulated, though not necessarily in words, by a prior understanding and interpretation that guide and determine them and so bring them to fulfillment. In discussing simple sense intuition, Husserl tentatively observes, "I *see* white paper and *say* 'white paper,' thereby expressing, with precise adequacy, only what I see,"[21] and then adds that the matter is not so simple because of the compresence of categorial intuition. Because of the apriori presence of categorial structures, it would be more accurate to maintain that we see what we say rather than say what we see. Even the simplest perception is already expressed and interpreted by the prior understanding we have of it, which determines *how* we perceive. This is not

[21] Paragraph 40, the Sixth Logical Investigation. This text was also discussed in the seminar at Zahringen: cf. *Questions* IV, p. 314.

necessarily a bias that we impose on our perception; it just *happens* to
be the way we perceive. On the one hand, language overlays our
experience and sometimes obscures our access to it, as in idle everyday chatter; on the other hand, the articulations of experience
underlie language and optimally manifest themselves through it.
This is the double-edged lesson that Heidegger reads in Husserl's
discovery of categorial intuition. Categorial intuition is the simple
apprehension of the categorial element operative in our experience,
an element in which we live without regarding it thematically. As
such, the categor*ial* is not yet formulated into categories, but provides the basis for such formulation. We are already caught up in
meaning, and only later capture it in part for ourselves in and
through concepts. Thus Heidegger repeatedly tries to point below
our conceptual grasping and logical defining to the *horismos*[22] of
meaning, which defines the scope as well as the limits of the human
situation, which is first of all given not through the senses or the
intellect but *in actu exercitu* of existence in the world. At this level
expression, in the sense of articulation of structures, still bears some
relevance to the existential movement of living the world, while
intuition becomes a very tenuous analogy for our first way of access
to such structures. Accordingly, "seeing" yields to an analogy of
"doing," the understanding "know-how" that comes from habitual
commerce with a familiar world.

Husserl approaches this domain of habituality in his discussion of
a familiar field of static unions between expression and intuition
where "the expression seems to be laid upon the thing and to clothe
it like a garment."[23] In a world that has already been talked over,
words have been worked into things and remain impaled on things.
On the other hand, by means of the proper reductive procedures, it
is possible to loosen the grip that our customary words have upon
things and thereby glimpse how the things themselves articulate
their own structures. Thus the early Husserl already points to the
tension between the habit of language and the disclosive structures
of experience, which becomes central in Heidegger's existential
framework. Husserl eventually identifies these structures as the ma-

---

[22]Existence "defines" structures which are chiaroscuro, more incipient, thus
"softer" in nature. "Conceiving in effect involves a gesture of seizure. By contrast, the
Greek *horismos* gently encompasses what the regard brings into view; it does not
conceive." *Questions* IV, p. 339.

[23]Paragraph 6, the Sixth Logical Investigation. One is reminded of the later Husserl's discussion in the *Crisis* of the scientific cladding of ideas, which cloaks and
obscures the lifeworld.

terial apriori of things and regions, another discovery rooted in the *Logical Investigations*, which Heidegger regards as a significant departure from modern philosophy, especially Kant. With this discovery, categorial phenomenality, first uncovered in the discussion of logical issues, manifests its ontological import, whereby categories become regional essences (for Husserl) and projective contexts of meaning (for Heidegger).

But Husserl adheres to the spirit of modern philosophy by placing the ultimate being of these intentional fields in an oriented consciousness. Heidegger, claiming a more faithful adherence to the principle of phenomenology, seeks to shift the locus of discussion from an oriented consciousness to a situated existence, where the question of the sense and the truth of being posed by the structures of intentionality and categorial intuition is to receive its answer in some as yet insufficiently named confluence of the world, the self, time, and language. Accordingly, despite the family ties that Heidegger wishes to maintain with Husserl, the transition from the immanent structures of intentional consciousness to the ecstatic structures of worldly existence constitutes a radical departure, which, to use a perceptual metaphor common in Anglo-American philosophy, amounts to a "Gestalt switch."[24]

[24]Jean Beaufret, *Dialogue avec Heidegger,* Volume III: *Approche de Heidegger* (Paris: Minuit, 1974) p. 117. In describing the transition from intentionality to ecstasis, Beaufret observes that, despite the fact that the first led to the second, the second is in fact incommensurable with the first, so that "to anyone who places himself in intentionality, the experience of ecstasis is inaccessible, just as relativity physics remains unthinkable from the point of view of Newton, even though Newton already espied the principle which Einstein was destined to develop."

PART III

Merleau-Ponty

DENNIS T. O'CONNOR

NINE

THE PHILOSOPHY—SCIENCE NEXUS
IN THE EARLY MERLEAU-PONTY

THIS ESSAY WILL FOCUS ATTENTION on a dimension of Merleau-Ponty's thought, which is often either overlooked or treated in a cursory manner—his concern for and indebtedness to scientific research. Our study covers the crucial period of the thirties. To fulfill this intention the scope will be restricted to a consideration of three texts, the first two of which are research outlines submitted to the Caisse nationale des Sciences in 1933 and 1934;[1] the third is Merleau-Ponty's *La Structure du comportement* (1938).[2] These research outlines provide valuable insight into the author's philosophical-scientific project in the early thirties. Too, they serve as an invaluable introduction to a reading of *The Structure of Behavior*.

The general claim advanced here is that we cannot fully appreciate the philosophical project of Merleau-Ponty unless we trace carefully the connection, as he saw it, between scientific studies and philosophical reflection. More specifically, we hope to justify the claim that the 1938 work requires that we read it as (a) in large part a series of intrascientific critiques that are stunning in their detail, scope, and incisiveness; (b) an introduction to a philosophy of scientific consciousness; and (c) an attempt to show, rather than merely assert, that the relationship between scientific research and philosophical investigation must be one of reciprocal influence.

While full justification of these claims is clearly beyond the scope

---

[1] These documents, "Projet de travail sur la nature de la perception" (April 8, 1933) and "La Nature de la perception" (April 21, 1934), are available to us in Theodore Geraets' marvelous study *Vers une nouvelle philosophie transcendentale* (The Hague: Martinus Nijhoff, 1971). They will be cited hereafter as "Projet" and "Nature."

[2] Maurice Merleau-Ponty, *La Structure du comportement* (Paris: P U F, 1942); *The Structure of Behavior*, trans. Alden Fisher (Boston: Beacon Press, 1963). Page references to these texts, hereafter cited as *SC* and *SB* will be to the sixth edition and second edition respectively.

of the present essay,[3] it is hoped that enough of an indication will be given to justify a reading of Merleau-Ponty, which is long overdue.

PART ONE

1. "PROJECT DE TRAVAIL"

In this brief research outline what we find is a justification for a project that will focus on the problem of perception, and particularly on perception of the body-proper, in an attempt to establish a tentative synthesis between recent experimental studies in the sciences and recent philosophical suggestions. There are four points of interest for us in this outline.

First is Merleau-Ponty's insistence that recent experimental studies in neurology, psychopathy, and psychology of perception make it worthwhile, indeed necessary, to reconsider classical philosophical theories of perception. Second is the insistence that the research carried out by the Gestaltists in Germany threatens both the intellectualist conception of perception[4] and the empiricist doctrines of associationism and sensation, by indicating that (a) perception is not an intellectual operation; (b) it is impossible to distinguish in perception between matter and form; and (c) the notion of "sensations" in classical theory is a wholly gratuitous hypothesis. Third is the suggestion that if these scientific studies can be confirmed we will be obliged to join with certain philosophers in the Anglo-American tradition of realism[5] in insisting that sensible concrete relations are not reducible to intellectual relations and that the universe of perception is not identical to the universe of scientific objects. The fourth point that merits recognition is that in suggesting the necessity for significant conceptual reform Merleau-Ponty makes no reference to phenomenology.

This outline indicates that Merleau-Ponty's early attitude toward the relationship between philosophy and science was that the reflective method of the former and the experimental method of the latter are essentially complementary; and that he was engaged quite early

---

[3] I have attempted a detailed, systematic study of these themes in an unpublished doctoral thesis, "The Structure of Behavior: An Analysis and Critique" (Saint Louis University, 1972).

[4] The main representatives Merleau-Ponty has in mind here are Lachelier, Lagneau, and Alain.

[5] Geraets suggests (p. 11) that the allusion to Anglo-American realists refers to James and Whitehead whom Merleau-Ponty knew through Jean Wahl's *Vers le concret* (Paris: Vrin, 1932).

in his philosophical development in efforts to move beyond the tradition of critical thought (as represented by Brunschwicg and others) because of its failure to account for perceptual behavior.[6] And finally, it suggests that while Merleau-Ponty had been introduced to phenomenological thought as early as 1928,[7] this latter—especially in the figure of Husserl—had no strong influence on him until the period between April, 1933 and April, 1934.[8]

2. *"La Nature de la Perception"*

In this three-part document, which is concerned with summarizing a year's research on the physiology, philosophy, and psychology of perception, there are two items that immediately catch our attention: (a) the new concern with phenomenology; and (b) the underlying motif that no one of these three approaches to perception (i.e., from the points of view of physiology, philosophy, and psychology) can reach maturity except in relation to the other two. While each discipline has its special and distinctive methods, no one of them can be fully conceptualized or precise without the others.

Whereas a detailed treatment of this document is beyond the scope of the present essay, it would be informative to summarize briefly some tentative lessons that Merleau-Ponty has drawn from each of the areas of research. These "lessons" bear a strong relation to the first two chapters of *The Structure of Behavior*.

a) PHYSIOLOGY AND PATHOLOGY

Merleau-Ponty begins his summary of this research by saying that he had thought it would permit him to clarify the relations between sensible knowledge and the intellect. What he discovered, however, was that while certain advances can be pointed to in neurophysiology that have produced suggestive directions for future experimen-

[6]On the imposing figure of Brunschwicg see Merleau-Ponty's own recollections in "La Philosophie de l'existence," *Dialogue* 5,3 (December 1966), 307–322. "Vers 1930 quand je finissais mes études de philosophie, . . . on peut dire que deux influences, et deux seulment étaient dominates, et encore la premiere des deux est-elle beaucoup plus importante. La plus importante des pensées philosophiques de l'époque en France était celle de Léon Brunschwicg. . . . Il était, parmi nous étudiants, absolument célébre et á bon droit . . . " (p. 308).

[7]From Gurvitch's Sorbonne lectures on contemporary German philosophy (Husserl, Lask, and Heidegger) in 1928, 1929, and 1930 as well as the four conferences given by Husserl himself in February of 1929 entitled "Einleitung in die transzendentale Phaenomenologie," *Husserliana* l, pp. 3–39.

[8]That the period between 1933–1934 was decisivie vis-á-vis Husserl's influence on Merleau-Ponty can be inferred from the fact that no reference to Husserl is contained in "Projet," while the philosophical section of "Nature" is concerned solely with Husserl.

tation, there is still little in the way of specialized research that could support the contention that brain physiology can render comprehensible the psychology of perception. All that one can conclude from the present research is that (a) these studies lend no support to a psychology that would make of normal perception either a brute given (*une donée brute*) or an entirely mental activity ("Nature," p.2); and (b) the first task for psychopathology is to give morbid behavior exact description; this description must precede interpretations in terms of supposed physiological mechanisms.[9]

b) PHILOSOPHY OF PERCEPTION

Merleau-Ponty begins this section by remarking that it has become increasingly clearer that the eludication of problems related to the psychology of perception can be accomplished only by recourse to a *philosophy* of perception. Psychologists continually introduce notions (e.g., "sensations," "mental images," "the understanding,") that appear to be innocent enough but that are, on reflection, highly charged with philosophical presuppositions. He finds it necessary, therefore, to dedicate a certain amount of attention to seeking a philosophy that meets two essential criteria: (a) it must provide a viable way for demarcating between philosophy and psychology; and (b) it must allow for reciprocal influence between the two disciplines. It is in this context that the phenomenology of Husserl recommends itself.[10]

According to Merleau-Ponty that which allows Husserl to establish a clear distinction between phenomenological analyses of perception and psychological analyses is Husserl's continued insistence on the "reduction," by which one passes from the natural attitude, which is the attitude of all the positive sciences, to the transcendental attitude, which is proper to phenomenology ("Nature," p.3). But it is important to note that Husserl does not stop here. He goes on to give an example of a psychological analysis of perception as well as phenomenological analyses; and he shows that phenomenological analyses are not without consequences for psychological analysis, although neither can ever replace the other.

What Merleau-Ponty finds compelling in the Husserlian frame-

---

[9]This thesis was developed by Gelb and Goldstein in their classical treatise, *Psychologische Analysen Hirnpathologischer Faelle* (Leipzig: J. A. Barth, 1920).

[10]It is interesting that of the numerous articles and books cited under this section, all save one are by phenomenologists and all save one are by German philosophers. The single exception is M. Pradine, *Philosophie de la sensation* (Paris: Les Belles Lettres, 1932). No reference is made in this document to the Anglo-American realists referred to in "Projet."

work is that it can meet two essential criteria mentioned above. It allows for a clear demarcation between the eidetic method and the inductive, or experimental, method and it does this without ever contesting the legitimacy of the experimental method. At the same time the framework can renew psychology on its own proper terrain by providing analyses that determine the often obscure meanings of such essential structures as "representations" and "memory."[11] One could even claim that phenomenology has itself inspired important experimental research and that it leads more or less directly to an acceptance of Gestalt Theory.[12]

All of the above considerations led Merleau-Ponty to conclude the summary of this area of research by remarking that the scant attention that phenomenology has received in France is regrettable for the following reason. Phenomenology and the psychology that it inspires can help in the revision of the very important notions of consciousness and sensation, both of which are crucial to an adequate understanding of perception.

c) PSYCHOLOGY OF PERCEPTION

This part of the report is concerned with a summary and critique of recent experimental studies carried on by Gestalt psychologists in Germany. While there are a number of interesting points listed in the three earlier sections of this part, we will restrict our attention to a few comments of a general character that Merleau-Ponty makes at the outset and then turn to Section 4, which is concerned with the relations between Gestalt psychology and the theory of knowledge.

In the area of psychology of perception, Merleau-Ponty clearly thinks a decisive juncture has been precipitated by Gestalt research

[11]Merleau-Ponty cites in this context two works by Linke. The first is an article entitled "Phänomenologie und Experiment in der Frage der Bewegungsauffassung," *Jahrbuch für Philosophie und phänomenologische Forschung* 2 (1966), 1–20, which is concerned with representational consciousness; the second is a lengthy study of memory, entitled *Grundfragen der Warnehmungslehre* (München, 1918).

[12]This last point has its clearest and most sustained development in the work of Aron Gurwitsch, cf. especially Chapters 1, 2, 10, and 15 of *Studies in Phenomenology and Psychology* (Evanston: Northwestern University Press, 1966). In Chapter 4, "The Phenomenological and the Psychological Approach to Conciousness" (pp. 89–106), for example, Gurwitsch argues "One of the fundamental principles of Gestalt Theory, *viz., the dismissal of the constancy hypothesis*, lends itself to a phenomenological interpretation by means of which it may be disclosed as *an incipient phenomenological reduction*" (p. 90). One could argue that Gurwitsch's approach to the relationship between phenomenology and Gestalt theory, especially as seen in his "Quelques aspects et quelques développements de la psychologie de la forme," which was given as a lecture in 1933 in Paris and which Merleau-Ponty helped prepare for reading in French, serves as an excellent introduction to Merleau-Ponty's own development of this topic.

and by experimentation. In overthrowing the constancy hypothesis, Gestalt theory requires that we reject both the notion that sensations are "brute givens" of consciousness as well as the notion that perception is an intellectual activity—with the ancillary notion of the matter-form distinction. Because there is never in perception a matter without a form, but only more or less stable and more or less articulated organized wholes, the future of the psychology of perception lies not in atomistic analyses of sensations or bare impressions but in a progressively richer analysis of the basic "figure-ground" structure of perception. Everyday perception can no longer be thought of as a passive reception of impressions that are automatically, or mechanically, associated by the cerebral cortex before being presented to a mind for interpretation. Rather, it must be recognized as a spontaneous organization of a sensory field based on relations that are lived and seen rather than conceived ("Nature," pp. 4–5).

Following a sketchy outline of developments in Gestalt research concerning perception of space and motion and a brief section on developmental psychology, Merleau-Ponty concludes this document on the following note: Gestalt psychology presents a new notion of consciousness that has important consequences for a theory of sensible knowledge. But these consequences are still badly sifted out within Gestalt circles where this question receives little attention. One still finds, for example, Gestalt theorists adopting an attitude common to all psychologies: that there is a world of things and another world of immanent conscious acts. Furthermore, there is an effort to explain organization or structuration of consciousness by an appeal to physiological phenomena, the very existence of which this theory has in other respects so strongly contested. Because of this confusion within Gestalt theory, the problem of knowledge is still often posed in the same terms in which Kant poses it. For Mealeau-Ponty this shows that Gestalt theorists have simply not understood the significance of their own breakthroughs, for it is in and through a very difficult formulation of the problem of knowledge that we must turn our attention if we seek a satisfactory solution ("Nature," p. 8).[13]

While one must approach documents of the kind represented by

---

[13]Chapters 3 and 4 of *The Structure of Behavior* constitute Merleau-Ponty's first sustained effort at *reformulating*, in non-Kantian terms, the problem of knowledge. It is not accidental that this reformulation in initiated with a critique of Gestalt theory (*SC*, pp. 140–147; *SB*, pp. 131–137).

"Projet" and "Nature" with caution because they are explicitly tentative and all the more so because they were never intended for publication, we have chosen to treat them since one finds here themes quite relevant to our understanding of *The Structure of Behavior*. Six themes, or "suggestions" stand out in reading these two documents:

1. The author's conclusion that there is no *experimental* basis for supposing that the psychology of perception can be replaced by brain neurophysiology, or indeed for supposing that physiology can ever be fully conceptualized without employing concepts that are properly psychological.
2. The author's insistence, following Gelb and Goldstein, that no claims can be made for explaining normal behavior by reference to pathology or by reference to supposed physiological mechanisms until we can establish on a solid base a properly objective way of *describing* both normal and pathological behavior.
3. The author's insistence that there are good reasons for supposing that we must look for a kind of reciprocal development in philosophy and psychology with respect to theories or perception as well as his suggestion, following Husserl, that we can locate the distinction between the two disciplines in terms of methodology and "attitude."
4. The author's conclusion that there are fundamental problems in the psychology of perception that require the kind of reformulation and clarification that philosophy alone can and must provide.[14]
5. The author's suggestion that phenomenology can make, in a way that remains to be clarified, significant contributions to a psychology of perception and a theory of knowledge.
6. The author's insistence that Gestalt psychology has decisively undercut both the empiricist and intellectualist theories of perception—though this fact is unrecognized by Gestalt theorists themselves.

These six themes represent the essence of the philosophy-science nexus in Merleau-Ponty's earliest work.

---

[14]This seems to be so for two reasons: conceptually, because psychology must employ basic, descriptive concepts that are unavoidably charged with philosophical meaning; theoretically, because psychological genesis poses transcendental problems (i.e., a complete and accurate account of human behavior is possible only in a context that clarifies how human consciousness constitutes the behavioral environment according to its a priori structures).

PART TWO

The treatment of *The Structure of Behavior* that follows is guided by the belief that conventional scholarship has failed thus far to provide a detailed treatment of Merleau-Ponty's interest in, and indebtedness to, scientific research. His philosophical purposes, development, and priorities are somewhat obscured if we fail to see that *The Structure of Behavior* is, in large part, a series of intrascientific critiques; an introduction to a philosophy of scientific consciusness; and an attempt to *show*, rather than merely assert, that the relationship between scientific research and philosophical investigation can and must be a relation of reciprocal influence.

Proceeding by way of an investigation of what is called the book's "underlying organization" to a recasting of its argumentation, we shall attempt to show that the author was entirely serious when he claimed in his conclusion to Chapter 3 that "we have pretended to know nothing more about consciousness than was implicit in a scientific representation of behavior" (*SC*, p. 199; *SB*, p. 184).

The scientific study of behavior is decisive for Merleau-Ponty's replacement of the problem of the relationship between consciousness and nature with what will become the problem of perceptual consciousness. Merleau-Ponty believed that the former problem cannot be resolved or even adequately formulated until we reconsider the meaning of "objectivity," particularly scientific objectivity.

1. THE UNDERLYING ORGANIZATION

In his "introduction," Merleau-Ponty informs us that his goal is to understand the relationship between consciousness and nature but that this task is complicated by well-known disputes in the French philosophic and scientific communities with respect to determining the meaning of the two terms involved. A main focus of this dispute stems from the efforts to guarantee "objectivity" in designating the appropriate meaning of the two terms. Rather than resolving the issue, however, this search for objectivity has itself become extremely problematic. In the face of this, Merleau-Ponty insists that we must approach these issues "from below" (i.e., we must proceed in a methical, descriptive fashion investigating behavior as it is perceived in its progressively complex forms—physical, organic, psychological, social, etc.—all the while being on guard lest gratuitous assumptions or hypotheses be introduced). This procedure will be facilitated by adopting the term "behavior," since this term is neutral with respect to the classical distinction between the "mental" and the "physical" and it is employed by both the scientific and philosophic communities. The suggestion is that in proceeding in this way we can come to grips with the issue of "objectivity" and at the same time seek grounds for integrative dialogue between philosophers and scientists in answering the question concerning consciousness and nature.

Having given this general indication of his intentions Merleau-Ponty in opening Chapter 1, proceeds, to list a series of questions, three of which are especially crucial because they determine to a large extent the preoccupations of the first three chapters of *The Structure of Behavior*. He asks first whether or not the classical theory of the reflex is alone capable of constructing an objective and scientific representation of behavior. Secondly, he asks, "Has not mechanistic science misconstrued objectivity?" Thirdly he asks, "Can realistic, causal thought be amended or must we introduce instead a wholly new kind of analysis?"

Chapters 1 and 2 of the book together form the author's response to the first and second of these questions. Chapter 3 is Merleau-Ponty's response to the third question. What binds these three chapters together in a special way and sets them off from Chapter 4 is the author's continued emphasis on scientific, as distinct from philosophic, considerations. In these first three chapters we can discern two quasi-separable routes of analysis. The first, found in Chapters 1 and 2, is chiefly *intrascientific*. Most of the discussion here has to do with experimental studies and their accompanying problems of interpretation, methods, and so on. The second "route" is again concerned with scientific considerations but now at a level further removed. Here we find in broad outlines, a *philosophy* of science, or an analysis of scientific consciousness. This second route forms a bridge between the two early chapters and Chapter 4, where the focus is exclusively philosophical.

In Chapter 4 we see the author trying to situate the results of his prior analyses on a philosophical plane. His chief concern here is to show that a solution to the problem posed by classical modern philosophy—the problem of relationship between consciousness and nature—must await a deeper philosophical reflection on and clarification of the structure of consciousness itself.

1. We must discover how the intersubjective world is grasped through the field of lived perception, which is in a significant sense prior to conceptual or intellectual consciousness and is given only through a series of "profiles" (*SC*, pp. 235–236; *SB*, pp. 219–220).

2. We must formulate a notion of consciousness that surmounts the well-known contradiction that on the one hand consciousness appears as only a part of the world and on the other hand to be co-extensive with the world (*SC*, p. 232; *SB*, p. 215).

3. We must develop a method that allows us to formulate a theory of the intentional levels of consciousness in such a way that we can affirm the specificity of perceptual consciousness without rendering inconceivable its relation to conceptual consciousness (*SC*, p. 240; *SB*, p. 224).

2. DECISIVE STAGES OF THE ARGUMENTATION

An important consideration that must be addressed if we are to arrive at acceptable meanings for the terms "consciousness" and "nature" is the concern for guaranteeing objectivity. Merleau-Ponty recognizes that many contemporary thinkers take it as axiomatic that if there is to be objectivity in the analysis of behavior, this analysis must be founded on the classical theory of the reflex. The following passage from Bechterev's *General Principles of Human Reflexology* is representative in this regard:

> The study of subjective or conscious processes, which we discover in ourselves by introspection of self-observation . . . can nowise be regarded as a branch of natural science, for in any science the method of investigation is primary, and the method of natural science has hitherto been strictly objective. . . . Therefore, it may be said with certainty that the real—that is, the natural—scientific—study of human personality begins only when we introduce here a completely objective method, which gives reflexology its motivation as the science of the objective-biological study of human personality in the social environment. . . . The universe develops, changes continuously, and, at the same time, conforms to eternal, fundamental laws valid for the whole universe and each part of it. . . . That is the conclusion to which reflexology recognizes no independent study of the subjective side of man, unless objective data are taken into account.[15]

This approach troubles Merleau-Ponty for two basic reasons: (a) because this objective approach defines itself in opposition to "the givens of naive consciousness"; and (b) because it creates a vicious dichotomy between the universe of science and the universe of consciousness (even the consciousness of the scientists themselves!) so that each is sealed off entirely from the other. As a consequence of this thrust of objective analysis, science for Merleau-Ponty can no

---

[15]This is taken from the "Preface" to the second edition of V. M. Bechterev, *General Principles of Human Reflexology* (New York: International Publishers, 1932), pp. 19-21.

longer make sense of the experience either of the scientist or of human perceivers in general. This approach settles the question of the relations between consciousness and nature by assuming that it is simply that of part to whole. But this is done in an unsettling way because it implies that all true meaningfulness is that which is generated by and through our special and general scientific, methodological imperatives. The early stages of Merleau-Ponty's argumentation are addressed, then, to show why and how we can and must reject the dogmatism of objectivist analyses.

The first decisive stage in the author's argumentation is clarified if we consider the following quotation:

> It is clearly evident that, in speaking of a response "adapted" to the stimulus or of a succession of coherent movements, we are expressing relationships conceived by our mind, a comparison made by the mind between the "meaning" of the stimulus and that of the reaction, between the "total" meaning of the response and the partial movements which compose it (*SC*, p. 52; *SB*, p. 49).

The effect of this proposition is to show that, following a necessary "conceptual reform," when we speak of stimuli and response in a way that is descriptively accurate with respect to scientific observation, we are obviously expressing relationships conceived by our minds. What is essential here is the following: (a) the basic terms of reflex analysis ("stimulus," "response," "reflex circuit," etc.) are *essentially* mind-relational; (b) the meaning of behavior, far from being something that we must banish from scientific discourse, is the only conceivable foundation for science; (c) only a distorted and unreal notion of "objectivity" could carry with it a demand that we abandon "meanings"; and (d) we cannot rely on the form of analysis suggested by classical reflex theory if we want to validly clarify that which has been called "the cleavage between the subjective and the objective."

In Chapter 2, we find Merleau-Ponty continuing the above mentioned themes but now in relation to scientific studies of "higher behavior." A second decisive stage of the argumentation can be discerned in the section entitled "Proposal for Conceptual Reform," which immediately follows Merleau-Ponty's summary of contemporary research on the topics of spatial and chromatic perception and the physiology of language. The second stage is clarified if we turn our attention to those sections of *The Structure of Behavior* wherein we find articulated the following themes: (a) we must distinguish in scientific analysis between the "stimulus-in-itself" and its "presence-for-the-organism" if we want to account for the *de facto* elaboration of the world which effective behavior exhibits; (b) it is not the "real world" that constitutes the perceived world; (c) the living physiology of the nervous system can be understood only if we start with the phenomenal given; and (d) a physiological analysis of perception can never, *in principle*, be complete (*SC*, pp. 94–97; *SB*, pp. 88–92). What is decisive about these propositions is their import with respect to the notions of "objectivity," "behavior," and "realistic thought."

Concerning "objectivity," Merleau-Ponty feels that we can now conclude the following. An accurate description of the behavior of organisms indicates quite clearly that spatial and temporal relations are important at each level — syncretic, amovable, and symbolic — but that at each level they have a distinctively different meaning. It is only through an unwarranted form of anthropomorphic thought, then, that scientists attempt to constuct explanations of all forms of vital behavior in terms of the pure categories of "space," "time," and "relations." These categories have *objective* meaning only in relation to, and derived solely from, that structuration of the world that is properly and uniquely human. These categories are thoroughly "intellectual," and it is only anthropomorphically that we can construct the milieu of vital organisms out of them. Objectivity in scientific thought seems to have been fundamentally misconstrued by both empiricists and intellectualists insofar as they have tried to carry over into primitive modes of behavior structures that belong to a high level of abstractive thought.

Concerning "behavior," Merleau-Ponty feels that we must recognize that it cannot be conceptualized either as a thing (*en soi*) or as an idea-for-a-consciousness. Thus it cannot be incorporated simply as a part on the side either of "nature" or of "consciousness." It can be conceptualized only as a form, or concrete structure, though it remains to be shown precisely how this can be done. It is clear at this point, however, that the traditional analysis of behavior into "lower" and "higher" varieties needs to be fundamentally revised or rejected. Behavior is not a thing-in-itself but the projection outside of the organism of a possibility that is internal to it: it is a way of treating the world, of being-in-the-world, of existing (*SC*, p. 138; *SB*, p. 127).

Concerning "realistic" thought in general, Merleau-Ponty feels that the following comments are now in order. If it is the case that the orders of the "in-itself" and the "for itself" have as their loci of intelligibility the abstract realm of mathematical physics and the field of human intentionality, and if it is the case that we find relations of pure juxtaposition and pure interiority only at the level of symbolic conduct, then it is clear that these constructs of scientific and philosophic consciousness cannot be construed as constitutive of the organic milieu. These constructs are useful and necessary significations, but their legitimate signification is restricted to the context, scientific or philosophic, wherein they arise. They do not uncover the character of a reality-in-itself but rather the peculiar structure of scientific or philosophic behavior (i.e., the way human consciousness articulates itself in its various conceptual modes). These considerations strongly suggest that neither mentalistic nor materialistic realism can provide an adequate conceptual framework for the comprehension of behavior. For Merleau-Ponty a considera-tion of behavior in its unity and meaning calls into question realistic thought itself.[16]

What determines the character of the third stage of the argumen-tation is Merleau-Ponty's assessment of the failure, on the part of Gestalt theorists, to realize that which is entailed in a correct under-standing of the "theory of forms." We can summarize Merleau-Ponty's thoughts on this matter in the following way:

Thesis One: In a philosophy that would genuinely renounce the notion of substance, there could only be one uni-verse—the universe of form (*SC*, p. 144; *SB*, pp. 133–34).

Thesis Two: There can be no question of supposing any relation of derivation or causality between the various orders (*SC*, p. 144; *SB*, p. 134).

Thesis Three: In reality, matter, life, and mind must be understood as three orders of significations (*SC*, p. 147; *SB*, p. 137).

Merleau-Ponty's treatment of the three "orders" (physical, vital, and human) represents his effort to provide justification for the claim that the accurate description of scientific consciousness sup-ports and demands a noetic interpretation rather than a realistic one.[17] The main point that ought to be stressed here is that the

[16]There is considerable difficulty in making precise Merleau-Ponty's use of the terms "realism" and "realistic thought." It seems clear that in Chapters 2 and 3 of *The Structure of Behavior* these terms are almost synonomous with that which we might designate as any form of substantist theories, whether metaphysical or scientific. "Realism" takes on a more restricted meaning in Chapter 4.

[17]Merleau-Ponty attempts to justify the claim by showing how the notion of "form" can play a positive role in scientific analysis in physics, biology, and psychology. See especially his treatment of scientific objects as "concrete structures" or "concrete totalities" grasped through "ideal unities of signification" in three orders: physical (*SB*, pp. 143–145; *SC*, pp. 155–157), vital (*SB*, pp. 153–159; *SC*, pp. 166–172), and human (*SB*, pp. 180–184; *SC*, pp. 195–198).

primary task for a philosophy seeking objective foundations is to inquire into the character of "phenomena" as they are present in scientific awareness.[18] In other words, we must investigate consciousness itself as the ground of our knowledge. Rather than defining the physical, the vital, and the human as so many "realities" that together comprise "nature" Merleau-Ponty directs us toward a view in which external experience is that of a multiplicity of structures that can be comprehended and analyzed only in relation to the intentional character of human consciousness.[19]

What is necessary as a next stage, then, is an accurate, descriptive account of perceptual consciousness that, clarifying how phenomena are constituted by and for us, allows us to address the problem of the relationship between consciousness and nature. But it is at precisely this point that contemporary philosophy fails us:

> Philosophy does not possess an idea of consciousness and an idea of action which would make an internal communication between them possible . . . perception and action taken in that which is specific to them, that is, as the knowledge and modification of reality are rejected from consciousness (*SC*, p. 177; *SB*, p. 164).

To remedy this situation the author provides a brief descriptive outline of nascent perception from the point of view of an outside spectator.[20] This descriptive outline allowed Merleau-Ponty to draw out two sets of consequences, those for philosophy and those for psychology, which introduce the fourth decisive stage of his argumentation. Before considering the "consequences" let us note carefully that which the author finds crucial in the context of the descriptive account.

That which is crucial is that it is impossible to find exhibited in nascent perception any grounds for the classical distinction between sensible content and a priori form.[21] Instead what one finds are certain "material *a prioris*."[22] Merleau-Ponty cites as evidence in this

---

[18]The term "phenomena" is progressively clarified: *SC*, pp. 172, 215, 221, and 241; *SB*, pp. 159, 199, 205, and 224.

[19]See in this connection *SC*, pp. 156, 172, and 198; *SB*, pp. 144, 159, and 184.

[20]This first descriptive account of nascent perception (*SB*, pp. 166ff; *SC*, pp. 185ff) is from the point of view of an outside spectator. The second account (*SB*, pp. 185ff; *SC*, pp. 200ff) is from the interior of consciousness.

[21]This distinction is a secondary, or derived, one, which is applicable only to certain instances in the universe of natural objects constituted by adult consciousness.

[22]See *SB*, pp. 171–172, and 186. The term "material *a prioris*" is taken from Scheler, "Der Formalismus in der Ethik und die Materiale Werthethik," *Jahrbuch für Philosophie und phänomenologische Forschung* 1–2 (Halle: M. Niemayer, 1927), though it is used with a wider scope than Scheler himself suggests including the structure "expression-expressed" and "alter-ego" (i.e., linguistic consciousness and intersubjective consciousness, as well the moral consciousness (*sittliches Erfassen*) of Scheler.

context two important behavior patterns observable in infantile perception:

> ... child psychology precisely proposes the enigma of a linguistic consciousness and a consciousness of others which is almost pure and which is prior to that of sonorous and visual phenomena. . . . Speech and other persons, therefore, cannot derive their meaning from a systematic interpretation of sensory phenomena and the "multiple given." They are indecomposable structures and in that sense are *a prioris* (*SC*, p. 186; *SB*, pp. 171–172).

The reference to "material *a prioris*" is an attempt to account for that in infantile behavior by virtue of which the child is capable of responding to language (the structure "expression-expressed") and other persons (the structure "alter-ego") in a way that suggests the apprehension of an irreducible unity of meaning through visual, tactile, and sonorous phenomena. On the basis of these behavior patterns that accurate scientific description seems to uncover, Merleau-Ponty concludes that that which is necessary is a reformulation of the notion of consciousness.

The articulation of this reformulation in a series of psychological and philosophical consequences constitutes the fourth decisive stage of the author's argumentation, and the most significant aspect of this stage, for our purpose, is that it introduces into perceptual consciousness the distinction between the lived and the known.[23] Merleau-Ponty asserts that there is discoverable in infantile perception an active structuring of phenomena that cannot be attributed either to the activity of an epistemological subject in the intellectualists' sense or to the associating capacity postulated by empiricism. Just as we have discovered and described species-specific structurations in the scientific study of subhuman behavior, so now we can identify and describe structurations of the perceptual given which seem to be distinctively human. These structurations — "expression-expressed" and "alter-ego" — provide a major impetus for the formulation of a new notion of consciousness.

Whereas stage three of the argumentation showed that the concept of nature must be fundamentally revised, it is the thrust of stage four to show how and why the concept of consciousness must be

---

[23] It is important to note that it is precisely this extension of the notion of consciousness that allows us to relate consciousness to action. The distinction between the lived and the known and the inclusion of both in consciousness is decisive for Merleau-Ponty. Zaner quite rightly emphasizes the significance of this distinction in Merleau-Ponty's thought in *The Problem of Embodiment* (The Hague: Martinus Nijhoff, 1964), p. 154 but it is unclear how Zaner reconciles his statement that "Merleau-Ponty is unwilling to accept any notion of 'constitution' at the level of the body-proper," (p. 135) with the texts that we are presently considering.

treated likewise. At the base of these last two stages has been the author's insistence that we shift the priority of philosophical investigation. In stage three it was asserted that the primary task is not to construct "nature" out of those objects of analysis to which the sciences give special attention and meaning but to inquire into the character of phenomena of scientific consciousness. Thus there has been suggested a conceptual shift from ontological considerations to noetic-noematic analysis. In stage four the author argues that if we are to develop a notion of consciousness that has as a minimal qualification for acceptance the character of descriptive accuracy, we must:

> . . . stop defining consciousness by knowledge of self and introduce the notion of a life of consciousness which goes beyond explicit knowledge of itself . . . as well as describe the structure of action and knowledge in which consciousness is engaged (*SC*, p. 178; *SB*, p. 164).

Thus we discover at stage four as well a suggestion for a conceptual shift—from a single-minded preoccupation with the epistemological subject to a fuller consideration of the diversity of perceptual modes of lived engagement.

The view of "nature" that emerges is that of a multiplicity of "orders" (physical, vital, and human) of significations, the understanding of which is grounded in an analysis of scientific consciousness. The view of "consciousness" that emerges is that of a multiplicity of intentional levels and perceptual modes, some of which are primary and some of which are derived. The decisive questions for the next two stages of the argumentation should now be clear. The author must attempt to show (a) how he can positively conceive the relations between "orders," and (b) how we can positively conceive the relations between intentional levels of consciousness. These two concerns determine respectively the final two stages of the argumentation in *The Structure of Behavior*.

In stage five, Merleau-Ponty addresses the problem of the relations between orders in the following manner. He argues that that which we have uncovered in the analysis of orders are the forms of unity of behavior, not material or mental realities-in-themselves. Behavior in its unity and meaning of conduct is the only physical, biological, or psychological "reality" of which we can properly speak. We must acknowledge then, that behavior is a structure that belongs neither to the external world (i.e., nature-in-itself as *omnitudo realitatis*) nor to internal life (i.e., simply an idea for a consciousness). We must acknowledge, too, that the "external world" is conceivable only as a horizon for the totality of objects of consciousness and that "internal life" is inconceivable outside the concrete situations in which it is embodied.

The significance of these observations can be summarized in the following way. We can no longer treat the relations between orders as relations between substances. We must substitute a philosophy of form for a philosophy of substance and develop a *purely structural* conception of the relations between orders. Above all, we must recognize that the human order of consciousness does not appear as a third order superimposed on the others but as the condition of their possibility and their foundation. And finally, we must give priority to the kind of philosophical investigation that aims at clarifying the relations between intentional structures of perceptual consciousness since this clarification must precede any effort to construct an objective ontology.

The sixth decisive stage of the argumentation bears precisely on this last issue of how we can develop an adequate understanding of perceptual consciousness, and the first thing of importance is Merleau-Ponty's suggestion that the point of view of the "outside spectator" must be abandoned now, and we must seek a point of view somehow at the interior of consciousness (*SC*, pp. 214–215; *SB*, p. 199). The author states that up till now the argumentation has pretended to know nothing more about consciousness than was implicit in a scientific representation of behavior. Accordingly, consciousness has been treated only as "a region of being," or as a particular type of behavior.[24] The claim is now made that, if we are to truly comprehend perceptual consciousness in its immediacy, we must seek the benefits of an unconditional type of reflection (i.e., we must return to objects as they appear to us when we live among them without speech) (*SC*, p. 200; *SB*, p. 185). This is the only way that we can faithfully represent direct experience, and Merleau-Ponty's suggestion here is that we must give a kind of absolute primacy to that which is revealed by a descriptive account of naive or immediate perceptual consciousness.

That which we take to be the sixth stage of Merleau-Ponty's argumentation is his effort to show that if we are to remain faithful to the phenomena of naive or immediate consciousness, we must introduce as *fundamental* in our analysis the distinction between the

---

[24]These last comments represent our effort at clarifying what we take to be the *methodological* significance of Merleau-Ponty's "Conclusion" at the end of Chapter 3 (cf. *SB*, p. 184; *SC*, p. 199) as well as his comments at the end of the section in Chapter 4, concerned with "The Classical Solutions" (*SB*, p. 199; *SC*, p. 214).

lived and the known. This is necessary because we must distinguish between our *knowing about* the world and our *perception* of it. The perceptual consciousness of the "lived world as existing" is distinct from the intellectual consciousness of the "world as object of an infinity of true judgments." This is not to say that the "world" in the second sense in unperceived but that it is constituted in a fundamentally different way. The sensible mass in which we live, the "this" that our consciousness wordlessly intends, is not yet a pure signification or an idea—although it can serve, subsequently, as a base for acts of logical explication and verbal expression—but a concrete structure. We must acknowledge, then, a duality internal to perceptual consciousness and distinguish within consciousness itself "a region of individual perspectives" and a "region of intersubjective significations" (*SC*, pp. 231–232; *SB*, pp. 214–115).

That which is crucial for philosophy in this context is that it cease attempting to explain perception either as an event of nature or as a function of an "epistemological subject." The essential points here are:

1. It is no longer possible to define it (consciousness) as a universal function for the organization of experience which would impose on all its objects the conditions of logical and physical existence which are those of a universe of articulated objects and which owes its specifications only to the variety of its contents (*SC*, p. 186; *SB*, p. 172).
2. There will be sectors of experience which are irreducible to each other (*SC*, p. 186; *SB*, p. 172).
3. It is no longer possible to found all relations on the activity of the "epistemological subject"; at the same time that the perceived world is divided into discontinuous "regions," consciousness is divided into acts of consciousness of different types . . . there must be several ways for consciousness to intend its object and several sorts of intentions in it (*SC*, pp. 186–87; *SB*, p. 172).
4. To possess and contemplate a "representation" and to coordinate a mosaic of sensations—these are special attitudes which cannot account for all the life of consciousness and which probably apply to its more primitive modes (*SC*, p. 187; *SB*, p. 172).

To show that this is the case, Merleau-Ponty introduces two themes: (a) *perception can be understood only as a dialectical relation* (*SC*, p. 221; *SB*, p. 205); and (b) the major problem to which philosophy must address itself is that of the problematic structure of consciousness. It is clear to Merleau-Ponty that having come all this way we still face the problem of understanding:

> the lived relation of the "profiles" to the "things" which they present, of the perspectives to the ideal significations which are intended through them (*SC*, p. 237; *SB*, p. 220).

In short, we still face the task of clarifying the relations between intentional levels of perceptual consciousness. To complete this task, we must face and overcome the following major obstacle: it may turn out that our lived relations cannot be adequately grasped in, or expressed by, the ideal significations, which are constituted by, and proper to, intellectual consciousness.[25] Only through an attempt to trace the reflexive passage from immediate perceptual consciousness to intellectual consciousness can we hope to overcome this obstacle and settle the following question:

> Can one conceptualize perceptual consciousness without eliminating it as an original mode; can one maintain its specificity without rendering inconceivable its relation to intellectual consciousness? (*SC*, p. 241; *SB*, p. 224)[26]

In posing the last question, the argumentation of *The Structure of Behavior* ceases. No answer is provided in the 1938 work. Instead of an answer to the initial question of the relationship between consciousness and nature, we find the initial question profoundly transformed. Merleau-Ponty's response to the *new* question, "How can we clarify the relations between intentional levels of perceptual consciousness?" must be sought in his later works.

---

[25] Merleau-Ponty poses this obstacle in the following way: "Le passage réflexif á la conscience intellectuelle est-il une adéquation de notre savoir á notre être, ou seulement une maniére pour la conscience de se créer une existence séparée,—un quiétisme?" (*SC*, p. 240).

[26] To grasp the full import of this part of the question it must be recalled that the author has previously warned against confusing immediate consciousness with verbalized accounts of it, and has insisted that the distinction between direct perception and verbal account remain valid even if linguistic consciousness is in some sense underived or *a priori* (*SB*, pp. 185, and 246, footnote 1; *SC*, p. 200).

STEPHEN H. WATSON

TEN

MERLEAU-PONTY'S INVOLVEMENT
WITH SAUSSURE

I.

THIS PAPER WILL BE AN ATTEMPT to explicate Merleau-Ponty's work with Saussure's paradigm in linguistics. This is a paradigm with which he was increasingly occupied as his career progressed and which had, it shall be argued, considerable impact on both the form and substance of his later thought. This paper, however, will not involve first and foremost an attempt to judge Merleau-Ponty as a linguist, since his use of this model was not ultimately to be confined to the field of linguistics. Nor, for much the same reason, can it be an investigation of whether or not his use of the Saussurian text was a "faithful" one. While this writer thinks, as is indicated in passing, that there is a sense in which these issues can still be answered in a positive fashion, I shall be concerned here with tracing a path of enquiry that opens up in the *oeuvre merleau-pontyenne* in the middle forties and culminates in his final writings—a matter that consequently necessitates rather close attention to the texts themselves.

In the eighteen or so years since Merleau-Ponty's death, the name of Saussure has stood at the center of French thought. The works of the leading figures in this *theatrum philosophicum*, Foucault, Derrida, Barthes, Ricoeur, Kristeva, Lyotard, et al. have constantly revolved around issues germinated in Saussure's *Course in General Linguistics*[1], a work that, prior to these events, remained relatively unnoticed beyond the confines of linguistics. It has since been suggested that the *Course* accomplishes no less than the founding of the first real science in the murky set of disciplines that have been netted together

---

[1]Ferdinand de Saussure, *Course in General Linguistics*, ed. Charles Bally and Albert Sechehaye in collaboration with Albert Riedlinger, trans. Wade Baskin (New York: McGraw-Hill, 1959). Cited hereafter as *Course*.

in the domain of the "human sciences"—hence accomplishing a feat no less revolutionary than the events that have been tied to the name of Galileo in the natural sciences. What remains incontravertible, however, is the fact that the Saussurian text has stood pivotally involved in the contemporary problematics and polemics of the later developments of phenomenology and that which has come to be known as structuralism and now post-structuralism.

II.

Merleau-Ponty's work with Saussure begins as early as a decade before the high tide of these contemporary trends and, as Roland Barthes has noted in his 1964 book, *Elements of Semiology*, his work represents "probably one of the first French philosophers to become interested in Saussure."[2] The recognition of Saussure's importance can be traced to divergent sources during this period, to such areas as anthropology and the work of Claude Lèvi-Strauss and to psychoanalysis and the work of Jacques Lacan. In philosophy, however, Merleau-Ponty presents us with the first work in which Saussure's position is seen to be of fundamental and *general* theoretical significance.

Nonetheless this recognition in Merleau-Ponty's work was not one that stood constantly at the center of his philosophical concerns. Indeed no explicit reference is made to Saussure—or to his work—prior to 1947. Prior to this time the more prominent references on the theory of langauge to be noted in his work include the Gelb-Goldstein research into pathology in psycholinguistics, Cassirer's 1934 article, "Le langage et la constitution du monde des objets" (influential also for the early work of Lèvi-Strauss), and his *Philosophy of Symbolic Forms*, and the work of Piaget.[3] Yet at the same time it must likewise be said that by no means is Saussure totally absent during this period—notwithstanding that it is sometimes thought to be the case. Evidence of contact occurs, for instance, in Gurwitsch's reference to the Saussurian distinction between speech (*la parole*) and language (*la langue*) in a 1935 article on the psychology of lan-

[2] Roland Barthes, *Writing Degree Zero and Elements of Semiology*, trans. Annette Lavert and Colin Smith (Boston: Beacon Press, 1970), p. 24.

[3] Adhemar Gelb and Kurt Goldstein, *Über Farbennamenamnesie, Psychologische Forschung* (1925). Ernst Cassirer, "Le langage et la constitution du monde des objets," *Journal de Psychologie Normale et Pathologique* (January 1934); and *Philosophie der symbolischen Formen* (Berlin: Bruno Cassirer, 1929). Jean Piaget, *La représentation de monde chez l'enfant* (Paris: Alcan, 1926).

guage on which Merleau-Ponty assisted.[4] Further, Merleau-Ponty himself probably makes reference to this distinction in passing in his analysis in Chapter 6, "The Body as Expression, and Speech," of *Phenomenology of Perception:*

> It might be said, restating a celebrated distinction, that language (*langages*) or constituted systems of vocabulary and syntax, empirically existing 'means of expression,' are both the repository and residue of acts of speech (*parole*) in which unformulated significance not only finds the means of being conveyed outwardly, but moreover acquires significance for itself, and is genuinely created as significance (*PdP*, p. 229; *PoP*, p. 196).

Nonetheless, outside of this somewhat oblique reference, which is itself explicated in terms of the *parole parlant/parole parlée* distinction developed in this chapter, Saussure remains absent. Especially, it should be emphasized, the "diacritical theory of linguistic value," which arises in part II of the *Course* and which will later be taken to be almost synonymous with the Saussurian contribution, is by no means present.

III.

The first published discussion of Merleau-Ponty's work with Saussure occurs in the *Revue de Métaphysique et de Morale* in 1947, in an article that appeared likewise in *Sense and Non-Sense* as "The Metaphysical in Man." The form of this article itself, as shall be seen, is not unimportant for grasping the nature of the transition that Merleau-Ponty's work was undergoing at the time. It opens by mentioning the revolution wrought by Gestalt psychology in the human sciences. This revolution, it is claimed, is one that manifests a new metaphysical conception of man, one that emerges from a methodological basis that will be described a few years later as the "reciprocal envelopment of philosophy and science" (*Primacy*, p. 73). In a discussion of Koehler's work in animal psychology, Merleau-Ponty holds that what Gestalt theory has demonstrated is that we are excluded from the paradoxical attempt to "reject wholesale our human experience" (*SN*, p. 84) and separate "the radical subjectivity of all our experience from its truth value" (*SN*, p. 93). Behavioral processes are to be understood in terms of their internal organization instead of trying to find in them the results of an external combination of simple and universal processes. By so doing we are

---

[4]Aron Gurwitsch, "Psychologie de langage," *Revue Philosophique de la France et de l'Etranger*, Vol. LXX (1935), pp. 399–439.

led, it is claimed, beyond the classical dichotomies of subject and object, existence as thing and existence as consciousness, and invited to conceive knowledge in a new way—no longer as a way to break down these *typical* ensembles but rather as "an effort to embrace them and to understand them by reliving them" (*SN*, p. 86).

Nonetheless, as Merleau-Ponty proceeds to make clear, the advances in the human sciences in his opinion do not return us to the conceptual stronghold defended by classical rationalism. For example, with regard to that which is central to this domain, knowledge of "man by man," he states:

> The sciences of man—not to mention the others—have made it evident that all knowledge of man by man, far from being pure contemplation is the taking up by each . . . [and] appropriating a structure . . . of which he forms no concept. Here we no longer have the positing of an object, the universality of knowledge is no longer guaranteed in each by that stronghold of absolute consciousness in which the Kantian "I think" was assured of being identical to every other possible "I think" (*Sens*, pp. 162–163; *SN*, p. 93).

What appears here is not a thought that finds itself soaring over its objects in acts of pure constitution, but one that arises only insofar as it is always already 'in the world'—within the limitations of a personal and historical facticity. The advances in the human sciences, then, return us to the "originary" realm of lived experience. Moreover they make possible a "descriptive science" based on this realm. They do so, however, only at the cost of giving up the classical model.

What can be said about the role that linguistics, and Saussure's work in particular, plays in the revolution which has been discovered in Gestalt theory? Saussure is cited specifically for recognizing that the sort of being that language has is not susceptible to a causal analysis that would "link each fact with a previous fact and thus spread language before the linguist like a *natural object*" (*SN*, p. 87). Such a viewpoint would make language largely external, a mosaic of absolutely unmotivated facts. Rather, the precepts of objectivism and mechanism must be abandoned. Language has an organismic character, surrounding the speaking subject with an instrument having "its own inertia," its own demands, constraints, and internal logic. This 'logic' is one that each speaker is compelled to use but which remains to some extent open to his initiative. To this extent Merleau-Ponty states, "Saussure's linguistics legitimates the perspective of the speaking subject who lives in his language (and who may in some cases change it)" (*SN*, p. 87).

Nonetheless, it should be noted that this 1947 document, despite its overt reference to and affirmation of Saussure, makes little more use of the specificity of his paradigm than did the implicit statements of *Phenomenology of Perception*. The general significance of Saussure's diacritical theory of linguistic value, for example, for metaphysics itself—in this article focusing on this subject—is not an issue. Nor is the relationship between *la langue* and *la parole* seen to be applicable in any manner beyond the confines of linguistics. Rather, Saussure's work is seen as an example of the new developments in the human sciences, one whose importance receives secondary status in this domain—that of reinforcing that which had already been gleaned more primordially elsewhere, in Gestalt theory. It serves here, therefore, as a sort of principle of verification. Hence its introduction in the article:

> It goes without saying that the example of one school and a school about which there is still disagreement can prove nothing by itself. However, the work of the school would become significant if one could show that in general each of the sciences of man is oriented in its own way toward the revision of the subject-object relation. Now this is just what we note in linguistics (Sens, p. 151; SN, p. 86).

IV.

These extensions, finding a certain generality to the Saussurian paradigm, await later events. The initial moves extending the paradigm to fields beyond linguistics can be traced in the writings of the late forties and early fifties. Immediately following "The Metaphysical in Man" Saussure took on a role of increased importance in Merleau-Ponty's course work, first in his 1947–1948 course at Lyon entitled "Language and Communication," then in a 1948–1949 course presented at the École Normale Supérieure, entitled simply "Saussure." Although we lack Merleau-Ponty's course notes for these lectures, authenticated notes for the 1949–1950 lectures presented at the Sorbonne, "Consciousness and the Acquisition of Language," are available and are indicative of the altered and more prominent role given Saussure in his thought.

Consciousness and the Acquisition of Language presents us for the first time with an analysis of the Saussurian paradigm in its specificity. Language is essentially understood as a diacritical phenomenon; words are not to be taken as finite units of signification, the offspring of some sort of naming process or nomenclature (*CAL*, p. 96). The archetypal linguistic act is not that of a pure baptismal denotation in which pure thoughts are paired off with their objects. The power of language, as he was to put it shortly afterward, "does not reside in the *tête à tête* it conducts between our minds and things" (*Prose*, p. 58; *PW*, p. 41).

This attempt to plug thought directly into things longs, he says, for "a golden age of language in which words once adhered to the objects themselves" (*PW*, p. 6). Language here would be absolutely clear since thought is not left trailing behind a signification that transcends it. It would be the "double" of being; thought, the internal word, would be the standard for the external word. There would be nothing in language that the speaker did not put into it. Thought would escape the contingency, the mediation, the risk of the system of signs. It would be, therefore, a language more created than learned; and the result would be a system whose economics was rigorously delimited by its intentions and referents. Easily coupled with this view, moreover, is that of language as algorithm and the project of a universal language—transforming natural languages into homogeneous objects for thought. Here again, "in the purity of the algorithm, signification is disengaged from all interference with the unfolding of signs which it rules and legitimates" (*PW*, p. 121). Such a stance involves a revolt against the confusion and heterogeneity of everyday language, and hence against finitude. "In the name of this spiritual model human thought puts order into the chaos of historical languages" (*PW*, p. 5).

As the 1949–1950 course makes clear, however, words do not carry meaning as much as they separate themselves out from one another. "Each linguistic phenomenon is a differentiation of a global movement of communication" (*CAL*, p. 96). To know how to speak is not to have a number of pure signs and significations at one's disposal. The speech act is not merely a purely expressive act embuing signs with meanings; nor is it an act replacing a perception with a conventional sign" (*Prose*, p. 7; *PW*, p. 3). It involves "taking up" a position in the play of difference, which constitutes language as a domain of articulation and makes possible moves within it. Meaning is always the function of this mediation or, as Saussure put it, "it is only a value determined by its relation with other similar values, and without them the signification would not exist."[5] Signification, in short, is a function of a total system of values. The speech act becomes, then, much more complex than the classical theory dreamt. Among other things, as Merleau-Ponty says in a marginal note, "we must get rid of

[5]*Course*, p. 117.

(*défaire*) the illusion of possession through saying" (*Prose*, 97 n, *PW*, p. 69 n).

Because of the speech act's involvement in this 'global movement' Merleau-Ponty states, following Saussure, that "language is not the function of the speaking subject" (*Bulletin*, p. 257; *CAL*, p. 97).[6] The speaking subject is not the proprietor of language, being dependent on an institution that always antedates his participation in it. This means, again following Saussure, that language is always only "relatively motivated."[7] Each speaker is reintegrated into the collectivity of speaking subjects and undergoes its contingency. In a sense then, the speech act is burdened with a certain risk and undecidability. "Expression is like a step in the fog—no one can say where, if anywhere, it will lead" (*SN*, p. 3).

Nonetheless, if language is not the function of the speaking subject it also "is not a transcendent reality with respect to all speaking subjects" (*CAL*, p. 97). While it is out of the question to found linguistic practices on the basis of any empirically specifiable speaker, it would be no less mistaken to create a sort of linguistic platonism holding them to be distinct from the usage of the community. As Saussure had realized, language is not a separate reality. Behind language there is not some sort of reified transcendent thought. This means, moreover, that language is not just a principle of classification that speakers would reproduce. Rather the relationship between speech and language inherently holds an "original conception of the relationship between mind and object" (*CAL*, p. 99).

While it is noted that for Saussure "everything in language is psychological,"[8] Merleau-Ponty adds that "what is mental is not individual" (*CAL*, p. 98). Individual idiolects do not present phenomena sufficient in themselves to exhaust the function of language. "In language the consciousness of signification is not exhaustive" (*CAL*, 96). Rather an analysis that would start at this point would put the cart before the horse. The subject is instituted in phenomena that transcend it and can be founded only on the global will to communicate. It is this intersubjective motivation that sustains linguistic coherence and intelligibility. "Order and system are

[6]cf. *Course,* p. 14.
[7]cf. *Course,* p. 131.
[8]cf. *Course,* p. 66. Jacques Derrida, who will later claim that Saussure's work opens the field of a general grammatology, emphasizes with regard to this text that it is the acoustic image and not the material sound that is Saussure's object, obtainable, Derrida argues, only by a phenomenological reduction. See, for example, *Of Grammatology,* trans. Gayatri Chakrovorty Spivak (Baltimore: The Johns Hopkins University Press, 1976), p. 63.

reestablished by the thrust of speaking subjects who want to understand and to be understood" (*CAL*, p. 101).

This intertwining between system and individual in the speech act
demonstrates the integral relation between language and thought.
Their separation, as has been intimated, was a necessary condition
for the classical model and the attempt to provide it an absolute
foundation in pure thought. But such a separation is, at best, an
abstraction. Rather, quoting Saussure, Merleau-Ponty states,
"There is 'neither a materialization of thought, nor a spiritualization
of language'; language and thought are only two moments of one
and the same reality" (*CAL*, p. 99).[9]

Drawing on an insight that had been gathered as early as *The
Structure of Behavior*, this mediation might be explicated by stating
that the speech act (*act de parole*) involves both "a principle of slavery"
and "a principle of liberty" (*SB*, p. 245 n). On the one hand we are
tied to the 'grids' of language, the rules of that which can be said or
that which can be meaningful. For example, even if Chomsky is right
in declaring that most of the sentences uttered are novel sentences[10],
they must still count *as* sentences. If 'grammaticality'[11] is an ambiguous notion, *that* there are limits between meaningful and nonmean-
ingful sentences in specific contexts — however obscure — is unchal-
lengeable. On the other hand, despite these constraints (or in a sense
just because of them, since they function as a necessary condition of
linguistic intelligibility), nothing forbids the transformation of that
which has been said (i.e., utterances in ordinary language are free to
be 'novel,' even if in an ambiguous sense they are condemned to be
meaningful). It is perhaps because of this play in usage, the fact that
language involves an open situation, "constituting a background to
either a confirmatory or transformatory decision" (*PoP*, p. 438), that
Saussure wrote of the synchronic laws of usage that they were "general, but not imperative"[12] and that "speaking is characterized by
freedom of combinations."[13]

This conception of the relationship between mind and object and
its mediation through the structures of language furthermore
forces us to revamp our notion of rationality. Already in the preface
to *Sense and Non-Sense* Merleau-Ponty had written, "We are born into

[9]*Course*, p. 112.

[10]See Noam Chomsky, *Syntactic Structures* (The Hague: Mouton, 1957).

[11]See Noam Chomsky, "Some Methodological Remarks on Generative Grammar,"
Word, No. 17(1961). For an opposing view, see Roman Jakobson, "Boas' View of
Grammatical Meaning," *American Anthropologist*, Vol. LXI(1959).

[12]*Course*, p. 92.

[13]*Course*, p. 124.

reason as into language" (*SN*, p. 3). In the Sorbonne lectures Saussure is seen as providing the key to an understanding of how this takes place. "What Saussure saw is precisely this masking of chance and order, this return to the rational, the fortuitous" (*CAL*, p. 101). What Merleau-Ponty found in Saussure was a sort of 'living rationality' that could account for the nature of concrete practices. Here, as the latter realized, "one must consider everything that deflects reason in actual contact between individuals."[14] Individuals are not endowed with the absolute freedom to enact intentions that arise *ex nihilo*. Instead these acts are made possible by the structures to which they belong. Nor, on the other hand, can it be said that individuals are the mere effect of these structures, their acts being the result of external constraints. On the contrary, the exchange between system and event that has been disclosed, denying the separation of reason and fact, introduces "the idea of a kind of blundering (*trébuchant*) logic in which the development is not guaranteed" (*Bulletin*, p. 259; *CAL*, p. 101).

In the closing paragraphs of *Consciousness and the Acquisition of Language* Merleau-Ponty's concerns with the Saussurian paradigm move beyond the confines of philosophy of language and linguistics proper. The analysis of language will now be taken as a key for the elucidation of major problems throughout the domain of the social, including initially those of history. In his analysis of the speaker's involvement in the usage of the community Merleau-Ponty had already seen that "Saussure elucidates the enigmatic relationship linking the individual to history by his analysis of language" (*CAL*, p. 97). On a broader scale now it is asserted that "the Saussurian *conception, if generalized*" could find "*application* to the Philosophy of History" (*Bulletin*, p. 259; *CAL*, p. 101).

Under the auspices of this move we would be able to escape both the position that history is the sum of independent chance events and that history is providential. Neither in fact is the case, for, in a sense, history is both—completely accidental and completely rational. There is no system that does not originate in some particular accident, and no accident becomes historical except insofar as it is capable of cohering to a system. "That which we call the logic of history is a process of elimination by which only the systems which are capable of taking the situation into account subsist" (*CAL*, p. 102). The fortuitous and the rational then do not constitute two

14*Course*, p. 78.

different *historical* orders. Nor does the systematic aspect of history, its 'logos,' stand outside change:

> The principle of historical rationality does not eliminate chance. It turns chance or uses chance. As Saussure might say, it converts the accidental into systems; it surrounds the pure event without eliminating it (*CAL*, p. 102).

V.

It is evident, therefore, that the Saussurian paradigm, and philosophy of language in general, had ceased to be merely 'regional problems' and had taken on a position of wider significance in Merleau-Ponty's thought. Further evidence of this generalized affirmation would be shortly forthcoming. The paper presented at the Brussels colloquium in 1951 on contemporary problems in phenomenology, "On the Phenomenology of Language," presents a clear statement regarding the priority of language as a philosophical problem and can be viewed, perhaps, as an expression of a turning point in French thought.

The opening paragraph of this paper explicates a program for contemporary philosophical thought (one rightly or wrongly finding its roots in Husserl). Against the philosophical tradition in which language does not pertain to 'First Philosophy,' Merleau-Ponty claims that in Husserl we find it moved to a central position. Further, because of its priority, it is claimed that this problem provides us with our best basis for "questioning phenomenology and recommencing Husserl's efforts" (*Signs*, p. 84). It soon becomes evident, however, the the philosophy of language holds importance not just for its methodological importance *vis à vis* Husserl. In considering the consequences of his descriptions for phenomenology, Merleau-Ponty is in fact quite clear. Having explained that phenomenology is not just an adjunct to philosophy, he proceeds to state:

> This is particularly clear in the case of the phenomenology of language. More clearly than any other, this problem requires us to make a decision concerning the relationships between phenomenology and philosophy or metaphysics. For more clearly than any other it takes the form of both a special problem and a problem which contains all others, including the problem of philosophy (*Signs*, p. 93).

The problem of the nature of language, then, moves to the forefront in philosophy. But why? The reasons explicit in 1951 appear to differ little from the 1947 article, which first manifested his interest in Saussure: it is a key in the attempt to "reflect upon the object's mode of presence to the subject" (*Signs*, pp. 92–93). But, as becomes evident, likewise, in contradistinction to the earlier work, it no longer merely verifies that which had been established in another domain. Now *more* clearly than any other it takes the form of a special problem that contains all others. The precise sense in which this is the case, however, will not fully emerge until the final writings.

It is in the 1951 paper that Merleau-Ponty presents what has become a somewhat controversial characterization of Saussure's speech/language distinction, claiming that the distinction is one between "a synchronic linguistics of speech and a diachronic linguistics of language" (*Signs*, p. 86). This characterization appears, *prima facie*, to contradict the definitions of Chapter 3 of the introduction to the *Course* in which it is claimed that the object of linguistics excludes *la parole*.[15] Linguistics has for its object, rather, the homogeneous, systematic artifact of concrete usage—versus the discrete multi-faceted character of *la parole*.

VI.

If Merleau-Ponty has in fact simply confused or misunderstood this issue, then (in addition to a major blunder in understanding Saussure) he would be open to his critics' charge that he never really accounted for the discursive constraints exercised by language (i.e., *la langue*) on speakers. This is a criticism, moreover, that has been formulated both by later phenomenologists such as Ricoeur[16] as well as by writers more strongly influenced by structuralism, for example, Lyotard.[17]

In *The Prose of the World*, nonetheless, Merleau-Ponty states that "We need to learn to reflect on consciousness *in* the hazards of language and as quite impossible without its opposite" (*Prose*, p. 17). This reflection implies, as has been seen, a general deconstruction of the position that has been overriding in classical thought, both with

---

[15]*Course*, pp. 14–15.

[16]See Paul Ricoeur, "The Question of the Subject," trans. Kathleen McLaughlin; in *The Conflicts of Interpretation*, ed. Don Ihde (Evanston: Northwestern University Press, 1974). Regarding this analysis in *Signs*, Rocoeur states: "The fact that the notion of language as an autonomous system is not taken into consideration weighs heavily on this phenomenology of speech" (p. 249).

[17]See Jean François Lyotard, *Discours, figure* (Paris: Editions Klinksieck, 1971), "Merleau-Ponty is able to think language as expression . . . but he is not able to think language as discursive" (p. 93 n) (my translation).

regard to the subservience and effacement of the sign before consciousness (and indeed consciousness itself, since "to be conscious is
to constitute"; *Signs*, p. 93) and in relation to the supposed primal
connection the sign has with "the world."[18] It would be simply mistaken to hold that Saussure was not a catalyst in this reappraisal.

At the same time, however, it would be equally remiss to claim that
the resulting account does not challenge that which Barthes has
called the "Durkheimian"[19] reading of the *Course*, which takes *la
langue* and *la parole* to be radically distinct and *la parole* to be a mere
efflux of the former. It might also be said that in this he antedates
Barthes' own move from "a semiotics of the message" to a "semiotics
of the interlocuter."[20] A parallel text from *The Prose of the World*
explicates what Merleau-Ponty has in mind.

> Alongside the linguistics of language (*la langue*), which gives the
> impression, in the extreme, that language is a series of chaotic
> events, Saussure has inaugurated a linguistics of *speech* (*la parole*)
> which would reveal in it at each moment an order, a system, a
> totality without which communication and the linguistic com-
> munity would be impossible (*Prose*, p. 33; PW, p. 23).

To mark off the speech/language distinction in effect is immediately
to set off a 'dialectic' between the two perspectives.

If there is a criticism on Merleau-Ponty's part here it involves the
necessity of recognizing that "since synchrony is only a cross section
of diachrony, the system realized in it never exists wholly in act but
always involves latent or incubating changes" (*Signs*, p. 87). In a
sense, however, this demands of Saussure only that he make good

---

[18]This deconstruction occurs more and more as Merleau-Ponty's career progresses.
Compare, for example, the critique of the *cogito tacite* presented in the working notes
of *The Visible and the Invisible* (VI, pp. 170–171; 175–176). The appeal—which this
notion involves to a level that "conditions language" (*PP*, p. 404) or a "pre-expressive
stratum," to use the language of Husserl's *Ideen I*—inaugurates a problem regarding
the subject's adherence to language that could not be settled at this level. Indeed the
cogito tacite is labeled "impossible," since to return to immanence and to the consciousness of . . . it is necessary to have words." Less and less, therefore (doubtless aware of
the failure it implied), Merleau-Ponty felt obliged to search out such an originary
"text which our knowledge tries to translate" (*PP*, p. xviii). And, as Jacques
Taminiaux has quite rightly demonstrated, this 'deconstruction' that occurs within
the evolution of Merleau-Ponty's thought coheres with (and antedates) the deconstruction practiced by Jacques Derrida on Husserlian phenomenology in *Speech and
Phenomena*. See Taminiaux's article, "Experience et expression" in *Le regard et l'excédent* (The Hague: Martinus Nijhoff, 1977).

[19]Roland Barthes, "intervention" in *Prétexte: Roland Barthes: Colloque de Cerisy* (Paris:
Union Générale d'Editions, 1978), p. 408.

[20]Ibid., "intervention," p. 30. This move is also reflected in Barthes' Inaugural
Lecture at the College du France, *Leçons* (Paris: du Seuil, 1978). (my translation)

what amounts to a promissory note. In discussing the mutability of the sign, he states:

> The causes of continuity are a priori within the scope of the observer, but the causes of change in time are not. It is better not to give an exact account at this point, but to restrict discussion to the shifting of relationships in general.[21]

The point never comes, however, when the *Course* puts forward "an exact account" of this process. In the conclusion to his discussion of the distinction between static and evolutionary linguistics Saussure does say somewhat parenthetically that

> . . . once in possession of this double principle of classification, we can add that everything diachronic in language is diachronic only by virtue of speaking. It is in speaking that the germ of all change is found.[22]

But, the *Course* never really completes these indications. The fact is that Saussure's attempt to rule out bad theories about the nature of language, which doubtless surrounded him at the time, kept his own from being complete. What Merleau-Ponty demands is that change be accounted for and that an account of the speech act in its specificity be provided.

There is a danger, however, to such an attempt, and Saussure is quite right here. The danger is to revert back to a point at which language once again becomes nothing more than a naming process, and the system becomes swallowed up in intentions, expressions, pure significations, returning the workings of language back to the "universal stronghold" of a constituting consciousness. The positive effect of Saussure's contribution in this regard has been, as has been seen, to recognize the 'derivative' character of these entities and their facticity, their dependency on the "speaking" of language itself (*Prose*, p. 102).[23]

The 'universality' that the classical account sought is not to be found in a point prior to the diversity of existing languages, but will

---

[21]*Course,* p. 77.

[22]*Course,* p. 98.

[23]The notion of the "speaking of language" is Heideggerean in origin (*"Die Sprache spricht," Unterwegs zur Sprache:* Pfullingen: Neske, 1958, p. 13). This is a text to which Merleau-Ponty returned several times in his later period (eg., *TL*, p. 121; *VI*, p. 250). At the same time, however, Merleau-Ponty's concerns still (or perhaps already) emphasized the attempt to formulate an account of the speaker within the perspective that this paper sets out in detail above. This is a necessity that Heidegger recognizes in the above work, but delays: "At the proper time it becomes unavoidable to think of how mortal speech and its utterance take place in the speaking of language as the peal of the stillness of the di-ference." trans. Albert Hofstadter in *Poetry, Language, Thought* (New York: Harper & Row, 1975), p. 208.

always be defined by the laterality of value to value, Merleau-Ponty holds. Here it is the symbolic context itself that determines this universality. Universality is achieved only by a contingent passage from one context to another, "the two languages (and ultimately all given languages) being contingently comparable only at the outcome of this passage" (*Signs*, p. 87). Rather than subjecting the heterogeneity of existing practices to a reduction to pure linguistic forms, or a pure grammar, as Husserl, for example, had done in the *Fourth Investigation*,[24] here the analysis of usage remains at the level of the concrete.

It is just this concern for the specificity of concrete usage—one that refuses to reduce language from below (by turning that which is essentially a mental phenomenon into a natural object) or from above (by 'returning' it to the pure expressive foundations of a constitutive subject)—that manifests an explicit affinity between the two projects. And it is precisely this affinity that leads Merleau-Ponty to claim of Saussure's approach, in the manner perhaps in which he had of his own, that it "emphasizes the necessity of a phenomenology of speech" (*Bulletin*, p. 150).[25]

From the phenomenological approach that results, Merleau-Ponty describes the speech act's radical inscription in its symbolic context. Usage is, he says, "recommended" by its morphological, syntactical, and lexical archive. These patterns jointly comprise that which von Humboldt referred to as the *Innere Sprachform* in which the 'archive' contributes a perspective or mode of access to the world. Organized signs have an immanent meaning in this structure that I do not constitute or need to represent to myself in order to use them. This phenomenon he describes as a "languagely (*langagière*) meaning of language which effects the mediation between my as yet unspeaking intention and words, and in such a way that my spoken words surprise me myself and teach me my thought" (*Signs*, p. 88). To express, therefore, is "to become aware of," the speaker does not express just for others but also to know himself. Thus the classical view in which complete 'inner' thoughts gets translated into 'external' signs (or "mentaleze" gets translated into signs) will not do. The picture we have of thought encoding and decoding signs (which, for

[24]See Edmund Husserl, *Logical Investigations*, trans. J. N. Findlay (New York: Humanities Press, 1970).

[25]This text does not appear in Wild's translation of *Les science de l'homme et la phenomenologie* (published in Primacy), which was prepared from the version issued by the Centre de Documentaire Universitaire (1961). (The *Bulletin* text is my translation.)

example, any semiology of 'messages' or 'codes' is based on) breaks down. It falls along with the classical foundation according to which thought reigns over language. If thought only arises in the midst of the play of the symbolic context, then "the reason why thematization of the signified does not precede speech is that it is the result of it" (*Signs*, p. 90). The subject, then, no longer stands outside the play of language. In this heterogeneity self-expression and self-transcendence are no longer radically distinct. It becomes a "speaking subject" or a *sujet en proces*.[26]

Earlier in the *Phenomenology of Perception* Merleau-Ponty had analyzed this notion of meaning immanent in the significative system at another level with regard to the "lived body" as the "gestural meaning" of the sign. And here again the ability of signs to delineate their own meaning, to catch up and organize my intentions, this "action at a distance," as he puts it following Sartre,[27] remains understood as "an eminant case of corporeal intentionality" (*Signs*, p. 89). Just as I have an awareness of my body, which allows me to maintain my relationships with the world without thematically representing to myself the objects of my dealings, so likewise, he reasons, the spoken word is "pregnant" with a meaning that can be read off in the texture of the linguistic gesture. Again, the speaker's mode of access to the intersubjective field and the symbolic context is not based on pure thought, a foundation that resulted inter alia in the problems that arose in classical phenomenology with regard to the alter ego. Rather the lived body, like the sign itself, is always already constituted in an intersubjective field. Indeed the speech act is itself a mode of behavior demonstrative of the body-subject's inherence in an intersubjective field. "Speech is evidently an eminent case of those 'ways of behaving' which reverse my ordinary relationship to objects and give certain ones of them the value of subjects" (*Signs*, p. 94). Nonetheless, even this foundation for language in the lived-body, or "carnal generality," is not without a certain instability, as a note to *The Prose of the World* indicates: "This foundation does not prevent language from coming back dialectically over what preceded it and transforming the purely carnal and vital coexistence with the world and bodies into a coexistence of language (*coexistence langagière*)" (*Prose*, p. 29 n; *PW*, p. 20 n).

[26]This notion belongs to Julia Kristeva's description of the speaker's involvement in the "heterogeneity of significative practices." See her *Polylogue* (Paris: du Seuil, 1977).

[27]See Jean Paul Sartre, *Being and Nothingness*, trans. Hazel E. Barnes (New York: The Citadel Press, 1968), p. 350.

VII.

Two years later, in his inaugural lecture at the Collège du France, Merleau-Ponty again enlarges the parameters of his considerations on Saussure. This discussion occurs at the end of the section on history in which it is stated that Saussure's model "could have sketched a new philosophy of history," surpassing even that of Marx and Hegel in its ability to account for historical meaning (*IPP*, pp. 54–55). Here Merleau-Ponty begins to integrate its functioning into a general "symbolic space." The various "systems or symbols" for which the Saussurian position can be seen to be exemplary have now begun to be integrated into one general conception. Regarding these various matrices, he states:

> We were asking ourselves *where* they are. They are in a social, cultural, or symbolic space which is no less real (*réel*) than physical space and is, moreover, supported by it. For meaning lies latent not only in language, in political and religious institutions, but in modes of kinship, in machines, in the landscape, in production, and, in general, in all the modes of human commerce. An interconnection among all these phenomena is possible since they are all symbolisms, and perhaps even the translation of one symbolism into another is possible (*Eloge*, pp. 65–66; *IPP*, p. 56).

Moreover the symbolic structure within this space is all-pervasive. This means that the event in which it is disclosed must likewise be placed within it.

> Each philosophy is also an architecture of signs. It constitutes itself (*se constitue*) in close relation with the other modes of exchange which make up our historical and social life (*Eloge*, p. 66; *IPP*, p. 57).

Nonetheless, the discursive practice that constitutes philosophy still receives a distinction in this explication since, "for the tacit symbolism of life it substitutes, in principle, a conscious symbolism; for a latent meaning, one that is manifest (*IPP*, p. 57). In disclosing his involvement it remains possible for the theoretician to enter consciously into this play and transform it.

There emerges then in the Inaugural Lecture an attempt to explicate a polymorphic space where the symbolic matrices to which the Saussurian paradigm remains applicable can be mapped out. That which remains outstanding here, however, is the recognition that this space itself—in a sense *logos and* being—can be explicated in terms of the same sort of diacritical paradigm. We can find perhaps just such a recognition at work in the final writings of Merleau-Ponty's career.

VIII.

The developments that have been followed out here can be seen to be precisely mirrored in the introduction written for *Signs* in 1960. Having introduced the concept of language that has been traced out above he states, "We ought to think of the historical world according to this model" (*Signs*, p. 20). And, once again the question of the site for this model and its instances arises, as it had earlier in the Inaugural Lecture. However much there may be a truth to nominalism ("nominalism is right' the significations are only defined separations"; *VI*, p. 238), an endless play of signs will not suffice. Again, it must be questioned where the site that this model structures is located. Here with regard to history we are given a more complete reply:

> Where is history made? . . . It is of the same order as the movement of Thought and Speech, and in short, of the perceptible world's explosion within us (*Signs*, p. 20).

But if this is the case, if it is the same order that is in question here, then it would not be wrong to claim that this model holds not only with regard to history and to social institutions in general, but likewise in opening the 'space' of the perceived world itself. In all cases it could be said that the entities in question have a sort of "languagely (*langagière*)" existence.

That which has been discovered here, Merleau-Ponty states, amounts to "a dimension in which ideas obtain their true solidity," one in which the play of differences—which the notion of the laterality of value announced, "the swarming of words behind words, thoughts behind thoughts, this universal substitution"—is recognized to constitute a sort of ontological stability (*Signs*, p. 20). In the working notes to *The Visible and the Invisible*, written about a month earlier than the initial work on the introduction to *Signs*, Merleau-Ponty speaks of that which underlies this stability as "my being set up (*mon montage*) on a universal diacritical system" (*Visible*, p. 287; *VI*, p. 233). In this system has already been found a new perspective on rationality, on history, and culture in general—one that recognizes a 'flesh' to them, a living field for which Saussure's model provides one of the keys. But the final move generalizes this concept of universal substitution even further. He asks, "But are the visible things of the visible world constructed any differently?" (*VI*, p. 126). Here the sensible landscape itself becomes understood as a manifestation of the universal matrix that had been found in language; and it too involves the disavowal of the sign-signification positively that resulted:

> What is proper to the sensible (as to language) is to be representative of the whole, not by a sign-signification relation, or by the immanence of the parts in one another and in the whole, but because each part is torn up from the whole, comes with its roots, encroaches upon the whole, transgresses the frontiers of the others (VI, p. 218).

Visible things are always behind what I see of them; "no thing, no side of a thing, shows itself except by actively hiding the others, denouncing them in the act of concealing them" (*Signs*, p. 20). It can be said, then, of the sensible landscape, just as he would in a Lacanian fashion of "vision itself" and "thought itself," that it, too, is "structured like a language, articulation before the letter" (*VI*, p. 126); and the textual path that has been traced or followed out here can be affirmed to lead not only to *logos*, but to being—more precisely, to the recognition of their intertwining:

> The Saussurian analysis of the relations between signifiers and the relations from signifier to signified and between the significiations (as differences between significiations) confirms and rediscovers the idea of perception as divergence (*ecart*) by relation to a level, that is, the ideal of the primordial Being, of the Convention of conventions, of the Speech before speech (*Visible*, p. 255; *VI*, p. 201).

All of this calls up the reaffirmation of the central position of language in philosophy. The close of the chapter entitled "Reflection and Intuition" in *The Visible and the Invisible* reexplicates that affirmation, perhaps now more fully aware than ever of that which it involves. Language receives here a double priveledge in this explication. This involves in the first place its role as the medium of philosophy (i.e., as was noted earlier in the Inaugural Lecture, philosophy is an architecture of signs). The philosopher's act is a linguistic act; specifically an act of writing, a task that a text from the same period describes:

> (T)he writer's work is a work of language rather than "thought." His task is to produce a system of signs whose internal articulation reproduces the contours of experience; the reliefs and sweeping lines of these contours in turn generate a syntax in depth, a mode of composition and recital which breaks the mold of the world and everyday language and refashions it (TL, p. 25).

Philosophy is a move in this symbolic space, an operative language, and he who makes this move must believe that "language is not the contrary of truth or coincidence" (*VI*, p. 125). But at the same time, through his work with the philosophy of language, and Saussure in particular, Merleau-Ponty had gleaned a great deal of what this language would need to be like:

> It would be a language of which he would not be the organizer, words he would not assemble, that would combine through him by virtue of a natural intertwining of their meaning, through the occult trading or the metaphor—where what counts is no longer the manifest meaning of each word and each image, but the lateral relations, the kinships that are implicated in their transfers and their exchanges (*VI*, p. 125).

It would therefore be "more like a sort of being than a means" (*Signs*, p. 43). And as such its importance became almost *archetypal*, as he likewise said of perception (*VI*, p. 158). In this second sense, in the case of living language, for which, as has been seen, Saussure's work had acquired a significance that was "primordial," it can be said that it provides us with a theme that is "universal." Indeed, he states that "it is the theme of philosophy," again raising it above the status of a merely "regional problem" (*VI*, p. 126). It is precisely because of this double priviledge that in a move echoing Husserl and his own Preface to *Phenomenology of Perception* (one demonstrative of the distance he had put between himself and both) Merleau-Ponty states: "It is by considering language that we would best see how we are to *and* how we are *not* to return to the things themselves" (*VI*, p. 125).

ROBERT D. ROMANYSHYN

ELEVEN

UNCONSCIOUSNESS AS A LATERAL DEPTH:
PERCEPTION AND THE TWO MOMENTS
OF REFLECTION[1]

I. INTRODUCTION

PHYSICS IS AN IMPLICIT PSYCHOLOGY, and a theory of things is also already a theory of the body. Uncritically adopting its conception of the world from the natural sciences, modern psychology has more or less understood the body as a thing and as a consequence thereof has more or less either ignored consciousness as an illusion[2] or treated it as a derivative of biological processes. Mind, then, has been reduced to brain until this reductionism is forced back upon itself and a dualism of mind *and* body reemerges.[3] Such a view is the line of development of modern psychology: the body is conceived in the image of things, and consciousness is derived from this image of the body.

Psychoanalysis, however, seems to be an exception to this view, and Freud's work appears to offer an understanding of body, things, and consciousness that radically differs from psychology's vision. Recognizing and developing the symbolic character of things, Freud also transforms the meaning of the human body. "The body is enigmatic" in psychoanalysis, Merleau-Ponty says, and with Freud's work "Mind passes into body as, inversely, body passes into mind".[4] Mind or consciousness, therefore, is also changed, and Freud recovers "between the body's anonymous life and the person's

---

[1]This paper was originally read at the Society of Phenomenology and Existential Philosophy, Chicago, Nov. 1976, and in an altered version at the second annual Merleau-Ponty Conference, Athens, Ohio, October 1977.

[2]B. F. Skinner, *Beyond Freedom and Dignity* (New York: Knopf, 1971).

[3]Wilder Penfield, *The Mystery of the Mind* (Princeton, New Jersey: Princeton University Press, 1975) p. 13.

[4]Maurice Merleau-Ponty, *Signs*, trans. Richard C. McCleary (Evanston: Northwestern University Press, 1964) p. 229. (Hereafter incorporated into text as *Signs*).

official life" (*Signs*, p. 229) a consciousness that neither fully knows its ignorance nor is fully ignorant of its knowing, an *unconsciousness* that Merleau-Ponty calls the "Protean idea in Freud's works" (*Signs*, p. 229). But just when psychoanalysis seems to be an exception to much of modern psychology, it becomes the very epitome of its expression. Unconsciousness becomes the repressed, and the Cartesian consciousness, whose influence Freud has rightly circumscribed,[5] reappears *beneath* consciousness as a silent but all-knowing witness of life's forbidden wishes. Thus it is small wonder that Merleau-Ponty says that "we have only to follow the transformations of this Protean idea . . . to be convinced that it is not a fully developed idea, and that . . . we still have to find the right formulation for what he [Freud] intended by this provisional designation" (*Signs*, p. 229).

Merleau-Ponty's work offers a possible direction for a reformulation of this notion of unconsciousness. Beginning with perceptual consciousness, he challenges Freud's protean idea, but in such a fashion that a challenge is also offered to the notion of the Cartesian *cogito*. Perceptual consciousness offers a critical consideration of "Freud,"[6] which moves toward "Descartes," but toward a "Descartes" that is also critically reunderstood in a movement toward "Freud." Indeed Merleau-Ponty's thesis of the primacy of perception provides an understanding of human subjectivity that integrates the notions of the lower and the higher into a dimension of *lateral depth*.

In this paper the meaning of this dimension of lateral depth shall be discussed. This discussion involves three points. First, it will be demonstrated how this notion is already implied in the double movement of Merleau-Ponty's thought. Hence parts two and three of this paper will show respectively how Merleau-Ponty's critical considerations of consciousness and unconsciousness from the side of perception converge toward this notion of lateral depth. Second, part four of this paper will indicate how this theme of lateral depth means a deepening of the meaning of reflection, and how the double sense of the meaning of reflection already reformulates the

---

[5]Sigmund Freud, "The Ego and the Id," *The Standard Edition of the Complete Psychological Works of Sigmund Freud*, XIX, trans. James Strachey et al. (London: Hogarth Press, 1961) p. 16, note 1. (Hereafter incorporated into text as Freud, volume, date).

[6]Names in parentheses indicate that Merleau-Ponty's considerations refer as much to a way of thinking as they do to these particular thinkers themselves and/or their specific works.

meaning of unconsciousness. Third, part five will consider how this reformulation of unconsciousness as a failure of the first moment of reflection adequately handles Freud's notion of repression.

II. FROM CONSCIOUSNESS TO PERCEPTION
[*The Phenomenology of Perception*]

The chapter, "The Cogito" in the *Phenomenology of Perception*, is Merleau-Ponty's first attempt to work out the ontological consequences and implications of his thesis of the primacy of perception. While some of his thinking in this chapter will later be revised and/or abandoned, its position in the work bears witness as to how the thesis of perception radically alters the notion of the *cogito*. For example, having already provided phenomenological descriptions of the perceived world and the body, Merleau-Ponty says: "What I discover and recognize through the *cogito* is not psychological immanence, the inherence of all phenomena in 'private states of consciousness,' [and] . . . not even transcendental immanence, the belonging of all phenomena to a constituting consciousness, the possession of clear thought by itself."[7] On the contrary, what perceptual consciousness reveals about consciousness in general "is the deep seated momentum of transcendence which is my very being, the simultaneous contact with my own being and with the world's being" (*PP*, p. 377).

Immediately, however, Merleau-Ponty challenges himself because maybe the case of perceptual consciousness is unique and maybe it prejudices this reconsideration of the *cogito*. Are there not, he asks, instances that sustain the absolute privilege of consciousness, instances such as one's awareness of "psychic facts," which demonstrate consciousness' transparancy to itself? Do not experiences like love and will, for example, show consciousness in full possession of itself and, if not these, then surely does not the case of pure thought demonstrate that consciousness is identical with its own self-awareness?

Using the example of the feeling of love, Merleau-Ponty considers that while one may be mistaken about the object of his love he can never be mistaken about his feeling of being in love. "A feeling, considered in itself, is always true once it is felt" (*PP*, p. 378). Here, like the Cartesian thinker, we seem to be within "a sphere of absolute certainty in which truth cannot elude us" (*PP*, p. 378). And if in time

---

[7]Maurice Merleau-Ponty, *Phenomenology of Perception*, trans. Colin Smith (New York: The Humanities Press, 1962) p. 377. (Hereafter incorporated into text as *PP*).

one discovers that he *was* mistaken about his feelings of love, then two "solutions" seem possible: either he may say *now* that *then* he already knew he was not in love or he may say that *then* he was fully deceived.

But neither solution is acceptable for Merleau-Ponty because they force a choice between everything and nothing, between absolute knowledge and absolute ignorance. In the first instance one's love was from the very beginning never true love and hence *now* there can be no question of an earlier mistake. And in the second instance one was so deceived about his loving from the very beginning, that *now* one cannot be certain about not being currently deceived about that earlier deception.

In opposition to these apparent solutions, Merleau-Ponty affirms on the one hand that one could not have fully *known then* that his love was mistaken, for then he would not have loved. Hence he says that "it is impossible to pretend that I always knew what I now know, and to see as [always, already] existing, a self-knowledge which I have only just come by" (*PP*, p. 380). On the other hand he adds that one could not have fully *not known*, for then he could never love or know the difference from deception. In opposition to these apparent solutions he affirms, therefore, neither a Cartesian vision nor a Freudian blindness. On the contrary, he says that the "love which worked out its dialectic through me, and of which I have just become aware, was not, from the start, a thing hidden in my unconscious, nor was it an object before my consciousness, but the impulse carrying me towards someone . . . a matter of experience not knowledge from start to finish" (*PP*, p. 381).

Perceptual consciousness, therefore, is not a special case for Merleau-Ponty because even 'psychic facts' such as this feeling of love, reveal a consciousness that knows itself only through the world and over time. Indeed Merleau-Ponty says that in this work he has restored a "temporal thickness" (*PP*, p. 393) to the *cogito*, which is after all only another way of saying that a consciousness knows itself through its participation in the world. "Presence to oneself and presence in the world" are linked together, he says, and "the *cogito* [is identified] with involvement in the world" (*PP*, p. 433). In Sallis' terms, Merleau-Ponty has radicalized "the bond between presence to self and transcendence so as to integrate the former into the latter."[8] Hence if "the primary truth is indeed 'I think'," then this is

---

[8]John Sallis, *Phenomenology and the Return to Beginnings* (Pittsburgh: Duquesne University Press, 1973) p. 66.

true "only provided that we understand thereby 'I belong to myself while belonging to the world' " (*PP*, p. 407).

Merleau-Ponty's analysis of the *cogito* suggests, therefore, another meaning of consciousness or subjectivity, a meaning that to be sure still exists side by side with a notion like the "tacit cogito," that "retreat of non-being" (*PP*, p. 400) that still haunts the *Phenomenology of Perception* and remains with Merleau-Ponty until *The Visible and the Invisible*. But in spite of this spectre of "Descartes," the consideration of perceptual consciousness has already forced a new beginning— even if this *explicitly* comes later. The thesis of the primacy of perception lowers consciousness back into the world and in such a way, moreover, that "Descartes" is infected with "Freud." An echo of "Freud" haunts these criticisms of "Descartes," and if consciousness is not transparent to itself it is "because the subject that I am, when taken concretely, is inseparable from this body and this world" (*PP*, p. 408). It is no accident; nor is it surprising therefore to find *after* the *Phenomenology of Perception* increasing references to and considerations of Freud and psychoanalysis since these first suggestions of another meaning of consciousness and subjectivity seem already to be foreshadowed in Freud's work.

The movement from "Descartes" toward "Freud" is not however without its consequences for Freud, and Merleau-Ponty's consideration of perceptual consciousness is not a mere affirmation of Freud. On the contrary, he says himself that phenomenology is the *latent* meaning in Freud's work, "the philosophy implicit in psychoanalysis itself."[9] Hence as much as Merleau-Ponty admits that "Freud is sovereign in his ability to listen to the hushed words of life" (*Preface*, p. 30), as much as he praises Freud's "increasingly clear view of the body's mental function and the mind's incarnation" (*Signs*, p. 230), he still warns that "Our age is as far from explaining man by the lower as it is by the higher" (*Signs*, p. 240). The "idea of a form of consciousness which is transparent to itself, its existence being identifiable with its awareness of existing" he says, "is not so very different from the notion of the unconscious" (*PP*, p. 380). His critique of Cartesian thought is therefore simultaneously a critique of Freudian thought and indeed his critical reconsideration of the *cogito*, of that which he calls "high altitude thought,"[10] already affects his consid-

[9]Maurice Merleau-Ponty, "Preface *L'Oeuvre de Freud*, by A. Hesnard," *Existential Psychiatry*, 28, 1970, p. 31. (Hereafter incorporated into text as *Preface*).

[10]Maurice Merleau-Ponty, *The Visible and the Invisible*, trans. Alphonso Lingis (Evanston: Northwestern University Press, 1968) p. 13. (Hereafter incorporated into text as *VI*).

eration of the unconscious, or what one may call low-altitude thought. Indeed reading Merleau-Ponty in this way it is difficult to avoid the suspicion that "Freud" is a "Descartes" of the depths as "Descartes" is a "Freud" of the heights. In fact, if we recall how on the night of November 20, 1619, Descartes dreamed his three fateful dreams, then it seems justifiable to say that Freud has reasoned the dream as much as Descartes has dreamed a new reason. It may even be the case in fact that "Freud" is "Descartes' " dream. Be that as it may, however, the next part of this essay takes up this consideration of the unconscious from the side of perception, this second movement in Merleau-Ponty's thought.

III. FROM UNCONSCIOUSNESS TO PERCEPTION:
[*The Visible and the Invisible*]

In the working notes to *The Visible and the Invisible* Merleau-Ponty says that "perception *qua* wild perception is of itself ignorance of itself, imperception" (*VI*, p. 213). Perceiving effaces itself in favor of the perceived, much like "Expression fades out before what is expressed" (*PP*, p. 401). Like speaking, therefore, perceiving, which Merleau-Ponty calls a "nascent logos"[11] "promotes its own oblivion" (*PP*, p. 401). Between perceiving and the perceived there is a kind of natural unconsciousness, an unconsciousness at the heart of perception.

But this natural unconsciousness is not a total ignorance because if *I* am not present to the birth of my own perceiving still in another sense I must be there in order to perceive. "I do not perceive any more than I speak — Perception has me as has language" (*VI*, p. 190), Merleau-Ponty says. But then most importantly he adds that "As it is necessary that all the same *I* be there in order to speak, *I* must be there in order to perceive" (*VI*, p. 190, his emphasis). The perceiving subject, like the speaking subject, is *present* to his perceiving and speaking because he is also *absent* from them. His absence is a kind of presence, just as his presence is through this absence. This natural unconsciousness is therefore a question of another kind of knowledge.

It is "as *one*" (*VI*, p. 190, his italics) that the perceiver is present and absent to his perceiving, and Merleau-Ponty illustrates this point with the following example. A woman who is walking in the street

---

[11]Maurice Merleau-Ponty, "The Primacy of Perception," *The Primacy of Perception* (Evanston: Northwestern University Press, 1964), p. 25. (Hereafter incorporated into text as *Primacy*).

suddenly grips her coat together because she feels that others are looking at her breasts. But she is not able to say what she has just done or tell us why.

With this example Merleau-Ponty wants to suggest that the *one* who perceives is the embodied perceiver. He wants to suggest that it is the sensitive body that can know that which *I* do not (want to) know, that this body can be a knowing that *motivates* ignorance.[12] Through her body this woman is present to the gaze of others, and it is her hand that testifies to this presence. Yet *she* is herself absent from this presence. She cannot say what her hand has just done. The body, therefore, is for Merleau-Ponty not simply his equivalent of the Freudian unconscious; on the contrary it is a structure of conscious-unconsciousness, a structure of absence-presence. It is, however, this notion of the body as a conscious-unconsciousness which must be more precisely understood.

In his last work Merleau-Ponty suggests, according to Lingis, that "the invisible substructure of the visible is the key to the unconscious structure of consciousness" (*VI*, p. liii). Considering, therefore, how Merleau-Ponty understands the invisible, we can begin to understand the body as a conscious-unconsciousness.

The invisible, Merleau-Ponty says, "is not the contradictory of the visible" (*VI*, p. 215), a negative defined in its opposition to the positive. Nor is the invisible a potential visible, a "possible visible for an other" (*VI*, p. 229). Neither a category nor an inference from the visible, as Freud's unconscious is at times presented and justified as a inference from the data of consciousness, the invisible is rather "the

---

[12]The sentence is written with the parentheses to call attention to an important point that will be discussed below. This is the notion of repression. Placing the words "want to" in brackets indicates that while the structure of habit is a different relation between I and my body than the structure of repression, the two structures have the same source. In each case it is a question of a knowing by not knowing, but in the one there is a *motivated* "ignorance." In one case, therefore, this "mindful-body" gives itself over to the world, while in the other case it chooses a world to give itself over to. In each case it is a different relation of activity/passivity.

Indeed Merleau-Ponty himself speaks of repression in this way when he discusses the phantom limb. "The phenomenon of the phantom limb is absorbed into that of repression . . . (*PP*, p. 82)" he says, and just as one's body can project and sustain habitual situations, it also can project and keep alive previous intentions, phases of one's history that are no longer supported by the world. There can be, in other words, a "phantom history" just like there is a phantom limb, because this body through which one perceives, this sensitive flesh, is a history, and this history is embodied. Indeed what Merleau-Ponty's consideration of repression suggests is that in the human psychological world the dichotomy of a biological organism *and* an historical subject is erroneous. Considered psychologically the human body, this *one* who perceives, is neither biological nor historical nor a combination of the two. Considered psychologically the biological-historical distinction has to be rethought.

secret counterpart of the visible . . . the Nichturpräsentiebar which is presented to me as such within the world" (*VI*, p. 215). The invisible, therefore, is the visible's only way of being visible; it is "an urpräsentation of the Nichturpräsentiebar" (*VI*, p. 254), the "*other side* or the *reverse* of sensible Being" (*VI*, p. 255, his emphasis). Like the light, the invisible is a level or system of levels that are not *what* we see but are that "*with which, according to which,* we see" (*VI*, p. li, his emphasis).

Now the unconscious of consciousness is like the invisibility of the visible. Unconsciousness is not *that which* we see but that through which there is the perceived. Speaking of consciousness, Merleau-Ponty says that "*what* it does not see it does not see for reasons of principle, [and that] it is because it is consciousness that it does not see" (*VI*, p. 248, his emphasis). In other words, *because* consciousness does not see itself seeing, or because it never fully touches itself touching, it sees (and touches) the world. Or, said in a positive way, consciousness is consciousness because it sees itself only in seeing things, because in touching things it manages to touch itself. There is, therefore, in principle a central blindness of consciousness, but a blindness that is insightful. Indeed the only way for consciousness to be consciousness is by not being conscious of being conscious of the world. Consciousness is not an act, Merleau-Ponty says, but a being at the world.

Unconsciousness is the other side of consciousness, like the invisible is the other side of the visible. As an explicit illustration of the latter, consider the phenomenon of depth. It is not the visible, and yet as invisible it has no other way of appearing except as *of* the visible. The painter, for example, who paints depth must paint things, and it is between and among things that depth appears. The depth of a thing is not that which is inside it but that which the thing is in and through its existence among other things, which leads Merleau-Ponty to speak of "a reflexivity of the visible" (*Primacy*, p. 168), or a "radiation of the visible" (*Primary*, p. 182). "All flesh," he says, "and even that of the world, radiates beyond itself" (*Primacy*, p. 186). The depth of something, therefore, is "what there is in it of reflection of other things, allusion to other things."[13] Not a fact in itself or an idea for consciousness, the thing is an axis upon which hinge the visibility of the surface and the invisibility of its depth.

But in much the same manner is the human body an axis upon

[13] Jose Ortega y Gasset, *Meditations on Quixote* (New York: W. W. Norton & Co., 1961) p. 88.

which consciousness and unconsciousness hinge, and its depth, like the depth of things, is not inside it but through its engagement in the world with others. Hence for that woman in the street, her body is a hinge or pivot around which knowledge and ignorance revolve, and her consciousness of the other's gaze is simultaneously her unconsciousness of her own behavior. It is the other who is her depth, and if in that depth she does not find a reflection of her sexuality, then it is because she does find there another reflection, a reflection perhaps of the guilt and the shame of sexuality. The other's gaze already disrobes her because between her hand, which unknowingly closes the coat, and this gaze there is already a silent communion.

The unconscious is not an index of the subject's ignorance any more than it is an index of a division *within* himself. On the contrary, Merleau-Ponty's remarks on the unconscious from the side of perception suggest that unconsciousness is a register of the subject's relations with others, a register of the way his being present to others is also an absence from himself. Indeed a radical sociohistorical interpretation of the unconscious in place of Freud's biological-instinctual interpretation is implied by these remarks, just as a notion of *lateral depth* in place of Freud's intrapsychic vertical depth is seen to emerge. In the next section of this essay this theme of lateral depth shall be considered. To conclude this section, however, we might say that if Merleau-Ponty's critical consideration of Cartesian consciousness brings that which is above life back into the world, then this critical consideration of the Freudian unconscious restores that which is below life to its place in the world. *Unconsciousness is in the world between us,* and hence it "is to be sought not at the bottom of ourselves . . . but in front of us, as articulations of our field" (*VI*, p. 130).

IV. PERCEPTUAL CONSCIOUSNESS AND REFLECTION

In a paper written in 1912, titled, "A Note on the Unconscious in Psychoanalysis," Freud justifies his concept and use of this term within the context of a definition of consciousness. He says: "Now let us call 'conscious' the conception which is present to our consciousness and *of which we are aware,* and let this be the *only* meaning of the term 'conscious' " (Freud, XII, 1958, p. 260, my emphasis). Beginning with this definition, which equates consciousness with its awareness of itself as consciousness, Freud is correct in *inferring* that there is more to psychological life than meets the mind. But beginning in this way, Freud already accepts a Cartesian image of consciousness and thereby infects his own beginning. As Descartes' *cogito* already presumes a Galilean world,[14] so too does Freud's unconscious presume a Cartesian *cogito* as the previous sections have indicated.

We have seen, however, that Merleau-Ponty's work offers another understanding of unconsciousness, which is contained in the notion of lateral depth, and, in his essay "Eye and Mind" we find an interesting meditation on this theme. The painter, he suggests, struggles to capture not the world as it is for profane vision, and his effort is not to portray on canvas a representation of that world. Indeed to the extent that the painter achieves this *representation* of the visible, to that same extent does he fail to paint, since the achievement of painting is that "It gives visible existence to what profane vision believes to be invisible" (*Primacy*, p. 166).

But what does profane vision believe to be invisible? One of the examples that Merleau-Ponty uses in the text provides the best illustration of an answer. Looking at some water in a pool, he acknowledges that that water inhabits that space, and yet it most certainly is not contained there, because "if I raise my eyes toward the screen of cypresses where the web of reflections is playing, I cannot gainsay the fact that the water visits it, too, or at least sends into it, upon it, its active and living essence" (*Primacy*, p. 182). What the painter sees but what profane vision forgets is this water that is in the pool because it is not there, this water that is in the pool because it is also in the trees. It is this relation of *reflection*, this relation of mirroring in which a thing is that which it is by virtue of the others that surround it, "this radiation of the visible" (*Primacy*, p. 182), which painters such as Matisse in his early canvases paint, but which everyone does not see.

Moreover this relation of reflection, this "dehiscence" of the visible, this "system of exchanges" (*Primacy*, p. 164) also includes the painter himself because his body, which sees the spectacle, is also of the visible. "The painter 'takes his body with him'," Merleau-Ponty says, and "it is by lending his body to the world that the artist changes the world into paintings" (*Primacy*, p. 162). But that which the painter lends, the world borrows, and indeed it is this borrowing by the world, a being possessed by it that Merleau-Ponty means. The things of the world are already "encrusted" into one's flesh and painting's interrogation of the world "looks toward this secret and feverish genesis of things in our body" (*Primacy*, p. 167). Hence

[14]Edmund Husserl, *The Crisis of European Sciences and Transcendental Phenomenology*, trans. David Carr (Evanston: Northwestern University Press, 1970) p. 70.

Merleau-Ponty quotes the artist, Paul Klee, when he says that "Perhaps I paint to break out" (*Primacy*, p. 167), and he adds himself that "There really is inspiration and expiration of Being, action and passion so slightly discernible that it becomes impossible to distinguish between what sees and what is seen, what paints and what is painted" (*Primacy*, p. 167). A circularity of sorts, a circular depth, exists, therefore, among things and between the painter and the world, and there is a human body and a human world when, "between the seeing and the seen, between touching and the touched, between hand and hand, a blending of some sort takes place" (*Primacy*, p. 163).

The painter *recovers* that which profane vision forgets, this "metamorphosis of seeing and seen which defines both our flesh and the painter's vocation" (*Primacy*, p. 169). Lights, shadows, reflections, and especially, Merleau-Ponty says, the image of the mirror all betray a circuit of reflection that exists among things and in which man himself is involved, a relation of reflection that defines a lateral depth. The metamorphosis of seeing and the seen means that the seen is the depth of the see-er, in much the same way that the reflection of the water in the trees is the depth of the water in the pool. In a painting by the Fauvist artist, Raoul Dufy, entitled "Old Houses at Honfleur" (Fig. 1)[15] we have a particularly good illustration of this lateral depth between things, or what Merleau-Ponty calls the "labor of vision" (*Primacy,* p. 168) within things. The houses in the distance have their depth and come alive through their reflection in the water, and in fact it is only through their reflection that they have a place in the world. The reflection allows those houses to become human houses, places in which to dwell. The reflection gives them their distance, a distance moreover that is an absence (the houses are over there, far away) *and* a presence (the houses are nevertheless also here, in the water). Indeed what would those houses and their distance be without these reflections? Imagine the painting exactly as it is but with no reflections of the houses in the water. Would not the distance now seem too great? Would not the distance in fact now seem like an inhuman distance, and would not these houses lose their place in the world? Would they not lose their anchorage in the world and simply float away? What the painting teaches us, therefore, is precisely what profane vision forgets: the reflection of things and of the see-er through the seen *matters* as much as that which is

---

[15]John Elderfield, *Fauvism: The "Wild Beasts" and Its Affinities* (New York: Oxford University Press, 1976).

Figure 1. Dufy: *Old Houses at Honfleur.* 1906. Private Collection, Switzerland. (Reproduced with permission).

reflected. Indeed a thing is that which it is only through its reflections. The water is the depth of the houses, their inside—their unconscious as it were—made visible.

But that which is true of the reflection of things, and of the see-er through the visible, is also true of two see-ers. "Man is [a] mirror for man," Merleau-Ponty says, and the "mirror itself is the instrument of a universal magic that changes . . . myself into another, and another into myself" (*Primacy*, p. 168). For the woman in the street, therefore, the eyes of others are a mirror that reflects who she is. Their gaze is her unconscious made visible. These others and their looks are the depth of this woman's sexuality, and like one's own image in the mirror, which reflects how one is present to others and absent from himself, these others reflect an absent-presence. They reflect, like one's own mirror image, a subject who is present to herself only at a distance. They reflect, again like the mirror image, a *familiar-stranger.*

Merleau-Ponty's philosophy presents a notion of lateral depth, which allows one to revision unconsciousness as a phenomenon of the mirror, as a phenomenon of reflection. It is a view that appears both in his early work when he says, for example, that "it is through my relation to 'things' that I know myself" (*PP*, p. 383), and in his last work when he says that there is "an *einfühlung* and a lateral relation with the things no less than with the other" (*VI*, p. 180). As such, therefore, unconsciousness does not refer to a subject layered within himself but rather to a subject whose *absence* from himself in that moment of *reflection* when he is *given back by* others, and the world intersects with a presence to himself in that moment of *reflection* when he *bends back upon* himself. Two moments of reflection, related as the concave is to the convex, this view of unconsciousness envisions the subject as an axis of knowledge and ignorance, just as it envisions the human body as a pivot of I and the Other. This view of unconsciousness envisions finally a subject whose unconsciousness is from the very beginning the face of the world.

Merleau-Ponty's work describes a natural unconsciousness, an unconsciousness that is the other side of consciousness. It is a description that offers an account of the possibility of a Freudian unconscious without, however, explicitly indicating how the unconscious appears. Stated in another way, Merleau-Ponty's account does not develop that which is most central about the Freudian unconscious, the notion of repression.[16] For Freud the unconscious is very much tied to the task of *becoming* conscious, a task moreover that is constantly beset by *resistance*, whereas, for Merleau-Ponty, becoming conscious seems to occur too easily. Indeed with Merleau-Ponty's view one seems to miss the sense of *effort* or of *work*, which is necessarily involved in overcoming resistance. One does not sense that there is a *labor of recovery* involved in becoming conscious. In terms of the examples used in this essay, Merleau-Ponty's "reflections" do not appear to distinguish sufficiently between the painter and the patient (the woman in the street). Each is absent from himself in being present to the world, but the painter recovers this absence in his creative *expressions* and thus returns to himself from the side of the world. His canvas, in the Freudian idiom, makes the unconscious conscious. But this recovery is precisely what the woman in the street

[16]Of course, Merleau-Ponty has not entirely neglected the issue of repression, and in the *Phenomenology of Perception* he says that repression is "the transition from first person existence to a sort of abstraction of that existence . . . " (*PP*, p. 83), a point that he demonstrates in suggesting that repression is like the phenomenon of the phantom limb. These remarks suggest that repression is an idea of one's life that is no longer supported by or reflected in the world, and it is this direction that is followed in this essay.

cannot do. Her sexuality is repressed and not expressed, and indeed her repression can be seen as a failure, or an absence of expression. The next part of this essay shall consider this issue and thereby further develop Merleau-Ponty's description of unconsciousness as a phenomenon of reflection.

V. REFLECTION AND REPRESSION

"I borrow myself from others" (*Signs*, p. 159), Merleau-Ponty writes, and to be unconscious is to be absent from oneself while being present in the world. This reconsideration of unconsciousness suggests that the initiative for repression is neither initially nor primarily with the subject nor on the side of the subject alone. Repression is not an intrapsychic event, a play of interior forces. It is on the contrary an activity initiated between a subject and his world, between me and you. It is a way of being with the other in which that which is lent does not reflect that which one intended to borrow. As such, and in terms of this essay, repression can be described as a failure, or breakdown, in the first moment of reflection.

As a failure of reflection, repression characterizes a condition of living in which a subject faces a world that offers no mirrors for this or that particular experience of human life. Consider, for example, that moment in September 1897 when Freud and the beginning science of psychoanalysis are thrown into a crisis because the stories of sexual seduction of the child by the parent are not actual events. It is a decisive moment because, while Freud reasons that psychology is not a discipline of the real but of the fictional (the child has not been seduced by the parent; on the contrary he has *wished* to be the seducer), he also transforms psychoanalysis from a science that finds psychological life in time and in the world to a science that now uncovers psychological experience in natural and universal conditions that are older than time and prior to any world. One month later, writing to Wilhelm Fliess, he introduces Oedipus, and with him he encloses the wish within a universal drama of incest and taboos. The child's wish, or actually the patient's imagination of the wishful child, is not an index of his relations with others; rather it has become a symbol of everyman's dilemma.

It would seem, however, that in this instance Freud misreads Oedipus, because his patient's tales do not necessarily repeat a universal drama of instinct and incest. Indeed Freud hears them in this way only because he already divides the real and the fictional, and the individual and the other. Given the Cartesian ground of his thinking, Freud is already predisposed toward the psychological as an individual rather than a relational phenomenon, and toward a notion of reality defined exclusively in empirical terms. Hence *either* the parent *really* seduced the child *or* the child *wished* to seduce the parent, and between these two alternatives there is nothing to choose. Within the context of his thought, therefore, it was not possible for Freud to hear his patients' stories as descriptions of the parent-child relations of his time, as indications of how relationships *between* people in that age concealed and did not reflect the sexual dimension of human life, as indications of how those relations reflected a false innocence masking human desire. Given this context, there was no way for Freud to hear these tales as a witness of the unconscious side of Cartesian consciousness (i.e., as an expression of how the life of passion finds no reflection in the Cartesian dream of reason). Within this context Freud was not able to understand these stories as an indictment against an age and a culture.

In "Eye and Mind" Merleau-Ponty notes that "a Cartesian man does not see *himself* in the mirror" (*Primacy*, p. 170). On the contrary, "he sees a dummy . . . which, he has every reason to believe . . . is not a body in the flesh" (*Primacy*, p. 170). The stories of Freud's patients describe this situation. Their tales of sexual trauma do not express a real, actual event—as Freud discovered; but neither do they express a forbidden, repressed instinctual wish—as Freud imagined. Rather they describe an intentional relation toward the world that finds no *reflection* in that world. They reveal a world in which the relations between individuals, as well as the things of that world (e.g., the styles of dress, of furniture, of architecture), conceal more than they reveal the flesh of the living human body. These tales reveal repression as a failure of this moment of reflection.

But that which is absent for reflection in this first moment is also unavailable for reflection in its second moment; thus repression also characterizes that condition of living in which experiences, which find no anchor in and/or reflection by the world, slip away from the world and are buried beneath it. Of course, this is where Freud begins—with the *maintainence* of repression; and this is where the strength of psychoanalysis lies. His patients' stories do reveal that a passion that slips away from the world does reappear as a fantasy above life or as a symptom from below it. But, as we have already seen, his unacknowledged acceptance of a Cartesian context leads him to inquire about the *origins* of repression in a predetermined way. The origins are destined to be found *within* the individual rather than between himself and others, and as a consequence that

242 Part III: Merleau-Ponty

which is *below* life is destined to take on a priority over that which is
within life and in the world.

Ironically, however, the *praxis* of psychoanalysis seems at odds
with Freud's own *theory* of repression, and the praxis seems to support an understanding of repression more in line with this essay. For
example, there is a passage in one of Freud's works where he recommends that the analyst be like a perfect reflecting mirror to the
patient. But why should Freud use this image if there were not
already an intuition of the *origins* of repression as the absence of a
reflection, and further an intuition of the *maintainence* of repression
as the failure of reflection in its second moment? This recommendation therefore may actually be an implicit acknowledgment of repression as originating at the interface, or at the boundary, of two
worlds. As such, moreover, this recommendation may also be an
acknowledgment of the necessity for the analyst to bring to reflection in its first moment that which has slipped away so that the
failure of the next moment of reflection can be reversed. Indeed the
recommendation may in fact acknowledge that that which is recovered for reflection in the mirror of analysis becomes available for
reflection as *expression*.

But even if Freud's suggestions cannot be taken in this way, this
essay lends support to this direction. It may be said, therefore, that
repression is finally the other side of expression—both the failure of
expression and overcome by expression. As the failure of expression, repression is initiated by the absence of reflection in its first
moment, the consequence of a kind of dialogue between me and
others, which prohibits this or that particular kind of expression. As
such, therefore, repression is a conspiracy of two. It is constituted in
partnership.

But what is originally constituted in partnership is recovered in
partnership, albeit of a different style, and in this sense the repressed unconscious cannot be detached from the interpretative
work that defines the analytic situation. The praxis of dialogue in
the analytic situation, the procedure of interpretative recovery, is
not incidental to that which the repressed unconscious is, and in this
light it is well to recall that Freud himself admits that repression is an
inference from resistance. He met resistance in the work of recovering that which had slipped beneath life, but this situation does not
logically or phenomenologically mean that the patient has repressed
within himself that which is resisted. On the contrary, it shows that in
its origins and in the analytic situation repression is inseparable

from the dialogue. Indeed without the *work* of recovery, without the *effort* of overcoming the resistances, which defines the analytic situation, there would be no repressed unconscious. It is the labor of recovery that announces and overcomes the repressed, just as the patient originally repressed *in relation to* a situation of dialogue. Repression is the obverse of expression, therefore, and repression without the situation of dialogue presumes a subject apart from the world.

Earlier it seemed as though Merleau-Ponty's description of unconsciousness as a phenomenon of reflection might have given us the possibility of the Freudian unconscious without sufficiently indicating how the repressed unconscious appears. This writer has tried to suggest in these remarks how a development of Merleau-Ponty's notions, particularly along the lines of the two moments of reflection, can account for the appearance of a repressed unconscious. In more specific terms, this writer has tried to show how the development of Merleau-Ponty's notions gives an account of the origins of repression in relation to the world.

VI. CONCLUSION

This paper began with the notion that a theory of things is a theory of the body, which in turn leads to a theory of the psychological. In addition it has been suggested how Merleau-Ponty's notions lead to a radical sociohistorical interpretation of unconsciousness. Freud's psychology is the reflection of a particular world, and consequently the repressed unconscious is a historical phenomenon. Hence, when the world changes, unconsciousness changes. Today it is questionable whether or not things conceal the sexual dimension of human life, and hence whether or not there remains a sexual aetiology to neuroses. Indeed if one considers Husserl's *Crisis*, in which there is expressed a deep and abiding concern for the loss and/or absence of subjectivity in the modern world, then a different picture of unconsciousness emerges. The crisis of the sciences are most fundamentally the crisis of the psychological in the sense that the mathematization of nature and the human body leads to an *interiorization* of psychological life, to an image of the psychological as equivalent to the mental, and to an understanding of it as being on the other side of the world. Matter, it seems, no longer mirrors man, and it is questionable what we reflect in our relations with each other. Indeed, it seems that today we may be living in a situation in which there is a world without the psychological and the psychological without a world. Perhaps, therefore, unconsciousness today is the failure and the absence of the psychological. Certainly the very curious situation of a modern psychology without the psychological bears some reflection.

ELIZABETH A. BEHNKE

TWELVE

THE SEARCH FOR AN INVARIANT
OF SILENCE

ENTRANCE TO AN OPEN SITE

THE TITLE OF THIS PAPER refers to one of Merleau-Ponty's Working Notes from June 1960:

> Show that philosophy as interrogation (i.e. as disposition, around the this and the world which *is there*, of a hollow, of a questioning, where the this and the world must *themselves* say what they are—i.e. not as the search for an invariant of language, for a lexical essence, but as the search for an invariant of silence, for the structure) can consist only in showing how the world articulates itself starting from a zero of being which is not nothingness, that is, in installing itself on the edge of being, neither in the for Itself nor in the in Itself, at the joints, where the world's multiple *entrances* intersect.[1]

There are a number of ways to summarize this quotation, each steering us toward a different investigation. For the moment, let us focus it this way:

> Show that philosophy as interrogation (i.e., . . . as the search for an invariant of silence, for the structure) can consist only in showing how the world articulates itself starting from a zero of being which is not nothingness. . . .

Stripped of its paraphrases and parentheses, Merleau-Ponty's note is exposed for what it is—the statement of a task to be done, a thesis to be demonstrated. But for us this sentence can never become a study question referring to a text that we are supposed to have mastered. There can be no exegesis because the text was never written. What we have is a sketch of a project, an improvisation toward a

---

[1] Maurice Merleau-Ponty, *Le visible et l'invisible*, ed. Claude Lefort (Paris: Gallimard, 1964), p. 314; *The Visible and the Invisible*, trans. Alphonso Lingis (Evanston, Ill.: Northwestern University Press, 1968), p. 260 (translation slightly altered).

245

question that was not even clear to Merleau-Ponty himself. And if we take the word "silence" to mean some sort of absence, then we must conclude that the final stillness of death has irrevocably put an end to this improvisation. If we believed this, we would have to confine ourselves to the texts Merleau-Ponty did write, interpreting them as well as we could, while regretting that he did not live to formulate his question more clearly and to answer it.

According to the quotation itself, however, our task is not interpretation, but interrogation. And it is interrogation of a given: a given that escapes, or slides between, the great metaphysical categories, since it is neither being nor nothingness, neither presence nor absence, but rather silence. Let us assume, then, that the demonstration we seek is neither present in nor absent from Merleau-Ponty's thought, but rather is silent in it. We cannot assume, however, that our task consists of translating something "silent" into something said. "There would be needed a silence that envelops the speech anew," says Merleau-Ponty in another passage, and "this silence will *not be the contrary* of language" (*Visible*, 233; VI, 179). Such a statement suggests that by the time of *The Visible and the Invisible*, "silence" has become a technical term in the same way that "flesh" and "invisible" have. Thus a search for the invariants of silence—for the structural articulations according to which the world displays itself—implies an inquiry into what Merleau-Ponty means by "silence."

But this is a difficult project since the term is not employed consistently. At times Merleau-Ponty uses the word "silence" quite casually, in the accustomed sense of a lack of sound or as a metaphor for absence. Furthermore, the technical meaning not only shifts over time but resists final codification, remaining an open site. Hence we cannot accumulate a definition by collecting all Merleau-Ponty's references to silence, giving them all equal weight. Instead we shall attempt to trace two sorts of silence that appear in his writings: silence as the prose of the world—the tacit structures of the *Lebenswelt*—and silence as the poetry of the world—the articulation of latency in the genesis of meaning.

THE PROSE OF THE WORLD

One of Merleau-Ponty's working hypotheses seems to be the notion of silence as a tacit background. When we speak, for example, we are not conscious of language per se; it remains unthematized. Language itself becomes present only when speaking breaks down (e.g., when I can't recover the elusive word on the tip of my tongue, or when I can't understand someone through his heavy accent). Yet language cannot be said to be absent, either; it is the background of structures and possibilities against which my words and sentences are profiled. *La langue* is silent: it functions as an unthematized background that is neither present nor absent, but tacit. Language, however, is but one example of a tacit background; perception has its own tacit structure, an unthematized modus operandi haunting experience as *la langue* haunts *la parole*. Thus silence is not opposed to language or defined as its "other side," but serves as a more general term.

The invariant of this silence, the structure of the tacit, may be summarized with the word "cohesion." Cohesion implies joints and interjoining—the articulation of a network of connections and interconnections that hang together, that cohere as they intertwine. For example, the Heideggerean analysis of "equipment" (*das Zeug*) shows that a tool such as a hammer makes sense by referring to other equipment (e.g., the nail); to a certain kind of "manipulability" (*Handlichkeit*) (e.g., hammering); to the project that calls for its use (e.g., building a house); and to the natural environment, which provides in this case not only materials (e.g., wood), but also reasons for building a house (e.g., shelter from the weather). The house in turn may indicate such patterns of social organization as the isolation of the nuclear family or the gathering of neighbors in a place that is not only a house but a home. We could, of course, start with the house or with the nail; no matter what we pick to focus the field, we can unfold its implications in such a way as to show its insertion in a vast array of interconnected significations mutually capable of implying each other. In short, each thing opens onto a tacit background characterized by the cohesion of many intersecting horizons.

But these horizons are open horizons. There is always "quelque chose d'inachevé."[2] This is not to say that there are literally gaps or holes in the panorama; there is rather an ongoing perceptual task that calls me, like the bear in the song, to go look at the other side of the mountain. Each view promises more to be seen and each statement hints that more could be said. Words are pregnant with other nuances; each context suggests other contexts; there is always another side of things; and the significance toward which the things

---

[2]This phrase was borrowed from Philippe Jaccottet's French translation of Robert Musil's *The Man Without Qualities*. See *L'homme sans qualités*, 2 vols. (Paris: Éditions du Seuil, 1961), 2: 692.

point at the moment already implies other meanings, other uses, other valuations. "Everything, like ceramic pots, leaks" (Plato, *Cratylus*, 440), and yet there is an indubitable cohesion of the flesh of the world, a general coherence that is not invalidated by the perpetual incompleteness of perception and expression. Thus when we take silence to mean a tacit background, we are led to the invariant of cohesion: at the heart of the *Lebenswelt* we find an implicatory structure that holds everything together and yet ensures that nothing is ever totally closed.

The tacit structures of the *Lebenswelt* are, however, taken for granted in the natural attitude. It is only when the painter steps back from the familiar world of constituted things that he begins to catch the invisible play of light, shadow, and color which allows the things to appear; it is only in the philosophic reflection that the tacit, unthematized structures are seen for what they are. But in that case they have become thematic. We run into at least two problems: infinite regress and de facto transcendence. In the first place, no matter how eloquently I describe to you the tacit structures of *la langue*, I still presuppose another *langue* silently haunting the words with which I propose to explain this silence; no matter how intimate Cézanne may be with the shadows and planes out of which Mont Sainte-Victoire emerges, he does not see his brush, his easel, his palette, and his canvas in the same way. Another painting would be required, and even this second revelation of the invisible dimensions constituting the visibility of the painter's gear ignores the tacit structures involved in *its* production. Similarly, when the poet Jean Tardieu tries to write about language, he finds that it evades him; it refuses to become an object of investigation, for it is the very means of investigation, and its tacit manner of operation decomposes rather than yielding up its secrets:

> I'm going to write a poem. On what subject?
> On language. This bizarre exercise, this bold
> venture, nevertheless requires that I express
> myself *in a language*!
> And so an amazing phenomenon appears:
> language will scrutinize language. Now in
> order to indicate the simple idea "My language
> will scrutinize language," it is obvious that
> I've used . . . what? None other than language!
> From which we get the following result: my
> language observes language contemplating language!
> But this is still not the end of it, since it's
> language that I've just used to say "My language . . ."
> —and so on, you see: the language of language of

language of language of language of language of language of
language
language
langwidge
languish
line-wish
lingo-which
link-wedge
language
language language language language language language. . . [3]

Hence the tacit is irrevocably one step ahead of us. And in the second place, the tacit structures are known to us only as they are raised to the level of description. It seems that we can never reach the silence of the prereflective, prelinguistic stratum; or, to put it another way, we find that the very definition of the tacit as "unthematized" leads us straight into a contrast with that which is thematic. We are caught in a dualistic system composed of a mute layer of "reality" and a layer of articulation that purports to bring the mute structures to expression, while admitting that these mute structures are known only in their "expressed" version and that there is no guarantee that the articulation adequately expresses the silence it assumes.

But we have arrived at this problem only because we have assumed a contrast between the natural attitude, which is a kind of unconscious maneuverability or operationality among the tacit structures of language and perception, and a philosophy of reflective consciousness, which extracts itself from the natural attitude to describe certain things as presently given significations, other things as tacit structures supporting these significations. Such a notion as "the unthematized" can arise only in terms of a consciousness that is centered upon and correlate with its objects, a consciousness that is the witness for whom there could be perception and then also apperception, a present given and then a silent background. Consciousness is the reference point at which some things are overt and others are tacit.

But even if we were to set aside the question of a privileged standpoint, operating in terms of the presence of a signification and the correlative silence of all that is required to constitute that signification, we would still find that the notion of the tacit is problematic. For the tacit is ubiquitous. We are at a loss to account for the emergence of something truly new, something neither contained

[3]Jean Tardieu, "Poème intraduisible," in *Obscurité du jour* (Geneva: Albert Skira, 1974), p. 47.

nor foreshadowed in the world we have inherited. Even schizo-
phrenia and culture shock are perceived as dislocations of a cohesive
whole; they are defined in terms of their lack of intimacy with a
network of tacit implications. The perpetual incompleteness of perception and expression provides only variations on a single cohesive
theme; whenever we think we have discovered something new, it
turns out, on closer inspection, to belong to the reticulation of the
familiar and the possible. It is as though everything is already silently prefigured, since the new does indeed cohere with the old and
hence must have belonged to the web of implications already silently
"there." All questions are then already pregnant with their own
answer; there is only a dialectic of the prose of the world, with no
room for an interrogation that would intertwine with the poetry of
the world. But these conclusions are the product of an analysis that
has defined the silent as the tacit and specified cohesion as its invariant. Merleau-Ponty's writings also yield a silence whose prime
invariant is latency. We shall approach this topic by way of what may
well be a limit case: the genesis of meaning in artistic creation. And
we shall begin with a problem borrowed from the novelist Henry
James.

THE FIGURE IN THE CARPET AND THE CLUE

The problem in the Henry James narrative called "The Figure in
the Carpet"[4] is one of interpretation. The story concerns a young
critic who reviews a work by a novelist called Vereker, only to hear
from the author himself that he has entirely missed the point. Vereker tells the critic that all of his books have in fact a single point—
"my little point," he calls it, admitting that it is indeed "something
like a complex figure in a Persian carpet," and adding, "It's the very
string that my pearls are strung on" (p. 33). The critic knows that
there's a figure in the carpet, for the novelist has told him so, but he
can't see it; it is not yet thematized in his reading of the works and
remains the novelist's secret. It would be the task of hermeneutics to
lend voice to this tacit pattern, to see and to announce the figure in
the carpet.

But the enterprise assumes from the start that there really *is* a
figure in the carpet, and that the task of hermeneutics boils down to

---

[4]Henry James, *Embarrassments* (New York: The Macmillan Company, 1897), pp.
3–82.

the trick of pulling it out of the intricate background. The problem is posed in such a way that the silence of the tacit pattern turns out to be a kind of presence to which we are simply not yet initiated. As Oscar Wilde pointed out in "The Decay of Lying" (1889), no one really saw the London fog until Impressionist painting opened our eyes to mist and haze. Yet we take it for granted that the fog was actually there all along. And we can argue that mountains have always maintained their thick and weighty visibility through the play of light, shadow, angle, and plane; it is simply that we did not realize this until we saw Cézanne's paintings, or perhaps until we encountered Merleau-Ponty's description of Cézanne's achievement. In short, we assume that the sense we are seeking is lodged in a silent text, whether this text is a painting by Cézanne, a novel by Vereker, or a region of the lived world.

The problem of the critic, then, the problem of hermeneutics, is to make sense of the figure in the carpet—to reveal the tacit meaning of a text we already possess. But another question suddenly troubles us: How did the novelist Vereker come into possession of his "little point"? Was it in any sense "there" before he wrote the novels? And that oblique gesture, that mountain thrust up from a textured plain—was it already "there" before Cézanne painted Mont Sainte-Victoire from the crest of Les Lauves? What is at stake is not merely a translation of the mute into the speaking, but also a question of time and ontology. Was the figure in the carpet *there*, was it *present*, before it was seen? And was it present *before* it was seen, was it there *all along*? Let us examine the original act of weaving the figure in the carpet rather than the hermeneutical problem of seeing it once we have assumed that it is already there.

One way of describing the process of artistic creation is as a passage out of latency into cohesion. (Here "cohesion" names both the structural unity of the finished work—its character of having no missing parts and no unnecessary ones—and the open horizons that permit us to interpret the work in more than one way.) The process can begin with a silent field that is tensed or focused by a clue, as when a single stroke of red on a blank canvas immediately reconfigures its homogeneous emptiness into a constellation of vectors and possibilities promising the final painting. The clue can act as a seed out of which the entire piece grows; hence it would seem to be the most important part of the work. In a television interview, Igor Stravinsky once confessed to experiencing a feeling akin to terror whenever he was about to start a new piece—the empty sheet of music paper, where anything was possible, was an abyss of freedom. However, his vertigo subsided after he had the first sonority or motif, since it would already invite repetition, variation, development, or contrast; the piece itself could begin to call for that which it needed to be completed. The clue thus introduces us to a silence that bristles and seethes with lacunae. And it is a very specific silence: the silence of this work and no other. A dance, for example, may resist the choreographer's attempt to graft on an ending borrowed from another context; a poem may insist on developing its own imagery, forcing the poet to abandon a favorite phrase or to set it aside as the clue to another poem. Jacques Barzun quotes Yeats as saying: "The correcting of prose is endless, because it has no fixed laws; a poem comes right with a click, like a box."[5] The poem can "come right" because the clue introduces the poet to the tacit laws of the finished work. Somehow the figure in the carpet participates in its own weaving; somehow the future poem calls across time and furnishes the prescription for its own genesis.

But the future has been conceived as that which is not yet. The future and the past are absent; only the now is present. We may conjure up the twin absences of past and future by way of mechanisms such as memory and expectation. But the memory and the expectation also occur right now, in the present, with its freight of being. It is unclear how a future, completed work, which is absent and as yet has no being, can compel the artist to perform the very gestures needed to bring the finished work into existence. We are tempted to jump to the conclusion that the problem is badly put when it is phrased in terms of presence and absence, and to substitute a theory of silence: more specifically, of a silence that is "a zero of being which is not nothingness."

However, our description of artistic creation as a passage from latency to cohesion calls for further qualification. There may, of course, be times when the choices that emerge at each stage of the work progressively clarify the shape of the whole, when the poem slowly comes into focus before coming right with a click. But the creative process does not always amount to the gradual realization of an end that was implied in its beginnings. Let us invent a simple illustration: When a filmmaker begins a movie, he might start with a single image or motif—his clue. The clue suggests other images, allowing a theme to emerge. The cameraman will undoubtedly

---

[5] Jacques Barzun, *Simple and Direct: A Rhetoric for Writers* (New York: Harper and Row, 1975), p. ix.

shoot more footage than the final film will contain; what the film needs, what the film itself demands, is not immediately evident to the filmmaker, but must be won in the editing room. When the filmmaker can see how the last shot fits perfectly into the montage, the work has assumed a "final shape." Presumably it was this final shape toward which everything was tensed; it was this answer that the clue demanded. But the question to which the movie is an answer may not be the initial question posed by the clue.[6] On the contrary, the last shot—the one that made the film come right with a click, which may or may not be the last frames of the movie—might radically change the meaning of everything else in the film, so that no image is left untouched, nothing is as it was before. The assumed presence of the hidden figure in the carpet—the inevitable cohesion of the finished work—arises only retroactively.

Furthermore, every shot in the film could become a seed, a clue with its own constellation of implications that were submerged in the project of the original movie, yet were not excluded from it. Photographers speak of the "latent image," the chemical alteration of film after it has been exposed and before it has been developed. But every image in the movie can be a "latent image" in another sense, and even a poem that has come right can remain an open labor: "Every phrase and every sentence is an end and a beginning . . . " (T. S. Eliot, *Four Quartets*, "Little Gidding," V). Hence the work is not the product of an irreversible passage from latency to cohesion but an inscription of their interplay.

Such a description, however, shifts the very notion of a work of art. It is no longer either an absent future—a *rien défini* toward which the gestures of its genesis converge—or a present object, but a style of concretizing silence, a style of cohering rather than an accomplished cohesion. The work displays silence—"a zero of being which is not nothingness"—in the act of self-articulation, and it does so by way of a dynamic interplay between two invariants of silence: latency and cohesion. We are very far indeed from the traditional concept of a work of art, and our description may be inappropriate for works created in conformity with that concept. Therefore we shall choose a contemporary work in open form as an example of the concretization and articulation of silence.

[6]"We are reminded of Valéry's saying that a felicitous line in a poem is the solution of a problem which arises only after it has been solved"—Victor Zuckerkandl, *Man the Musician,* trans. Norbert Guterman (Princeton: Princeton University Press, 1973), p. 326.

NOT WANTING TO SAY ANYTHING ABOUT MARCEL

Not Wanting to Say Anything About Marcel (1969) is a work of graphic art by the composer John Cage and the designer Calvin Sumsion.[7] "Marcel" refers to Marcel Duchamp, to whom the work is dedicated; he had died in 1968. The work is actually a series of lithographs and plexigrams, with each version produced in a multiple edition; chance operations were used in composing the pieces, so that each version is different.

The plexigrams, of which there are eight different versions, each consist of eight plexiglas sheets—some tinted and some clear—mounted one behind the other on a wooden base. The sheets may be rearranged in any order. Images in various colors have been silkscreened on each sheet; there are a few representations of objects or parts of objects, but letters, words, and fragments of words or letters predominate. Assorted typefaces are used, and the letters are oriented in many different directions. Since aleatoric procedures were followed in arranging the position of each element on each sheet, some letters cover or overlap others when all eight sheets are lined up. Hence the work is characterized by both transparency and obscurity.

The literal transparency of the plexiglas recalls Duchamp's works on glass, as well as Cage's concern for transparency in musical texture.[8] But some elements in the piece literally obscure others, making them hard to decipher. And the work is obscure and ambiguous in other ways. The title, *Not Wanting to Say Anything About Marcel*, already evokes that about which it proposes to say nothing; furthermore, some of the visual images may be taken as references to other Duchamp works. For example, one of the shapes in Plexigram III looks like Duchamp's *Chocolate Maker* (1914), and the appearance of a piece of rope or twine in Plexigram IV might be construed as a reference to Duchamp's *With Hidden Noise* (1916).[9] Barbara Rose

---

[7]For illustrations, see *John Cage*, ed. Richard Kostelanetz (New York: Praeger, 1970), plates 59 and 60, facing p. 143, and *Source* 4:1 (January 1970), which includes an acetate reproduction of Plexigram IV.

[8]See John Cage, *Silence* (Middletown, Conn.: Wesleyan University Press, 1961), p. 8. Cage is referring to music through which one can hear the sounds of the environment.

[9]*With Hidden Noise* is an assisted ready-made consisting of a ball of twine mounted between two metal plates. Inside the ball of twine is a small object that makes a slight noise when the work is shaken; the object was chosen and inserted by Duchamp's patron Walter Arensberg, and Duchamp never knew what it was—nor did he ever want to know.

remarks that the plexigrams and lithographs in this series "remind one of Duchamp—their suspended images creating a feeling of three-dimensional forms floating in free space reminiscent of Duchamp's experiments with perception and illusionism" (*John Cage*, p. 189). Hence the very look of the work may be taken as a comment on Duchamp after all.

But for the most part the work's ambiguity is the ambiguity of language itself. The words and letters I am using in this description become transparent, pointing beyond themselves to what I am trying to say. The words and letters in the plexigrams, however, are suspended just short of transparency; they persist in their opacity and impart no message. Yet they do not necessarily appear to be an indifferent jumble of signs. We find ourselves recognizing a word here or there, and each legible word suggests a cluster of possible interpretations. The tangle of letters that seems meaningless at first glance slowly begins to make sense as we examine the work. It begins to make sense; it hovers on the brink of making sense; it invokes our complicity in the activity of making sense, an activity that language usually seems to perform all by itself; but it never resolves into a text we can read through. The elements of language never efface themselves in favor of something said about Marcel. Instead, *Not Wanting to Say Anything About Marcel* greets the eye, not with the presence or absence of meaning, but with its genesis in a silence whose style of articulation consists of the interplay between cohesion and latency. By offering us a glimpse of latency in the act of cohering, the piece literally displays the transparent depth of silence.

A DANCE ON THE EDGE OF BEING

For the critic in the Henry James story, the figure in the carpet was there all along—he just couldn't see it. For us, the figure in the carpet is not necessarily there all along; it emerges in the act of creation. Some works of art are organized around this hidden figure, and these works invite interpretation. Other works, however, are woven of the event of creation: they are articulations of silence and demonstrations of interrogation. They are not expressions of a previously hidden meaning, but traces of an improvisation for two partners: the artist and the world that "articulates itself starting from a zero of being which is not nothing." With such works, "one enters a world that is held firmly open, imperfect until further notice, constantly breaking-up"—a world of continual genesis, of "the ever-new decision from the zero-point."[10] "Is this the highest point of reason, to realize that the soil beneath our feet is shifting, to pompously name 'interrogation' what is only a persistent state of stupor, to call 'research' or 'quest' what is only trudging in a circle, to call 'Being' that which never fully *is*?"[11]

But perhaps reason is no longer our only touchstone. The play of silence and interrogation is neither rational nor irrational but a clue to the style of the flesh of the world: a dance articulated "on the edge of being," a gesture improvised "at the joints, where the world's multiple *entrances* intersect."

[10]Henri Pousseur, "Outline of a Method," trans. Leo Black, *Die Reihe* 3 (English ed., 1959), p. 47; Friedhelm Döhl, "Sinn und Unsinn musikalischer Form," in Siegfried Borris et al., *Terminologie der neuen Musik* (Berlin: Merseburger, 1965), p. 68.

[11]Maurice Merleau-Ponty, "Eye and Mind," trans. Carleton Dallery, in *The Primacy of Perception*, ed. James M. Edie (Evanston, Ill.: Northwestern University Press, 1964), p. 190.

INDEX